CW00555094

LE FANU'S GHOST

LE FANU'S GHOST

Gavin Selerie

To Robert and family

with graphics
by Alan Halsey

with love and thanks
(see acknowledgment on
p. 352) for clerical detail
supplied

FIVE SEASONS PRESS · 2006

Gavin

7th Dec. 2007

Published July 2006 by
Five Seasons Press
41 Green Street
Hereford HR1 2QH, UK

www.fiveseasonspress.com
books@fiveseasonspress.com

Distributed in USA by SPD
1341 Seventh Street, Berkeley CA 94710-1409
www.spdbooks.org

ISBN 0 947960 44 9

Designed & typeset in Ehrhardt
at Five Seasons Press
and printed on
Five Seasons recycled paper
by Cromwell Press
Trowbridge, Wiltshire, UK

Acknowledgements: page 352

GRAPHICS by Alan Halsey
after Brinsley Le Fanu, George Cruikshank,
Phiz, Daniel Maclise and the many anonymous illustrators
who decorated the books and journals of the 19th century

FRONT COVER:
J. S. Le Fanu, *The Watcher and Other Weird Stories* (1894),
with design by Brinsley Le Fanu

BACK COVER:
portrait of author by Laura Lehman

*Five Seasons acknowledges
financial assistance from*

for Frances—
namesake
of the writer
of *Nourjahad*—
who has walked
some of these
trails

The fact is, Mr R., I have been nineteen years endeavouring to satisfy my own taste in this play, and have not yet succeeded.

R.B. Sheridan to James Ridgway, who wished to publish *The School for Scandal*, 1799

[PUDDOCK:] '. . . if I had your parts . . . and could write . . . I'd make a variation upon every play of Shakespeare, that should be strictly moulded upon it, and yet in no respect recognisable.'

[DEVEREUX:] 'A . . . young Venetian nobleman, of singular beauty . . . is seduced from his father's house, and married by a middle-aged, somewhat hard-featured black woman, Juno, or Dido, who takes him away—not to Cyprus—we must be original, but we'll suppose to the island of Stromboli—and you can have an eruption firing away during the last act.'

J.S. Le Fanu, *The House by the Church-yard*, 1863

. . . in Sheridan's Circle my wits repose, in black pitts of the pestered Lenfant he is dummed.

James Joyce, *Finnegans Wake*, 1939

CONTENTS

TWO

THREE

FOUR

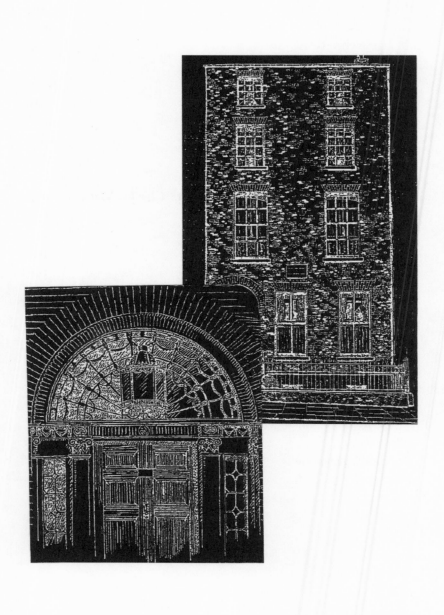

Prologue

HAUNTING HOUSES

O N THE DIAGONAL, facing north-west, in an area that was once fashionable: 12 Dorset Street, Dublin, birthplace of the author of *The School for Scandal*. Recent authorities state that the building has been demolished but it still exists, roofless and deprived of its top storey. All the windows are bricked up, grass and weed grow profusely on the steps, the front wall is sloping and jagged, corrugated iron shuts off the basement hollow. The brick of the mostly-surviving second floor is redder than that of the floors below, suggesting that the upper section was re-faced at some point. Only the arched doorway, with its two columns, shows any sign of the modest prosperity which an actor-manager and his bride enjoyed when they moved to this newly developed part of the city in 1747. Madeleine Bingham, writing in 1972, notes that the door-knocker 'is suspended from a wreath of bays and shows a hand grasping a roll.' This appropriate symbol has vanished. A monastery, forbiddingly solid, is set back from the road on one side. On the other, attached to number 12, is the Moy pub, which boasts a bright red-and-blue frontage; it has closed down and has a planning application attached to the entrance. Not even music and drink keep alive the adjacent space made for a great projector.

Across the Liffey, again on a diagonal, facing north-east: 70 (formerly 18) Merrion Square, home of the author of *Uncle Silas*. Now the head-quarters of the Irish Arts Council, this tall Georgian building exudes grandeur and stability. Adjacent to the sunken or excavated section of the park, the dwellings on the 'South' side rise up, with arched door-ways, balcony ironwork and great chimney stacks, from the spacious road and pavement. The first floor windows of number 70 are taller than those on the ground floor, an unusual façade variation within the collective design; as a result, light reaches the full depth of the library, at the front on this level. The front door is thick and massive, and the entrant proceeds through mahogany doors, under a second fanlight, to the inner hall and great staircase. From here one ascends, beneath elaborate mouldings, to three stages of living-space, capped by a huge attic that feels like an inverted ship. The basement, correspondingly,

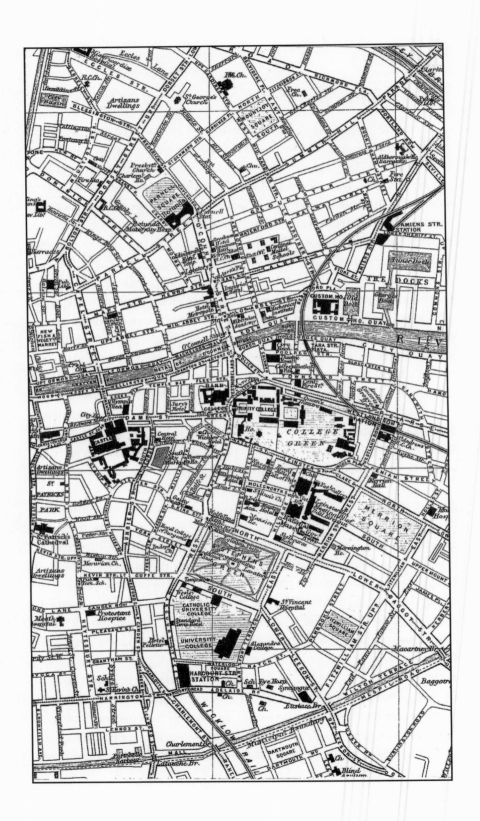

is a warren of chambers which echo at night as walkers tread the pavement. A passage at the rear leads up, via narrow steps, to the garden; on the side opposite the kitchen are the 'Dead Rooms', where files are now stored. The back of the house proper is curved, with four bow windows, aligned with decreasing height at each level. Beside these a back extension, with two floors, projects out a good way; on the upper level, which is a mezzanine between the first and second floor, light pours in from a cupola just beyond the landing. One room leads into another, which in turn gives way to a little recess with a window that looks down on the garden. A curious, ornate chimney juts into the sky above. These are the keynotes: grand spaces of light and ornament, and darker, plainer, semi-hidden spaces.

In between these sites, facing west, not far from Grattan Bridge: 27 Capel Street, home of the author of *The Art of Punning* (or, as Joyce has it, Panning). This area west of O'Connell Street is rather seedy but most of the older buildings survive intact. Once the mint of James II, number 27 is a three-storey building sandwiched between two narrower and slightly higher houses. At one point half of the premises was occupied by a shop called M. Wigoder, a name that surely would have appealed to a word-twirler. It is now the Longmile Furniture Centre, with red security grille and sign-board. One of the shops next door is called Irish Dance Wear; on the opposite side of the street stand Good Vibrations: Adult Pleasure Shop and a Credit Union office. The house is wide and deep; it would have been spacious inside, but it had to accommodate a large family and a school. Jonathan Swift acted as examiner and occasional instructor here. He used to have dinner with the principal in a small back parlour. According to a poem by the latter, the hall was 'All torn to rags by boys and ball', the parlour door 'Besmear'd with chalk, and carv'd with knives', the lock or handle always jammed, and the main chair, in response to weight, used to let the 'reverend deanship' down upon 'his bum'. The school was particularly noted for its performances of plays.

Richard Brinsley Sheridan's grandfather, the Rev. Dr Thomas Sheridan, was a friend of Swift, who called him 'the best instructor of youth in these kingdoms, or perhaps in Europe; and as great a master of the Greek and Roman languages'. Swift wrote parts of *Gulliver's Travels* at

Quilca, Dr Sheridan's country home in County Cavan, and it is possible that certain features in the book relate to this area and its inhabitants. Dr Sheridan's son Thomas became actor-manager of the theatres in Smock-Alley and Aungier-Street, Dublin and brought Garrick over for a triumphant season. His play *The Brave Irishman* (1743) helped to shape the stage type which recurs in such figures as Lucius O'Trigger (*The Rivals*). In 1747 he married Frances Chamberlaine, who wrote drama and fiction, notably the Oriental tale *The History of Nourjahad* (1767) and *Memoirs of Miss Sidney Bidulph* (1761/1767), the first English novel to present through its central characters the interlocking life of two generations. After a riot which despoiled the Smock-Alley Theatre, the Sheridans moved to England, eking out a somewhat precarious existence in literary and theatrical circles. London and Bath provided bases for new ventures in education and drama.

Of the next generation, two children lived in Dublin and two were based primarily in England. Richard married the singer Elizabeth Linley and followed his father into the theatre, initially as a writer and subsequently a manager. The dramatist derived crucial details of situation, character and phrasing from his mother's work. For instance, Mrs Malaprop is based partly on Mrs Tryfort (i.e. Try-for-it) in *A Journey to Bath* and the subplot of *The School for Scandal*—the testing of family members by a relative in disguise—is inspired by the Ned Warner episode in *Memoirs of Miss Sidney Bidulph*. Sheridan's elder bother Charles had a successful, if dull, career in Irish politics; selfish and aloof, he was seen within the family as the original of Joseph Surface. Alicia (Lissy) and Elizabeth (Betsy) both married sons of their father's Huguenot friend and banker, William Le Fanu. Alicia married Joseph, who had a post in the Irish Customs Office and wrote plays, including *The Hour before Marriage*, produced at Covent Garden. She and her husband shared a passionate interest in the theatre. Alicia wrote a comedy *The Sons of Erin* (1812), which provoked Lady Morgan's rhyme: 'Now [Dame Comedy] to her native spirit true/. . . treats us to a LAUGH ANEW.' Elizabeth married Henry, a Captain who had distinguished himself at the siege of Gibraltar in 1779. She wrote novels, such as *The India Voyage* (1804), and the letters to Alicia published (under William LeFanu's editorship) as *Betsy Sheridan's Journal* in 1960. This journal—called such by its author—had descended through the family, being held from 1845 to

1873 by J.S. Le Fanu. Betsy's daughter, Alicia (named after her aunt), wrote novels, poetry and a study of her grandmother's life and work, *Memoirs . . . of Frances Sheridan* (1824).

Richard Brinsley's son Tom married Caroline Callander, who published three novels including *Carwell, or Crime and Sorrow* (1830), which deals with the punishment meted out to those found guilty of forgery. Two daughters of this union continued the family writing tradition: Helen, Lady Dufferin (then Gifford) and Caroline Norton. Helen wrote songs and poems, including 'The Lament of the Irish Emigrant', alluded to by Joyce in *Finnegans Wake*. She is the dedicatee of Le Fanu's *Uncle Silas*. Caroline wrote poetry, novels and pamphlets on women's rights; she kept up a regular correspondence with the Le Fanus, and saw both J.S. and William in London and Dublin. Her works include an unpublished verse drama based on Beckford's *Vathek* (c.1836).

R.B. Sheridan's cousin Frances (Fanny) married Peter Le Fanu, the younger brother of Joseph and Henry. This created a third link and resulted in another literary legacy. Peter wrote a farce, *Smock Alley Secrets* (1778), and held private theatricals in his house. Frances's nephew, James Sheridan Knowles, became the leading tragic playwright of his generation and had many dramas produced in London between 1820 and 1840. *Virginius* and *William Tell* were considerable vehicles for the acting talent of W.C. Macready, both in English theatres and in Dublin. Knowles entertained J.S. Le Fanu on his first visit to London, providing him with tickets for Covent Garden. The playwright's son and grandson were also writers. *Glencoonoge* (1891), a novel by the latter, revolves around a quest for a lost relative; it is the recognition of a portrait which establishes identity by descent.

Peter and Fanny's daughter Alicia—born around the same time as her namesake, Betsy's daughter—married Captain William Dobbin, brother of Emma, J.S. Le Fanu's mother. William and Alicia's son, Rev. William Dobbin, married his second cousin Frances, daughter of Sheridan Knowles. The relationship between the Dobbin and Le Fanu families therefore has a complexity equivalent to the network outlined above. Emma (Dobbin) Le Fanu was a frequent contributor to magazines such as *Chambers Journal*, and one story, 'The Recollections of a Novel-Reader' (*Eliza Cook's Journal*, May 1850), uses the family portrait trope as an index of threatening forces which lead back to the subject's consciousness. Emma's cousin, Rev. Orlando Dobbin, published many essays in the *Dublin University Magazine*, including a study of macaronic literature.

Joseph Sheridan Le Fanu, grandson of Joseph and Alicia, was also fascinated by theatre. He worked at the writing desk which he had inherited from his great uncle, R.B. Sheridan. His novels and short stories reshape a series of recognizable narratives, characters and motifs. There is direct or implicit allusion to family events and artistic concerns, as when, in *The House by the Church-yard*, one character says 'the general's off to Scarborough' and another responds, 'I thought it was to Bath.' (*A Trip to Bath* is the original title of Frances Sheridan's play, while *A Trip to Scarborough* is R.B. Sheridan's adaptation of *The Relapse*.) The ancestor's portrait motif, which recurs throughout Le Fanu's fiction, is not only a standard Gothic device deriving from Walpole and Maturin but also a feature which is found, with less terrifying effect, in works from *A Journey to Bath* (c.1765) to Alicia Le Fanu the younger's *Strathallan* (1816) and, as indicated above, R.B. Sheridan Knowles's *Glencoonoge*. More prominently and wittily, *The Rivals* and *The School for Scandal* use the motif to gauge degrees of endowment and allegiance across generations (scenes 3.4 and 3.3-4.1, respectively). Beyond this, Le Fanu reworked his own tales, expanding and redefining the material to fit different publication contexts and, presumably, to provide an outlet for anxieties and obsessions. The short story 'Passage in the Secret History of an Irish Countess' (1838) becomes, with the removal of the frame introduction and a slight shift of names, 'The Murdered Cousin' (1851); this in turn, transposed to an English setting, becomes the novel *Uncle Silas* (1864).

William Le Fanu, brother of J.S., became one of Ireland's leading railway engineers and Commissioner of Public Works. Interestingly, in view of Joseph's writings about mental dislocation, the latter post involved scrutiny of Ireland's lunatic asylums. William's memoir *Seventy Years of Irish Life* contains vivid, witty anecdotes about famous people, relations and the rural peasantry. It is an important source of information about his brother, emphasizing the delights afforded by Phoenix Park, scene of their childhood, and the inspiration provided by the landscape and customs of Limerick. The record ranges from Sheridan Knowles's extreme absent-mindedness to the Phoenix Park murders. Although the book begins with the author's birth in 1816 and ends with some reflections about the state of Ireland in 1893, its progress is essentially non-linear. The narrative, with its loops and twists, retains an oral character. Joseph and William's sister Catherine published a single short story, 'The Botheration of Billy Cormack' (1840), before her early death. This, like the writings of her brothers, shows a keen sense of colloquial idiom and a lively narrative manner.

J.S. Le Fanu's niece (by marriage) was the novelist Rhoda Broughton, whose early work he fostered and published. *Cometh Up as a Flower* (1865) is dedicated to him. Some of her themes, such as the distinguished family shorn of its splendours and the woman trapped by devices, common enough in fiction, have particular parallels in the work of her uncle. The story 'Behold it was a Dream' (1872) contains an apparition, fortelling an imminent tragedy, which is reminiscent of Le Fanu's grotesque and psychologically acute tableaux. Again, events are shifted from Ireland to England, though this is revealed by the narrator at the close. There are correspondences between the work of Broughton and that of her cousin, Eleanor (Ellie), J.S. Le Fanu's elder daughter. The latter published three novels under the pseudonym Russell Gray before becoming an army wife in India. Gray eschews the sensational and does not have Broughton's vigour of expression, but she provides a strong sense of female reality within the romantic medium. Like her father and her cousin, she has a feel for landscape and domestic decor. The main location for the first novel, *Never—For Ever*, seems to be a thinly disguised version of Beaumaris, where the family went for holidays and which also features in J.S. Le Fanu's *The Tenants of Malory* and *Willing to Die*.

Eleanor's last novel, *Up and Down the World* (1869), is a story of divided attachment in which the heroine marries one painter (her cousin) but loves another. Ellie's brother Brinsley, Le Fanu's youngest child, trained as an artist in Dublin, London and Paris, at one point working in Lutyens's studio. He lived in London for the rest of his life, in Chelsea and Lavender Hill. Brinsley illustrated his father's books and provided anecdotes which are relayed by A.P. Graves and S.M. Ellis in early accounts of the novelist. Apart from his work for the publisher Downey, he was the main illustrator for William Stead's 'Books for the Bairns' series. Issued monthly, these popular penny booklets ranged from fairy and folk tales to abridged classics. Thousands of children in the years 1896 to 1927 would have gained their first experience of visual art from this source. David Jones, who illustrated *The Ancient Mariner* in 1929, first encountered this text in the Le Fanu / BFB version, heavily influenced by Doré (no. 97: Mar. 1904). Brinsley's more sophisticated work, as in *The Watcher and Other Weird Stories* (1894) and Downey's *The Little Green Man* (1895), catches an eerie or fantastic atmosphere with fidelity to the word but avoidance of mere duplication. A distinctive feature is the extension of an image beyond the theoretical frame into a circle or curved space.

William Le Fanu recalls in a letter to Lord Dufferin how he first visited Clandeboye, the latter's estate in County Down, in 1854. His brother stayed there with Ellie and Emmie in 1866, and was probably a visitor in earlier years. Helen Sheridan, Dufferin's mother, was cousin to the Le Fanu brothers. Much later another writer, a direct descendant of the Blackwood–Sheridan union, grew up at Clandeboye. This was Caroline Blackwood, whose novel *Great Granny Webster* (1977) draws on her experience of the 'big house' in the 1930s and early 1940s. Dunmartin Hall, as it is termed in the book, is a place of decaying splendour 'doomed by the height of its . . . ancient colonial aspirations.' Blackwood does not mention pictures, but the narrator describes how her grandfather's whole sense of himself has 'become inseparable from the burden of maintaining his inherited possessions.' Humorously treated, this is the dark side of a culture that involved not only exploitation and stagnation but also an intensity of artistic purpose born of those very tensions.

Not all the people listed above were great practitioners of their art. Despite memorable climaxes and the strong portrayal of parent–child relationships, Sheridan Knowles's pseudo–Elizabethan tragedies seem stilted; it is only in a comedy such as *The Love-Chase* or a melodrama such as *The Daughter* that inspiration seems fully operative. Moreover, it is important to distinguish levels of privilege and differences of background and approach within what may appear to be a common family cluster. If the Sheridans became part of the Ascendancy, they were originally 'native Irish' and Catholic. The Le Fanus, though absorbed within an elite Anglo-Irish group, must have been all too aware of the blight cast on the Huguenot cloth industry by English import restrictions—a situation glancingly evoked through reference to the run-down area of the Liberties in J.S. Le Fanu's 'The Fatal Bride'. Struggle, rather than comfort, is the dominant feature of these lives and, as W.J. Mc Cormack has remarked of Victorian Ireland, 'the language of success was often a mask'. Different writers have different takes on the culture: Fitz Edward in Alicia Le Fanu's *The Sons of Erin* is intended to reverse the type of the stage Irishman, so vividly realized in her father's play, and the final form of her brother's Lucius O'Trigger certainly softens the stereotype. Nevertheless, the thread of endeavour has a cumulative force which resonates down to the present.

OUTSIDE IN

The connexion between the work of these blood relations is paralleled by that between the friends and associates who operated within the narrow spectrum of the mostly Protestant power structure in Dublin. Lady Morgan, whose novel *The O'Briens and the O'Flahertys* was a significant influence on *The House by the Church-yard*, was a friend and protégé of Le Fanu's grandmother Alicia. Charles Maturin, whose novel *Melmoth the Wanderer* had a profound effect on Le Fanu's work, was a friend of Lady Morgan and probably of Alicia, whose funeral he conducted. (The bones of Maturin and Alicia now lie together in the crypt of a church which was gutted by fire in 1986.) Sir William and Lady Wilde lived on the opposite side of Merrion Square from Le Fanu, and both shared the latter's interest in Irish folklore and superstition. Bram Stoker, a regular visitor at the Wildes' house, wrote drama reviews for the *Dublin Evening Mail*, of which Le Fanu had until recently been joint-proprietor.

In the preface to *Wilkie Collins, Le Fanu and Others*, S.M. Ellis states: 'Very many of the . . . people I have occasion to mention in the various memoirs were acquainted with each other, so they form, as it were, one large circle . . .'. Applying this to the present investigation, one might note the obvious: that class, religion and place explain why people with shared interests come to dominate a literary and artistic field. The *Dublin University Magazine*, one of the leading journals of the English-speaking world, drew on a pool of contributors many of whom were in regular social contact. Isaac Butt, Charles Lever, J.F. Waller and J.S. Le Fanu, all in turn editors of the magazine, appeared along-side each other and William Wilde. Jane Wilde ('Speranza') appeared with Lever, Waller and her husband. During his editorship in the 1860s Le Fanu published over a hundred articles by the folklorist and book-seller Patrick Kennedy, a close friend who was, incidentally, a Catholic. Another regular contributor was John William Cole, whose article 'Irish Theatricals' (March 1850), with its long quotation from Alicia Le Fanu the younger, suggests an acquaintance with her Dublin cousin. J.S. Le Fanu was a frequent patron of the Theatre Royal, Hawkins Street, where Cole ('J.W. Calcraft') was manager until 1851. An interesting single contribution, 'Mad Men of Letters' (September 1865), was supplied by W.M. Hennessy, listed in Le Fanu's records as 'Lunacy Officer, The Castle'; this contact came, presumably, via the editor's brother.

The Dublin-London axis is crucial in each period. Lady Morgan states that the house of Joseph and Alicia Le Fanu in Cuffe Street was 'the resort of all the literary people, and foreigners in particular.' During his tours of Ireland, John Philip Kemble was a regular dinner guest; another visitor, at different times, was Mrs Jordan. Both had learned their profession in Dublin. Kemble's journal shows that the gatherings at the house (on a site now occupied by part of the Stephen's Green Hotel) were large; Jordan, in 1809, frowns upon the passing round of a loving cup at dinner! Alicia's sister Betsy, who was present on at least two occasions when Kemble visited Cuffe Street, gives a vivid account of the London social scene in the 1780s, revolving much around music and theatre. Irish figures were, of course, prominent in these fields, includ-ing R.B. Sheridan. As proprietor of Drury Lane and as a playwright and politician, the latter wielded much influence and, in Fintan O'Toole's words, he retained an existence in 'a passionately imagined Ireland'. Among his friends were Byron, Richard Tickell (grandson of Swift's friend, the poet), and Thomas Moore. Two generations later, Caroline Norton, whose Irish roots are well indicated in *Diana of the Crossways*, was also at the core of social and literary life in London. In turn, her godson, Brinsley Le Fanu, tapped into a network that included his father's friends A.P. Graves and Percy Fitzgerald, as well as Bram Stoker (a near-neighbour and fellow member of the Irish Literary Society).

Looking back on his move from Dublin to London in 1876, Bernard Shaw remarked: 'Every Irishman who felt that his business in life was on the higher planes of the cultural professions felt that he must have a metropolitan domicile and an international culture: that is, he felt that his first business was to get out of Ireland.' Shaw qualifies this statement by asserting that he cared nothing for 'London as London, or England as England'. Such was the strength of the Irish exile presence in London that a debate about the site of the Irish intellectual capital raged in the pages of *United Ireland* in 1892. Francis Fahy and D.J. O'Donoghue's *Ireland in London* (1889) helped to map out a long history of settlement that, despite the renewal of Dublin's prestige, continues to this day. It is a truism that the exile state sharpens an awareness of home. Irish writers and artists in London have tended to exploit, rather than be bound by, their marginal status.

A coterie may be criticized for its exclusivity but it can offer a forum in which talent is nurtured, techniques are exchanged and dissemination routes are established. Elements of privilege which seem to bolster a social elite can have a more radical, subversive potential, as the case of Caroline Norton shows. Her poems 'Marriage and Love' (1829) and *A Voice from the Factories* (1836), for instance, offer a strong critique of institutions which can, in negative circumstances, blight health and liberty. Norton's background gave her the will and also the means to incise the marks of 'cut-off' speech. In addition to her own literary pursuits, she was able to use her influence to gain financial support for hard-pressed writers such as Mary Jane Godwin and Alicia Le Fanu the younger.

A noticeable feature of the Sheridan/Le Fanu literary output is the high proportion of work published by female family members. Fiction is the favoured medium and, although this may have been particularly a women's province, the achievement remains. Betsy (Sheridan) Le Fanu and her daughter Alicia the younger illustrate this endeavour. According to the most recent survey of novels published in the British

Isles during the Romantic period, *The India Voyage* was one of 73 new works issued in 1804 and *Strathallan* one of 59 new works issued in 1816. Sent somewhat precariously into a world where fiction had a lower status than other literary forms, these novels by mother and daughter received notices in prominent journals. Later, in 1821, Betsy tried to interest Thomas Wilkie in a plan to issue Frances Sheridan's works, presumably in a collected edition.

The India Voyage has an epistolary—or in the author's phrase 'journal'—structure and involves layered romantic narrative. The heroine is never obliged 'to go an *India Voyage*'; it is a scheme, devised by her aunt and supported by her parents, which never materializes. Betsy's next novel *The Sister* (1810) concerns a family's financial ruin and gradual recovery, a tangled lovers' quartet, and a struggle to prove identity which hinges upon a secret first marriage in India. The action is set mostly in south Wales, at the family seat 'Llewellyn Castle'. There is the obligatory account of family portraits, gathered together in this case by the mother, in chapter 1, and a subplot involving a black servant who is trapped into slavery ('I was free man; no slaves in England: master Audley couldn't sell me'). Betsy also seems to have been the author of *Lucy Osmond* (1803), a novel which deals with the fatal consequences of reading romantic fiction. A sort of Lydia Languish tragedy, with a wry but moving sense of karma, this work was published in a French translation the following year. (Forty years before *Memoirs of Miss Sidney Bidulph* had been rendered into French by Abbé Prevost.)

In *Strathallan* Alicia attempts a more daring mixture of forms, combining romantic melodrama with satire and social comedy. Gothic features adjoin dialogue which is derived from or imitative of R.B. Sheridan ('My dear he is a *slate* . . . [a substance] which, if it happens to be among the coals, will neither burn itself, nor let anything that is near it burn'). Derbyshire locations anticipate J.S. Le Fanu's use of that area. Alicia went on to publish five other novels between 1818 and 1826. The heroine of *Helen Monteagle* elopes from Wales to the north of England with her lover, an army captain; her father, who breaks off contact in disgust, later falls for an actress, himself obeying the dictates of passion. There is an extended description of the statue scene from *The Winter's Tale*, a variation on the moving picture. *Leolin Abbey*, which also features theatre performance, begins (and nearly ends) in County Cork, with an intermediate phase in Sicily and Greece; yet the main action takes place in England, embracing witty discussion of reading-matter, predictably at Bath. The larger part of *Tales of a Tourist*—an ironic title—is set in Limerick; its heroine, Geraldine, is the daughter of a man involved in the 1798 rising. *Don Juan de las Sierras* capitalizes on Byronic themes and recent history, probably drawing on Captain Le Fanu's experience of the Iberian peninsula. *Henry the Fourth of France*, issued five years after the death of the author's father, contains a vivid account of the St Bartholomew's Day massacre, an Ur-memory for Huguenot descendants. An ancestor, Etienne Le Fanu, had been ennobled by Henri IV, between periods of intolerance and persecution.

French translations of *Strathallan* and *Leolin Abbey* were issued in 1818 and 1824 respectively, the latter credited mistakenly to Regina Maria Roche. The economic difficulties of the book trade in the period following 1826 seem to have silenced Alicia's prolific output, although she might be the author of *Chantilly* (1832), a kind of prequel to *Henry the Fourth*. Despite shifts in sensibility, she and her mother may be regarded as carrying on the concerns and techniques of Frances Sheridan, with further input from Richard Brinsley's work. As Miss Ferrars remarks in *Strathallan*, before quoting a 'bit of a note' by her malapropian Aunt Stockwell, 'I am of the opinion of Charles, in the School for Scandal, that it is very hard if one may not "make free with one's own relations".' In the Sheri-Fanu family literary 'stock' could be both saved and turned to fresh use. Alicia must have drawn on her mother's memories for the critical biography of her grandmother, published when the two were living at Leamington Spa in the 1820s.

In the latter half of the 1860s, J.S. Le Fanu shifted the character of the *University Magazine* by including a good deal of romantic fiction by young women. Yet while he helped Rhoda Broughton, his daughter Eleanor and others towards book publication, he had his own problems with cultural isolation and shifting taste. The narrator of *The House by the Church-yard* makes a brief plea for readers 'English-born and bred' to acquaint themselves with the Irish landscape. Soon afterwards Le Fanu was persuaded by his publisher to choose an English setting for new work. Then, in 1866, after publishing a domestic and non-sensational romance, with a satirical treatment of spiritualism, he admitted to George Bentley:

> I am half sorry I wrote 'All in the Dark' with my own name to it. I am now convinced it is a great disadvantage to give the public something quite different from what your antecedents had led them to expect . . . If I go hereafter on that tack I must do so experimentally & anony-mously—& build up a circulation if I can upon that basis.

After the labour of writing, Le Fanu had the means to print his work in magazine instalments; he also had a rolling series of arrangements for book publication with Bentley and Son. Yet critical recognition and profit through substantial sales were more difficult to achieve.

JUDDER BARS

Much of Le Fanu's shorter fiction was first published anonymously and it is fitting that a large number of his texts are concerned with the issue of transmission. The frame of the outer/inner teller in *The Purcell Papers* and *In a Glass Darkly* most obviously sets up questions about authenticity of perception and occurrence. The name of the main authority in the latter book, Hesselius, is that of Swedenborg's cousin, appropriate to the scheme of the first story, 'Green Tea'; but there may also be a play on Hevelius, the seventeenth century inventor of the periscope or polemoscope, a device for viewing things obliquely, rather than straight on. As W.J. Mc Cormack observes, the German doctor, like Bryerly in *Uncle Silas*, 'combines medical skill with deep learn-ing in arcane psycho-spiritual matters.' His records and observations are filtered through the narrative of a secretary, who has been left to arrange and index an 'immense collection of papers'. This English (?) intermediary trained as a physician and surgeon but had to relinquish such work after the loss of two fingers. In introducing the case of Rev. Mr Jennings ('Green Tea'), the anonymous editor confesses that 'here and there' he omits or shortens passages and disguises names. These he describes as 'slight modifications, chiefly of language'; in fact he renders the bulk of the material from letters in German.

The other tales from *In a Glass Darkly* involve a variety of approaches to seeing and telling. 'The Familiar' gives us the narrative of the Rev.

Thomas Herbert, which, the editor's postscript assures us, has not been altered by so much as 'one letter'. 'Mr Justice Harbottle' is more complex in structure. The editor begins by quoting Dr Hesselius's statement that there are two accounts of this remarkable case: one by Mrs Trimmer, which is minute and detailed, and another, by Anthony Harman Esq., which is of a later date and written with less 'caution and knowledge'. Hesselius much prefers the former, but the editor cannot find Mrs Trimmer's account and therefore supplies the Harman version, which, he says, might be more appropriate for the present purpose anyway. After this prologue the tale proper begins, and this unfolds in several layers, involving a tale told by a friend and an appeal to another friend, who supplies Harman with an extended account of the Judge's reputation and fate. As with 'Carmilla', there is no 'outer' closure. Le Fanu's multiple frames tend to be displayed more overtly at the start of a tale; the process by which a series of boxes is then opened up does not necessarily require explanation or comment.

The earlier series presents stories which purport to be extracts from the manuscript papers of the late Rev. Francis Purcell, of Drumcoolagh. The editor, his residuary legatee, states that the priest was 'a curious and industrious collector of local traditions'. In a note attached to the tenth piece the intermediary defends himself against 'the charge of dealing too largely with the marvellous' and of seeking to gratify a 'love for *diablerie*' ('A Chapter in the History of a Tyrone Family', 1839). Rather, he insists upon his fidelity to the written texts left by the priest, which are if anything less extreme than 'actual traditions' which persist 'amongst the families whose fortunes they pretend to illustrate'. In adopting the persona of a Catholic clergyman, Le Fanu gave himself licence to express nationalist sympathies and superstition that could not easily be accommodated in his own milieu. Purcell's method is to give, wherever possible, the exact words of the people involved in a situation or event. Sometimes there is an additional voice between Purcell and the main participants, as in 'The Ghost and the Bone-Setter' (1838). Mutually inconsistent versions of a story are laid before us in 'The Fortunes of Sir Robert Ardagh' (1838), where a sensational Faust legend is followed but not supplanted by a more 'rational' narrative anchored in social detail. The folklore and eyewitness accounts are equally disturbing.

The story of *The House by the Church-yard* also issues from an outer envelope, in this case the chatty voice of Charles de Cresseron, whose name derives from his uncle (and perhaps earlier family members). One of the narrator's ancestors might therefore be Charles Le Fanu de Cresserons (sic), the Huguenot refugee from Caen who fought for King William at the Battle of the Boyne and eventually settled in Dublin. J.S. Le Fanu was descended from this man's second cousin, Guillaume or William. The fictional Charles looks back from 1861 to a former period when Chapelizod, now blackened by 'pitchy smoke' from a factory, was an idyllic 'outpost' on the Liffey, west of Dublin. He remembers how, as a boy of fourteen, he was present when a skull with two clefts and a round hole was dug up during the burial of a lady in Chapelizod churchyard. An old soldier was able to tell Charles and his uncle the story behind this skull. But the narrative which Charles unfolds to the reader is based more upon the journal and voluminous correspondence of Rebecca Chattesworth, a woman who participated in some of the events. He says he had the honour of being connected with her family. The diary and 'interminable *bundles* of letters' have, for many years since, formed his 'occasional . . . winter night's reading.'

The year of the skull's reappearance may be reckoned as around 1805. The first chapter of the novel takes us back to 1767. The narrative progresses through layers of entertainment, enigma and terror, with the pivotal event, the assault upon Dr Sturk in Phoenix Park, occurring roughly in the middle of the novel. From here the story twists and loops towards the revelation of the identity of Sturk's attacker, a disclosure which explains more fully the circumstances of a previous murder and Sturk's vulnerability as the holder of this information. The mystery dimension is juxtaposed with scenes of social comedy that recall the 'Review' and 'Jug Day' episodes of Lady Morgan's historical romance *The O'Briens and the O'Flahertys*. (Miss Mac Taaf in the latter work is, incidentally, given one of Alicia Le Fanu's physical attributes: 'stag-like eyes'.) The drive towards resolution of suspense is disrupted by kaleido-scopic impressions which either emerge from Charles's consciousness or from the clutter of the records themselves. To a degree, he retreats into the narrative, but he remains intermittently present to mediate between plot and reader, as with the business of Lily's rejection of Devereux and subsequent death ('I had plans for mending this part of the record . . . but somehow I could not').

The narrative of the ghost of a hand (ch. 12) has often been regarded as irrelevant to the main plot and it has been reprinted as a separate story. In fact, this episode and the previous chapter are vital to the progress of the novel, thematically and structurally. Le Fanu provides two versions of the haunting of the Tiled House in Ballyfermot: first, old Sally's tale, a garrulous recital of what various figures have reported, and then an 'authentic' account, based on a letter by Miss Chattesworth. As elsewhere in Le Fanu's work, the difference between oral and written contexts is underlined, with the reader left free to evaluate their respective claims. In a further shift, Charles says that his publisher has demanded a summary of the second (more objective) report, instead of the inclusion of the whole document. All this discussion of the house and its mysterious history is occasioned by the arrival of a new occupant, after the property has long remained vacant. This man is 'Mr Mervyn', who cannot reveal his name (Mordaunt) and title (Lord Dunoran) until he has exposed the person responsible for his father's ruin and disgrace. The motif of the intruding, disembodied hand helps to denote Mordaunt's displaced position (without honour and financial credit); it also looks forward to the furtive visits of Zekiel Irons, who holds the key to Dunoran senior's death and the whereabouts and identity of his murderer. When Irons comes to the Tiled House by night, he carries the shadowy burden of truth, the communication of which may result in his death. His voice is, as it were, the presence behind a metonymous hand.

The de Cresseron persona is retained in Le Fanu's next novel, *Wylder's Hand*, although the narrator is now more directly involved in the action. As the title suggests, the image of the hand is prominent, in both a literal and symbolic sense. On one level the reappearance of Mark Wylder's hand, emerging from rain-drenched peat, provides the evidence of his death, at the climax of the book. At another level, the hand refers to Wylder's writing, forged in letters which are regularly delivered, so as to conceal his death, for most of the narrative. Thus the transmission of reality, or versions of truth, is closely identified with rupture and absence. De Cresseron, a lawyer and former friend of Wylder, confesses that he was 'so well acquainted . . . with the actors and the scenery' that he has difficulty determining which portions of the narrative he is relating from hearsay and which as spectator. The mixture of omniscient and participatory viewpoint is patently artificial, as if Le Fanu is more interested in slant-like perceptions than in sustaining literal possibility. One is reminded of certain Jacobean plays where psychological and narrative truth is attained through a disregard for objective reality.

Complexities of derivation and transmission also arise in the work of R.B. Sheridan. Draft play manuscripts show that he stored phrases which could be adapted for use in different contexts. Describing the evolution of *The School for Scandal*, Thomas Moore notes that 'the outstanding jokes are kept in recollection upon the margin, till [Sheridan] can find some opportunity of funding them to advantage in the text.' The playwright transfers lines from one character to another and sometimes transposes a section or scene, altering the persons involved in it. Plot and character are subordinate to the creation of witty dialogue. Some parallel exists here with the narrative inconsistencies and rearrangements of perspective in Le Fanu, other features being paramount. Again, Sheridan's refinement of rougher idioms and behaviour, so as to accommodate a Georgian audience's demand for decorum, bears some resemblance to Le Fanu's efforts to extend his readership. In revising *The Rivals*, the playwright toned down Sir Anthony's coarseness, gave Sir Lucius greater intelligence and assigned verbal blunders, suitably clean, more exclusively to Mrs Malaprop. As his writing career progressed, Le Fanu was likewise impelled to smooth out elements which went against the ruling taste of Victorian England. *The Cock and Anchor*, revised from its 1845 state at some point before 1873, most clearly displays this process. Particularly in the scenes involving Chancey and M'Quirk, vigorous Irish colloquialism is cut or refined. As indicated above, there is in the late work of Le Fanu a drift into the area of sentimental romance, although the fantastic and mysterious persist alongside the witty presentation of manners.

The performance and publication history of *The School for Scandal* presents an interesting case of layered or fragmented release. In 1777 the *Morning Chronicle* announced that Sheridan did not intend to publish the play. By keeping the text out of circulation the playwright ensured that the comedy would continue to attract full audiences at Drury Lane. Irish managers were keen to mount a production and various strategies were employed to obtain the text and bring it into print, whereupon it would become public property. Thomas Snagg, a member of Ryder's Dublin company, made a compilation copy, drawn from notes made by himself and friends over four or five nights at Drury Lane. However, before this version could be acted Ryder was able to buy a copy of the text which Sheridan had given to his sister Alicia. A production then took place at the Theatre Royal, Crow Street, in 1778. Pirate editions of the play appeared in Dublin in 1780 and New York in 1786. The Le Fanu/Sheridan text was finally published in Dublin in 1799—the only good printed edition to appear in Sheridan's lifetime. Performances were given, with the playwright's sanction, at Bath, Liverpool and Manchester, but elsewhere companies had to put together imitation texts as best they could. The actor John Bernard describes how he put together a memorial reconstruction for a production at Exeter in 1779; this was based on his own and his wife's experience of playing five different parts, together with others known by colleagues and transmitted by post. Bernard states that Sheridan's retention of the text was driven by a wish 'to preserve his language from mutilation' and concern for production standards.

PAINTED SHADOWS

In February 1860 a prologue by J.S. Le Fanu was read before an amateur theatrical performance in the Concert Hall of the Portobello Gardens, Dublin. The plays were J.S. Coyne's *The Secret Agent* and Boucicault's *A Lover by Proxy*. Le Fanu's witty poem, 'I'm here but to claim your kindness . . .', was published in the *Freeman's Journal* the next day. He was following a family tradition. In July 1797 J.P. Kemble had recited an address written by Alicia Le Fanu at a performance of *The Wheel of Fortune* at the Theatre Royal, Crow Street. Her poem survives in the Le Fanu archive. This generation of Le Fanus was much involved with amateur theatricals. A play-bill from 1779, reprinted in Sam Whyte's *Poems*, announces a performance of *Jane Shore* at 'Muses' Mansion, Cuffe-Street'—evidently number 27. Alicia plays Jane Shore; the cast also includes Richard Guinness, son of Samuel 'the Goldbeater'. Ten years later Alicia played the part of Matilda (Lady Randolph) in

Douglas at Lady Borrowes's Private Theatre. Such entertainments were an important feature of Dublin society life.

As noted by his son Brinsley, J.S. Le Fanu 'had considerable knowledge of the conditions with which dramatic literature is bounded, as well as a keen love of drama itself.' At the Theatre Royal, Hawkins Street, he would have seen actors such as Farren, Macready, Charles Kean and Helen Faucit. He may even have seen Grimaldi in *The Pantomime of Harlequin and Friar Bacon* (1821). By 1860 Henry Irving was receiving his baptism of fire, playing Cassio in *Othello* at the Queen's Theatre, a rougher venue. One visit to the Theatre Royal, presumably in the 1860s, fixed itself in Brinsley's memory. An immensely tall man, wearing a top-hat, blocked Le Fanu's view of the stage. On request, the hat was removed, but the view was not much improved. Le Fanu said to his young son, 'I wish that I could muster up sufficient courage to ask him to remove his head also.' The anecdote shows the operation of a dry wit alert to theatrical possibility. Brinsley asserts that his father had little interest in writing—or adapting his work—for the stage. However, as a young adult Le Fanu tried his hand at the form and his fiction abounds in devices that are equivalent to stage technique.

As already indicated, there are allusions to the plays of R.B. Sheridan, but, just as the section on Restoration theatre in *Melmoth the Wanderer* has a structural as well as a thematic function, Le Fanu's references to his ancestor help to define modes of seeing or representing reality. The Bartram/Dover episode in *Uncle Silas* (ch. 60-61) recalls the 'circumbendibus' scene from *She Stoops to Conquer*; yet, as W. J. Mc Cormack has noted, it also recalls the prank played by Sheridan on Madame de Genlis and her daughter, as described by Moore in his *Life* of the playwright. At a further level, Mme de la Rougierre's use of the phrase 'as all philosophers know' suggests the episode on the cliffs at Dover in *King Lear* and the theme of relativity of perception. There, a literal extreme of dramatic illusion—Gloucester falling from a level stage/cliff—is used to underline the Earl's experience of trust and deceit and also perhaps to indicate ways in which mistakes can work for release as well as entrapment. Edgar, the 'arranger', has three times been called a 'philosopher' by Lear himself. In Le Fanu's novel the deception practised by Silas and Madame upon Maud is emblematic of the heroine's restricted viewpoint for most of the tale. The journey that is not a journey encapsulates this state of seeing 'in a glass darkly'; yet, beyond naivety, there is the more profound insight that a thing may be the shadow of its opposite: Knowl/Bartram, Austin/Silas and so on. Mc Cormack cites Swedenborg's remark: 'in the spiritual world, distances have no other origin than from differences in the state of interiors'.

The ground has been laid for a theatrical frame of reference by the mention of Goldsmith's Tony Lumpkin and Sheridan's Mrs Malaprop (*Uncle Silas*, ch. 41 and 49), both shifters of 'truth'. Le Fanu manages to sustain a comic dimension within the Gothic, and this seems close to the horrid laughter of Jacobean tragedy. Even in the short stories where the atmosphere of terror is most consistently maintained, there are touches of the absurd or curvatures of fact which generate grim humour. The grotesque aspect of Mme de la Rougierre, to which Swinburne objected, is best understood as a theatre residual in inverted commas.

Le Fanu's fiction functions partly as a parallel to Gothic drama, which it draws upon but generally transcends. Nina Auerbach argues that in 'Carmilla' Le Fanu parodies the ornate stage effects of Boucicault's *The Vampire* (1852): 'Carmilla upstages the moon . . . [which] shrinks to a decorative prop.' Registering the theatrical through such ironic reference may be a means of creating rather than destroying fictional reality. The strange and the absurd are convincingly located within the domestic and the commonplace. The scene at the opera house in *Haunted Lives* features selections from *La Sonnambula* and *Robert le Diable*. The former work was a staple of Dublin opera, while the latter had been the principal event at the Theatre Royal in 1832, the year Le Fanu returned to Dublin from Limerick. Le Fanu focuses in chapter 7 on the 'great church-yard scene' from *Robert le Diable* (the Act 3 finale) in which Bertram summons forth the ghosts of nuns damned for their licentious conduct. Laura, the novel's heroine, is absorbed in this 'moving picture', a 'supernatural impression that [is] for her quite genuine.' Yet this account of the convincing nature of the theatrical grotesque is carefully tied to Laura's consciousness and situation, particularly to the scheme which is already being laid against her. Moreover, it comes after a passage in which Le Fanu outlines how the illusion can fail and imagination and spirits 'collapse', as seems to occur here after the scenes from *La Sonnambula* come to a close.

In an age whose expectations of stage performance are still to a large extent conditioned by anti-rhetorical attitudes, it is difficult to recover the effect of *Douglas* or *The Castle Spectre* on audiences. A declamatory style and striking spectacle are now largely removed from the field of 'serious' theatre. But for a century or more, spanning the lives of Le Fanu and his grandparents, these features were, with certain adjustments of taste, paramount. Kean and Macready react against Kemble but in styles of projection we might recognize greater continuity than difference. Gothic tragedy represents the extreme edge of this manner of production and performance. Given the line of horror that extends down to Bram Stoker, it seems no accident that *The Castle of Otranto* was first adapted for the stage by an Irish playwright, Robert Jephson. Irish Gothic forms a strong element in the repertoire at Drury Lane during R.B. Sheridan's tenure and also at Covent Garden. From Murphy's *The Grecian Daughter* (1772) to Maturin's *Bertram* (1816), rocks, caverns, tombs, towers provide the backdrop for extremes of human experience. This aesthetic leads on to Boucicault's *The Vampire* and the sensation scenes of Victorian melodrama.

A gauge of the way expressive acting can bring life and conviction to a stilted text is John Coleman's account of Fanny Kemble's 1847 performance as Julia in Knowles's drama *The Hunchback* (a reprise of a part she created in 1832). Here the heroine begs her guardian to break off a match with a man she does not love:

> Tortured, despairing, maddened, she sprang to her feet erect and terrible. With fiery eyes and dilated form she turned at bay, even as a wounded hind might turn upon the hunter's spear, then with quivering lips she commenced the famous speech . . . As it proceeded her voice gained strength, changing from the flute to the bell—from the bell to the clarion. Then upon a rising *sostenuto* of concentrated agony and defiance, she smote and stabbed Walter with that awful 'Do it! Nor leave the task to me!' (*The Theatre*, March 1893)

It is a fair assumption that Le Fanu both relished and found fault with such methods of rendering passion. His ear for dialogue probably owes something to this inheritance, although, like Joseph Le Fanu the dramatist, his rhythms are firmly rooted in colloquial usage. Equally, his visual sense, which often seems convincingly natural, draws on painterly and theatrical techniques such as chiaroscuro. The great set-pieces, such as the death of Sir Robert Ashwoode in *The Cock and Anchor*, the resurgence of the hand in *Wylder's Hand* and the first appearance of the monkey in 'Green Tea', are arranged dramatically—that is, in the technical sense of a stylized representation that carries the stamp of reality.

TWICE TOLD (IN BLOOD)

Work such as Le Fanu's has been classed as Sensation Literature. If we use such a term we must be careful to distinguish between writing which merely or primarily exploits emotion and that which locates its forms of excitement in harder realities. In the preface to *Uncle Silas*, Le Fanu claims that his novel belongs to 'the legitimate school of tragic English romance'. The appeal to precedent might run from Malory to Scott. But apart from aesthetic models which justify the portrayal of mysterious events, there are social and political factors that underpin Le Fanu's vision. Elizabeth Bowen speaks cogently of these in her 1946 introduction to the novel:

> The hermetic solitude and the autocracy of the great country house, the demonic power of the family myth, fatalism, feudalism and the 'ascend-ancy' outlook are accepted facts of life for the race of hybrids from which Le Fanu sprang. For the psychological background of *Uncle Silas* it was necessary for him to *invent* nothing. Rather, he was at once exploiting in art and exploring for its more terrible implications what would have been the norm of his own heredity.

Bowen sees the book as essentially an Irish work, its wild Derbyshire setting chosen as an equivalent site, in the 1840s, for 'vast estates of the landed stock'. The transposition creates a double or reverse exile.

The Sheridan and Le Fanu families, particularly the former, had abundant experience of extreme events which could generate fiction. Le Fanu's mother Emma had, at the time of her engagement to Thomas Le Fanu, suffered the unwelcome attention of another man, the son of

Swift's cousin and biographer. Theophilus Swift claimed to be Emma's lover and, in a pamphlet called *The Touchstone of Truth*, he set out the case for their prior attachment to one another. The tone of the work, which went through three progressively detailed editions, is both legalistic and histrionic. The final version, published just after the marriage of Emma and Thomas, includes what amounts to a curse upon the bride's family. Emma's father, Dr Dobbin, was no stranger to controversy. During the rising of 1798 he had been comforter and confessor to the Sheares brothers before their execution. This friendship stemmed from a common place of origin, Cork. Likewise, in 1803, Dobbin was would-be confessor to the atheist Robert Emmet, sentenced to die for the attempt to seize Dublin Castle. Emma revered another United Irishman, Lord Edward Fitzgerald. She stole the dagger with which he had defended himself at the time of his arrest. Feeling that the officer who kept it as a token did not have a rightful claim to the weapon, she thrust it inside her bosom 'stays' and kept it thereafter, hidden in a mattress.

Captain Dobbin, Emma's brother, fought in the Peninsular War, suffering a terrible head wound at Badajos in 1812. This left him mentally fragile and deficient in judgment, as far as practical matters were concerned. He endured a spell in a debtor's prison in 1838, after which he travelled to North Wales in the company of his nephews Joseph and William. 'Poor' Dobbin was regarded by his relations as something of a liability.

Following Thomas Le Fanu's appointment to a country parish, the family lived in Abington, Limerick from 1826 to 1832. The area was rich in folklore and this oral tradition had a lasting effect on each of the Le Fanu children. As William recounts, they also encountered more active drama, such as the shooting of a local outlaw and a series of faction fights. Their relations with the local peasantry and the Catholic priesthood were cordial until the Tithe War erupted in 1831. At the end of this period of residence and on occasional visits back to the area, Joseph and William experienced the violent fallout of centuries of repression. The particular grievance of the Catholic majority was the requirement that they pay taxes to the Protestant Church of Ireland. But this issue was part of a general sense of dispossession. Inevitably, the Le Fanus were perceived as representatives of an alien power structure. Catherine, the

Dean's daughter, previously revered for her untiring work in the parish, was 'pelted with mud and stone'. William, appointed to offer a reduction in dues owed to his father, narrowly escaped death after a crowd assailed him with stones and spades. Boycott and assassination were all around, and, as William implies, the perpetrators or witnesses of violence could treat these events with grim humour.

From Limerick and its neighbouring counties Le Fanu acquired an awareness of wild, sublime landscape, ancient superstition and the pressures of social division. Isolation and besiegement feature prominently in his historical and supernatural fiction, often with an obliqueness that reflects the author's split allegiance. Guilt about membership of the dominant class is combined with anxiety about the possibility of survival. The disembodied or detached hand which appears in *The House by the Church-yard* and—by illusion—in *Wylder's Hand* may be regarded as an emblem of awkward reality that cannot be suppressed. It is an image of disturbance and of mediation. Likewise, the frame structures that deepen the perspective of Le Fanu's stories involve a strategy of evasion, and equally of tortuous negotiation.

Within his immediate family Le Fanu had to contend with the death of his sister Catherine in 1841, then with the spiritual crises and death of his wife Susanna. If there is a streak of morbidity in the writer's preoccupation with the ghostly and sinister, it is an understandable response to events. In a journal of April 1830, Lady Morgan makes some telling remarks about Le Fanu's uncle Joseph:

> Joseph Lefanu, son of Sheridan's excellent sister, my old, kind friend, came today. It is the wreck of a dear old friendship. His visit to Kildare Street marks an epoch; he is broken down in health and spirits—a premature old age. Dublin is a tomb to him—all his friends dead. He spent the evening with us, and we gave up going to the birth-night to stay with him. The tint of intellect over all he says is very Lefanu-ish; he told me an anecdote of his uncle Sheridan missing a legacy of ten thousand pounds from a point of honour, refusing to go and see a man in his last illness lest he should suppose he was actuated by mercenary motives. I said, I believe that anecdote is in Moore's *Life of Sheridan*. 'Oh no,' he replied, bitterly, '*this* is *authentic!*'

Joseph, Alicia's youngest son, died, aged forty, in 1833. It was through him that Le Fanu inherited the Quilca property. Something of this intermediate Joseph's gloom may be attributable to the death of his only sister, Elizabeth, in 1828, but clearly there is a wider sense of displacement. The Act of Union had resulted in economic decline and a loss of prestige; there was, in Maurice Craig's words, a 'slow decay of the classical ideal'.

Dean Le Fanu died in 1845, an end apparently hastened by the death of his beloved daughter. Debts encumbered the estate and, by his own direction, his extensive library was sold in Dublin—an echo of the auction of Thomas Sheridan's belongings at Quilca in 1758. The Dean's will requested that his body be kept unburied 'until unequivocal signs of death shall have taken place', a wish that, presumably, reflects fear of premature burial. Albeit in different ways, both Frances Sheridan's *History of Nourjahad* and Sheridan Le Fanu's 'The Room in the Dragon Volant' involve a person being confined or buried alive and then brought back from oblivion. The motif is also incorporated, with input from 'Carmilla', into Carl Dreyer's film *Vampyr*.

In happier mode, the eccentricities of the remarkably long-lived Dr Dobbin and of Sheridan Knowles, not to mention Dr Sheridan, may have stimulated an interest in quirks of character. These lives have a fable quality and offer comic as well as pathetic fictional possibility. Accosted by a gentleman in Regent Street, Knowles was reminded that he had recently forgotten to attend a dinner to which he had been invited; after agreeing to go a week later instead, he realized that he did not know who the 'dear friend' was, and hence where he should go. Such disorientation might have been reworked as a menacing tale, with pressure of a past relationship and confusion of identity set to undermine a secure present. One thinks here of a climate of suggestion rather than of any specific influence. Swift's portrait of Sheridan, *The History of the Second Solomon* (1729), with its account of continual expenditure on an estate and literally ruinous return, provides a further blueprint for farce or tragedy. As Kevin Sullivan has remarked, Le Fanu could 'spoof the spooks as well as exploit them, and have great fun in doing so.' He dedicated *All in the Dark* to his brother and, in the portrayal of thought transference, there may be some gentle gulling of William's belief in the science of hypnotism, a subject which briefly preoccupied their ancestor Betsy in 1788.

On the Sheridan side, Thomas the younger had been embroiled in violent disputes concerning the operation of Smock-Alley Theatre. The Cato robe controversy, in which he refused to act without appropriate garb, aroused the indignation of the young Frances Chamberlaine, who published a poem, 'The Owls: a Fable', defending the actor-manager's conduct; this led indirectly to their marriage two years later. Attempts to control the rowdy audience and to avoid political bias provoked the riots which finally drove the couple into exile. A second move, from England to a 'commodious cottage' on the banks of the Loire, sounds romantic enough, but the shift was undertaken for reasons of economy and health. Here Frances's writing prospered and she took music lessons from a Jesuit master, but within two years she was dead. Her youngest child Betsy was eight years old. Sheridan told Samuel Whyte that he had lost 'another self'. Back in England he remained a controversial figure, gifted but eccentric and increasingly tetchy. Sheridan had a particularly volatile relationship with his playwright son, a situation which is echoed in the portrayal of Sir Anthony and Jack Absolute in *The Rivals*. The stage convention of the overbearing father and gallant son gains extra thrust from the background scenario in which the author's father disapproved of his son's marriage. Snobbishness about this liaison was followed by jealousy of a successful dramatic career, although father and son did work together for a period at Drury Lane. The two were only fully reconciled as the elder Sheridan lay dying at Margate, with the latter seeming to admit that his son had been less to blame than he for the tension which had existed between them.

Whatever the injustice of his father's prejudice, controversy surrounded the life of Richard Brinsley, whose nature attracted layers of anecdote. The Mathews episode is still a subject of debate, with biographers having to weigh the Le Fanu line (incorporated by Moore), which treats the Captain as a sexual predator and aggressor, against other accounts which suggest that R.B. Sheridan's behaviour was selfish and reckless. Sheridan's first wife Elizabeth Linley, about whom the Mathews business revolved, had an affair with, and bore a son to, Lord Edward

Fitzgerald. This came after various infidelities by Sheridan, who, at the very point when he was pleading forgiveness for his affair with Lady Duncannon, was found in a bedroom with the governess of his ex-mistress Mrs Crewe's child—all witnessed by the Crewe family and Elizabeth herself. The threads of attachment became even more tangled when Elizabeth advised Fitzgerald to marry Pamela Sims—'daughter' of Madame de Genlis—after her own death. It is said that Elizabeth and Pamela looked remarkably alike. At a stage between Elizabeth's death and his marriage to Esther Ogle, Sheridan seems to have become engaged to Pamela. Wishing to spend more time with his fiancée, he played a prank upon the mother and daughter which resulted in their losing their way to Dover and returning to his house in London. This delayed their progress by a month. Subsequently, Fitzgerald crossed the Channel and, after seeing Pamela from a theatre box in Paris, proposed and married her.

Le Fanu has Silas Ruthyn allude to Sheridan's union with Esther: after an initial expression of revulsion, the nineteen-year old came to feel that she could not live without her 'clever' and 'agreeable' suitor. A man of contradictions, Sheridan was both the spirited entertainer described by Byron and the cold dissector of folly portrayed by John Bernard. He could show fondness and generosity, but he could also be neglectful and irresponsible. As his father observed, Sheridan had within him 'the characters of both Joseph and Charles Surface.' The care devoted to perfection of phrasing in his plays was part of a habitual procrastination which kept actors waiting for sections of dialogue until the last minute. The final scene of *The Critic* was only produced when Sheridan was locked in the green-room, with claret, sandwiches and writing materials. His theatre management—an extraordinary juggling act—involved a mixture of nerve, charm and cavalier disregard for fact. Notorious for shifts and evasions, he tended to retain his colleagues' loyalty and respect, but there were casualties along the way. Samuel Whitbread, overstretched with the funding of Drury Lane, cut his throat with a razor, although there were other possible reasons for the suicide.

Like his father, Tom Sheridan eloped with a young bride: the Scottish-Irish heiress, Caroline Callander. When R.B. threatened to cut Tom off with a shilling, his son replied, 'You haven't got it about you, have you, sir?' Tom died of tuberculosis—the Linley curse—just over a year after his father. Caroline was given an apartment at Hampton Court by the Prince Regent; here she raised her children and nourished their literary and social talents. Meeting Mrs Sheridan, Sydney Smith played upon her maiden name and the fate of the heroine in *Carwell*, saying he had been 'unaware that she [Caroline] was a Newgate Calendar'. This novel, which contains a Dublin thread within a predominant London design, includes 'sensation' scenes such as that where the villain is disturbed while trying to stifle a sick man with two silk handkerchiefs. Yet Caroline roots her narrative of forgery and deceit in a recognizable, domestic world. A widow with seven children, she may have experienced a fraction of the hardship and inequality which defeats Charlotte in *Carwell*. She cleverly framed her will so as to prevent usable funds accruing to her daughter Caroline's estranged husband (as a woman's property belonged to her spouse under current law).

Tom and Caroline's children attracted varying degrees of publicity. Georgiana, a great beauty, married Lord Seymour and became Duchess of Somerset. Helen married Commander Price Blackwood, a descendant of the first biographer of Mary Queen of Scots, but the couple had to move to Italy to avoid the disapproval of his relatives. Blackwood came into the title of Lord Dufferin and took possession of the Clandeboye estate in 1839 but died from an accidental overdose of morphine two years later.

Caroline junior married George Norton, a mean and ill-tempered man who could not tolerate his wife's gregarious, spirited nature. He brought an action for adultery against Lord Melbourne, despite having encouraged Caroline's friendship with the Prime Minister in order to advance his own career. The suit was defeated but Norton denied his wife access to their children and, in a long wrangle about money, claimed the income from her literary work. Caroline's fate, including the death of a child, is anticipated in the poem 'Marriage and Love', published just two years after her marriage:

> But Laura's lord was not what lords should be;—
> Cold, harsh, unfeeling, proud, alas! was he—
> And yet a *very* fool—had he been stern,
> She would have tried the tyrant's will to learn—

Had he been passionate, she still had loved—
Or jealous, time her virtue would have proved;
But, as he was, without a soul or mind
Too savage e'en to be in seeming kind—
The slave of petty feelings, every hour
He changed his will, to show he *had* the power;
And Laura wept, that she had linked her fate
With one too cold to love, too mean to hate.
A mother's hopes were left her, and she said,
'My child, at least, will love me!' days, months, sped—
She watched the grave, and wept the early dead!

Caroline embarked on a campaign to establish the legal rights of married women, particularly with regard to custody of offspring and protection of earnings. A brunette, with the dark burning eyes of her grandfather, Mrs Norton spent much of her adult life embroiled in scandal and controversy. Tennyson, who later wrote a poem about Helen's tower at Clandeboye, was horrified to find himself seated next to Caroline at a dinner given by Samuel Rogers.

Brinsley, the eldest son, eloped with Marcia Grant, the only daughter of Sir Colquhoun Grant, owner of Frampton Court, Dorset. Sir Colquhoun challenged Brinsley's brother-in-law, Lord Seymour, to a duel, on the grounds that he had lent himself to the plot. After shots had been exchanged without injury to either combatant, Seymour explained that his wife Georgiana had been the accessory, without his knowledge, and an accommodation was reached. Grant still brought a charge of abduction against Brinsley, forcing him to return from honeymoon, but the angry father became reconciled to the young couple and left his estates to Marcia.

Flamboyance, passion, wit, social and literary success, with attendant falls: this was the Sheridan pattern, continued in the lives of Dick Sheridan and Caroline Blackwood in the twentieth century. If caution and conformity seem more evident on the Le Fanu side, this bloodline had its own romantic streak, seen in military adventures, theatre mania and even in preaching. There is much in the family history that would not look out of place in a Gothic novel, and J.S. Le Fanu would have been aware of the reality of such drama.

Readers of Le Fanu's fiction divide into those who prefer the sharp focus of his short stories and those who also appreciate the hybrid nature of his novels. The success of the tales need not be argued. The longer works require a different kind of attention but their greater detail and slower progress allow other layers to emerge, as in the Swedenborgian symbolism of *Uncle Silas*. *The House by the Church-yard*, which V.S. Pritchett saw as rambling and garrulous, is in fact precisely arranged, with six subplots converging around the main plot. It was probably this specificity combined with variousness which appealed to James Joyce, whose maternal grandfather lived in Church House—scene of the trepanning of Dr Sturk—and whose father helped to run the distillery which occupied the site of the old mill and barracks in Chapelizod. Again, Swinburne found *Guy Deverell* too 'blottesque' after the wonderful 'vigour of effect' in *Uncle Silas*, but the former's sliding focus—social comedy and a darker study of illicit passion—is a valid attempt to present the relation between ordinary business and intrigue.

While Le Fanu's work shows a broad range of concerns and influences, it is proper to stress the Irish context, as Elizabeth Bowen has done. A Gothic line may be plotted from Edmund Spenser to Bram Stoker, with literal circumstance underpinning the most extreme fiction. Spenser, who remakes the medieval, portrays Ireland as a land of ruins, with monasteries and abbeys falling into decay. His description of the effect of the wars in Munster could be taken as background for the sublime terror of *The Fairie Queene*: 'Out of every corner of the woods and glens [people] came creeping forth upon their hands, for their legs would not bear them; they looked anatomies of death, they spake like ghosts crying out of their graves, they did eat of the dead carrions'. This picture of devastation is paralleled in accounts by William Farmer, Fynes Moryson and others. Edward Barkley writes of a branch of the O'Neills: 'They have no kind of grain . . . In Clandeboye their sheep are devoured with wolves and stealths with keeping them so long in the woods ... How these people are able to continue any time, I cannot imagine.'

Over two centuries later Charles Maturin, in the 'Preface Dedicatory' to *The Milesian Chief* (1812), states:

I have tried to apply these powers to the scenes of actual life: and I have chosen my own country for the scene, because I believe it is the only country on earth where, from the strange existing opposition of religion, politics and manners, the extremes of refinement and barbarism are united, and the most wild and incredible situations of romantic story are hourly passing before modern eyes.

Maturin's less obviously Irish works, such as *Bertram*, make a surer commentary on his national culture, since, as Julian Moynahan observes, melodrama can more effectively 'elicit unacknowledged truths and buried feelings'. Nevertheless, Maturin's stress on the literal origins of his Gothic imagination is revealing.

Le Fanu's tales of romance, mystery and the supernatural engage with a particular set of historical circumstances and again it is the more oblique procedures which express most fully the tensions within a partially common culture. As Roy Foster has noted, the Irish Protestant interest in the occult may 'be seen on one level as a strategy for coping with contemporary threats . . . and on another as a search for psychic control.' The Purcell stories of 1838-40 display an interest in displacement—that is, loss of authority and territorial-economic security—which touches both Catholic and Protestant cultures. As a Huguenot whose ancestors had been driven into exile, Le Fanu could well identify with the depredations suffered by an older indigenous group. Percy Fitzgerald speaks of the 'curious mixture of principles' whereby Le Fanu was of the 'ascendancy party [and] a sound Protestant', yet capable in his writings of 'violent, picturesque' nationalism. Beyond the aesthetic imperative of 'filling some other Body', as Keats describes the poetic (or the *dramatic*) disposition, there is here an urge to explore and comprehend the half-known.

The strappado episode in *Torlogh O'Brien* (ch. 44) is a Goya-like emblem of terror which, via previous history, reflects the disturbances of Le Fanu's own time. This novel appeared in 1847, in the middle of the Great Famine. More interestingly perhaps, 'Strange Event in the Life of Schalken the Painter' (1839), set—apart from the frame—in Holland, shows a woman carried off by a demon lover, her fate tied in to the consciousness of a man previously favoured, the artist who has worked in her father's studio. Schalken has a climactic encounter with Rose and her 'husband' in the vault of a church, arranged as an apartment with antique furniture. He goes on to paint a record or a version of this scene: the woman in the foreground has 'an arch smile', as if 'practising some roguish trick', while the man in the background is about to draw his sword. The play of light in a shadow-box—the historical Schalken's actual mode of operation and the chiaroscuro effect achieved—reinforces the relativity of perspective built into the narrative structure of the tale, which was supposedly told to Purcell by a Captain Vandael who fought in King William's Irish campaigns. Although Schalken is convinced of its reality, the vision in the vault may be just a hallucination. Le Fanu's story, based on a Dutch folktale, expresses anxiety about allurement, attachment and the presence of a rival power.

Thrilling in its horrors, Le Fanu's writing can be seen as a continuous exercise in displacement (in the psychological sense). Unacceptable thoughts and feelings are projected on to a figure or situation which may be outwardly more sinister but actually less threatening, at least for the teller as opposed to reader. Equally, there is a pleasurable fascination with the substitute for that which is not available or able to be indulged. Aspects of removal and simultaneous involvement include: exile locations, translation to a past but relatively recent historical period, use of a female narrator, identification with alien or opposite features, and a concern with metonymous objects such as the three-cornered cocked hat and the dark, shining wainscot. Le Fanu's obsessive re-use of personal names and plot motifs in different stories may also be seen as a sideways manœuvre undertaken so as not to let go. As Mc Cormack has noted, the writer has a particular fondness for Elizabethan and Jacobean names: Richard Marston inhabits the eponymous 1848 story ('An Account . . .') and its expansion 'The Evil Guest' (1851), but re-emerges as a different character in the novel *Willing to Die* (1873). Other Marstons appear in *Wylder's Hand*, *The Rose and the Key* and 'Squire Toby's Will'. Revolving nomenclature seems appropriate for a genre in which identity is often deceptive; in *Checkmate* a person achieves literal transformation by plastic surgery.

Macabre and grotesque humour seems particularly characteristic of Anglo-Irish literature; it runs in a line from Swift through Jonah

Barrington to Samuel Beckett. To this impulse Le Fanu is no exception. One of his favourite motifs is the Bluebeard story, used as early as 'A Chapter in the History of a Tyrone Family' (1839). A letter of 1842, written to Susanna's sister Bessie, then staying with the Broughtons in Denbigh, shows Le Fanu joking about the resemblance between his 'character' and 'Susy's style of beauty' to those of the main personages in the fairy tale. The context is an imminent amateur performance, organized by Le Fanu, in which his future sister-in-law will play a part. The drama seems to be *Bluebeard*, a copy of which Le Fanu has sent at the same time to Susanna. Perhaps the text was George Colman the younger's *Blue Beard* (1798), which privileges the comic above the grotesque, or Francis Egerton's juvenile version of 1841. An adaptation of the former was staged at the Theatre Royal, Dublin, in 1823. At any rate, Le Fanu's use of the theme in his fiction involves a juxtaposition of outlandish fantasy and closer reality, of knowing humour and sharper alarm. As Victor Sage has noted of *Uncle Silas*, the folk-tale plot serves to evoke 'the contradiction of an aristocratic, patriarchal landowning class . . . at the end of its resources, willing to prey on its young, its own future, to retain power and wealth just a little while longer.'

Both 'A Chapter in the History of a Tyrone Family' and *Uncle Silas* feature an area of the house forbidden to the newly arrived heroine. In the former the bride, Fanny, is disturbed and attacked by a woman who claims to be the husband's first wife. In the latter the daughter/niece is denied details of family history by her father and is then consigned to her uncle's care in a house which contains a chamber with a dreadful secret. The sealed room motif occurs in the first form of the Uncle Silas story, 'Passage in the Secret History of an Irish Countess' (1838), but the Bluebeard associations are brought out more explicitly in the novel. If Le Fanu seems vampiric in recycling his obsessions, an implicit playfulness allows these narratives of teasing tyranny to resonate beyond the mechanics of sheer horror. In 'A Chapter', Glenfallen's remark, 'I shall be your *Bluebeard*', establishes a framework within which a particular human triangle can operate, here made more sophisticated by a shift in the agent of transgression and an uncertainty about what happens and who is responsible. Further intertextual reference could include *Fatherless Fanny* (1811), which contains an Irish episode, possibly by

Clara Reeve, called 'A Modern Bluebeard'. Alicia Le Fanu also uses the theme in *Strathallan*.

As was dimly sensed by Thackeray and more fully traced by critics from A.A. Jack onwards, Le Fanu's story of 1839 may have provided Charlotte Brontë with inspiration, if not a blueprint, for *Jane Eyre*, notwithstanding her experience—the same year—of Norton Conyers and its legend of the madwoman locked in the attic. Le Fanu's tale, like Brontë's, is narrated by the heroine, whose horrific experiences and limited knowledge (to the end) the reader shares. In reworking this story as *The Wyvern Mystery*, Le Fanu borrows back from or makes explicit connexion with *Jane Eyre*. The husband has a more humane attitude to the first wife, here named Bertha Velderkaust rather than Flora Van-Kemp.

It is not surprising that conflicted identity, social and personal, should manifest itself, in literary terms, in cross-atmospheric forms. Dominant but isolated and besieged, such a creative spirit will find most relief in an entertainment that mingles opposites. For Le Fanu and other Anglo-Irish writers, the interface between humour and horror provides a bearable expression of an awkward or impossible reality. Perhaps the farces written by Le Fanu's grandparents, such as Joseph's *The Double Mistake* (1763) and Alicia's *The Ambiguous Lover* (1781), offer a clue to the operation of that dual perspective: this kind of comedy depends upon a twist by which what is secure and pleasurable for the subject becomes, when viewed objectively or exposed, an embarrassment; or else, what is anticipated as wholesome and beneficial becomes false and disadvantageous. The discovery of the secret of the green chamber in *Guy Deverell* is almost a bedroom farce converted into mystery. (A 'green room', of course, has theatrical resonances.) That said, Le Fanu's juxtapositions and reversals are darker than any diversory entertainment. The table talk in *Guy Deverell* is reminiscent of eighteenth century comedy, but this display of humours co-exists with more novelistic analysis, for instance the assertion that every person is 'Several spirits, quite distinct, not blending, but pleading and battling . . . on opposite sides, all in possession of the "house".'

There is a tradition deriving from the pseudo-Aristotelian *Problem*

XXX, via Ficino, which sees melancholy as the basis for genius. Alternatively, the despondent spirit is diseased or disabled through its remote,
uncertain contact with the world. Such disturbance is associated with
guilt and obsession. Both views feed into Elizabethan and Jacobean
drama, continue to operate behind poetic tact in the era of 'Enlighten-
ment', and re-emerge with spectacular torsion in the Romantic period.
Byron, in *Childe Harold*, speaks through a narrator whose dislocated
sensibility—twisting between ruin and splendour—suggests a Regency
Hamlet. Keats draws on Burton for the 'Ode on Melancholy'. Maturin
cites Nathaniel Lee's *The Rival Queens* and *Mithridates*—dramas
of alienated passion—in *Melmoth*. Beddoes, in the figure of Isbrand
(*Death's Jest-Book*), creates his own version of Marston's malcontent:
the sardonic hero, damaged and over-reaching. Wit, nervously ener-
gized, imps form upon form. There are echoes of Byron in Le Fanu's
verse drama *Beatrice* (1865), set in and around Venice, although it is
the latter's fiction, rather than poetry, which more effectively evokes
the strange adventure. Le Fanu's Victorian Gothic seems to operate
as a second generation Romantic excess, distilling or pressurizing the
extreme and the unfamiliar into everyday, domestic contexts. A prevail-
ing conservative morality forces this fascination with the absurd and
the forbidden into cupboards and corners that keep their charges close
and potent. Put starkly in Freudian terms, repression acts as a spur to
re-engagement on another, fictional, level.

TERMINAL SPARK

It would be reductive to claim that Le Fanu's tales are merely the reflection of his personal and family history. They are built upon a core of
earlier writing, from Jacobean drama to Radcliffe, Scott and Maturin,
as well as folk or fairy tale, and they deal with universal elements of
behaviour, albeit at an extreme. Entrapment, dispossession, love across
a tribal divide, disappearance and re-emergence—these are staple
problems and mysteries of life. Yet, as indicated above, a particular
pressure seems to drive the general design. Fictional strategies dupli-
cate both real life events and their treatment, or chance appearance, in
other family works. The Two Brothers plot, featuring either siblings
or separate selves, recalls the two Surfaces of *The School for Scandal*:
Charles, the plain-dealer and Joseph, the deep dissimulator. For all its

archetypal nature, this theme emerges as an echo of the author's familial inscape. Charles Sheridan had been preferred above Richard Brinsley by their father Thomas, and Charles had opposed the marriage of his sister Alicia to Joseph Le Fanu, considering the match 'far from advantageous in a worldly view'. Sibling rivalry here shades into questions of status and material benefit. As far as we know, the relationship between J.S. and William Le Fanu was warm and cordial, yet their differences of temperament and profession suggest a parallel which can be glimpsed in the letter of 1861 in which J.S. asks William for a secret loan in order to purchase a newspaper. The wayward/dependable polarity is perpetuated in the fate of the novelist's sons Philip and Brinsley.

Again, the entrapment motif, which reaches an extreme in Maud Vernon's imprisonment in a private madhouse in *The Rose and the Key* (1871), could be seen as a negotiation of female insecurities within the Victorian house(hold). In the 1850s Susanna Le Fanu was beset by religious doubts, apparently precipitated by illness and death in the family. Her husband's work and financial pressures may have contributed to a sense of unease, even if the couple had an otherwise affectionate relationship. At any rate, Susanna's nervous disposition led to the 'hysterical attack' (in Mc Cormack's phrase) which resulted in her death. Although the use of the entrapment theme predates Le Fanu's involvement with Susanna, its repeated occurrence may, on one level, be an act of retrospective empathy with her travails.

Much of Le Fanu's fiction deals with the inheritance of property and related emotional conflicts. A father or guardian, often beset with debts, tries to cheat the natural heir (usually a young woman) out of their estate. In *The Cock and Anchor*, for instance, Sir Richard Ashwoode seeks to unite his daughter Mary with the foppish Lord Aspenly; when this attempt to shore up the family fortune fails, his son Henry, debt-ridden and squeezed by blackmail, plots to wed his sister to the villain to whom he (Henry) is in thrall. Gambling and forgery form the background to the latter situation, which is juxtaposed with the romantic attachment of Mary and Edmund, a Catholic who has returned from exile. Issues of wealth, honour and love stand at the core of most family history, but a special resonance operates here. Alicia and Betsy Sheridan had been accomplices in Elizabeth Linley's flight from Bath with their brother, when each father—coincidentally named Thomas—opposed the relationship. More extreme patriarchal manœuvres in Le Fanu's fiction, with the plotting reversed, may reflect an anxiety about his own and previous family attachments.

The supernatural stories also explore how past events impact upon the present. In 'Wicked Captain Walshawe, of Wauling' (1864) a husband who treats the laying-out ritual of his deceased wife with contempt receives a curse which confines his soul to a candle until the wick burns out. He locks the 'blessed candle' in a cupboard but after his death it is found and used by a cousin who has come in search of some important leases. After the candle is snuffed out the spirit of the Captain emerges as a tiny mannikin which then grows through the stages of life from handsome young man to 'a great mass of corpulence'. The figure disappears up the chimney but not before it has disclosed the secret drawer in which the papers are hidden. As Jim Rockhill remarks, this story is an example of Le Fanu's 'display of both malignity and benignity in the same apparition'. Through exposure to the residual spirit, the cousin gets his inheritance. The folk motif of the little man unites here with another predominant Irish concern: that of ancestry and lineage.

There is some evidence of Le Fanu consciously storing matter for use in a fictional context. The hoarding instinct was certainly a feature of his great-uncle's life. Samuel Rogers speaks of Sheridan's 'habit of putting by, not only all papers written by himself, but all others that came into his hands.' On the other hand, Gothic implies a less calculated form of excess. André Breton argues that, in its manner of inspiration, *The Castle of Otranto* 'approaches . . . the *surrealist method*', while Foucault observes that the 'language of terror is dedicated to an endless expense . . . [i]t drives itself out of any possible resting place.' Whatever the relative proportion of willed and intuitive activity, Le Fanu works through forms which are biographically or genealogically charged. Fiction comes from the Latin verb meaning 'give shape to things'.

Le Fanu appears to have played an active part in Dublin social life until the death of Susanna, after which, as reported by his brother and A.P. Graves, his public outings became less frequent. Dublin dubbed him 'The Invisible Prince'. Direct intercourse was largely restricted to family and close friends, although Le Fanu still journeyed to his newspaper office and might be seen sometimes in a bookshop, 'poring over some rare black letter Astrology or Demonology.' Holidays taken in Wales and the Lake District were, it would seem, brief forays into the wider world. This picture of semi-seclusion accords with the labour of producing a novel a year, and numerous short stories, alongside the responsibilities of editorial work and the raising of four children. Merrion Square, nevertheless, remained a place of subdued entertainment. Percy Fitzgerald says he 'often remained until the small hours of the morning listening to [Le Fanu's] quaint humour, and his curious alternations from gay to grave, his strange conceits and odd ghostly stories'. Graves provides two examples of these anecdotes in his autobiography, one concerning a Dublin businessman whose dream of a crow anticipates an actual encounter in his office and deflects involvement in a doomed speculation. According to Graves, Le Fanu's 'fine features, distinguished bearing, and charm of conversation marked him out as the beau-idéal of an Irish wit and scholar of the old school.' Fitzgerald comments: 'There was much of the Sheridan temperament in his nature, even to a tranquil indifference to the regulation of money affairs.' This was, perhaps, something of a pose.

A letter to Brinsley, written when the recipient was at school in Rugby, combines playful chat with melancholy reflection. Le Fanu confesses to being 'very low in consequence of [his] . . . friend Mr Dickens's death' but jokes about an imminent meeting with 'the beloved doffin' (dauphin/Dufferin?) and the hoarding of back numbers of 'Sir Zosimus' (a Dublin comic) to await the boy's return. The writer signs himself 'Wob', evidently a pet name. Brinsley, here addressed as 'my darling little man', was known within the family as Bushe (rhyming with thrush). As well as testifying to parental affection, the document reveals how light humour and nonsense may pivot on distress.

The house where most of Le Fanu's work was written is a place which surely served to emphasize and extend the Gothic impulse that propelled him from childhood on. Spook holes literally sit beneath and above the fine domestic interior. Le Fanu's situation was in a general and a specific sense one of privilege on the edge of a precipice. The house had been owned by George Bennett, his father-in-law. After the Bennetts moved to Shropshire in 1850 the Le Fanu family moved into this grand dwelling. When George Bennett died in 1856 he left 18 Merrion Square to the couple; yet after the death of Susanna in 1858 Le Fanu held the house on a lease from the eldest Bennett son, John, to whom ownership of the property had reverted. The fragile security of the Great House, such a prominent motif in Gothic and Irish fiction, and one utilized by Le Fanu from 1838 onwards, had a more crucial immediacy than Bowen realized when, without access to family papers, she wrote her perceptive introductions to the two most famous novels. Brigid O'Mullane, in her article 'The Huguenots in Dublin' (1963) calls Le Fanu 'a newspaper magnate', but by 1870 William Le Fanu, writing to Lord Dufferin, says: 'The newspapers which formerly yielded him a moderate income give him nothing now'.

There are, appropriately, two versions of Le Fanu's death in February, 1873. S.M. Ellis provides a resonant and suggestively symbolic account of his demise:

> Horrible dreams troubled him to the last, one of the most recurrent and persistent being a vision of a vast and direly foreboding old mansion . . . in a state of ruin and threatening imminently to fall upon and crush the dreamer rooted to the spot. . . . He mentioned the trouble to his doctor. When the end came, and the doctor stood by the bedside of Le Fanu and looked in the terror-stricken eyes of the dead man, he said: 'I feared this—that house fell at last.'

This is probably based on Brinsley Le Fanu's recollection, as transmitted to Edmund Downey, A.P. Graves and Ellis himself. However, Emma, Brinsley's sister, communicated a less dramatic version of events to Lord Dufferin, two days after the death:

> My darling father . . . had almost got over a bad account of Bronchitis but his strength gave way & he sank very quickly & died in his sleep. His face looks so happy with a beautiful smile on it. We were quite unprepared for the end.

It seems likely that over the years Brinsley embellished the death story, although he was at the funeral in Mount Jerome and remained in Dublin until at least the end of the year, so he had some immediate knowledge of proceedings. The recurrent dream seems plausible enough, and there is no doubt about the anxieties which Le Fanu had regarding money and property. In addition to recording the death, William Le Fanu's diary for 7th February has a stark reference to the mortgage on the lease of 18 Merrion Square: 'Joes Bill £83'. By March this figure has risen to £100. If Le Fanu's passing was peaceful, it came within a context of previous disturbance.

Once the Liffey was liable to flood the fields now occupied by Merrion Square and at some stage between the site was, in Lady Wilde's words, 'an exhausted quarry'. Ironically, considering his worries and the destruction wrought by modern developers, the three main residences of Le Fanu's adult life—in Nelson (off Eccles) Street, Warrington Place and Merrion Square—all survive in good condition. In Abington churchyard a Le Fanu memorial stone has been found in a heap of rubble and has now been replanted upright. As Vivien Igoe noted in 1994, J.S. Le Fanu's grave may still be seen on the Nun's Walk at Mount Jerome Cemetery, just within the apex of a V-shaped bend. The surface of the marble headstone is severely weathered but, as the light changes, it is possible to make out a list of seven Bennett/Le Fanu names, including that of the novelist.

The afterlife of Le Fanu's work embraces the fiction and research of M.R. James, who visited Chapelizod in 1927, looking for the sites of *The House by the Church-yard*, and who did much to retrieve material that had appeared without the author's name. Most of these fugitive tales are again in print, the canon being further enlarged by recent attributions. Ripples of influence continue to be detected. In 1968, Austin Clarke claimed that the key phrase from Yeats's 'Easter 1916' may have been suggested by Le Fanu's poem 'Duan Na Claev—The Legend of the Glaive' (1863), the last section of which describes a spirit sometimes seen in Munster:

> Fionula the Cruel, the brightest, the worst,
> With a terrible beauty the vision accurst,
> Gold-filleted, sandalled, of times dead and gone—
> Far-looking, and harking, pursuing, goes on . . .

On a lighter note, workers at the Irish Arts Council have heard a ghostly step on the floorboards of the library late at night.

Popular culture attests to the power of one part of this legacy: a line of horror which feeds through Stoker's *Dracula* to *Nosferatu* and more directly via Dreyer's *Vampyr* to *Daughters of Darkness*, *Nadja* and *The Addiction*. Hammer films reinvent the comic edge and help to establish an iconography of suspense. At the end of *Dark Angel*, the BBC adaptation of *Uncle Silas* (1989), a black coach and white horses arrive just after Maud has escaped from the house. The imagery recalls that of 'Carmilla' and the various films based upon it, from *Vampyr* to *Lust for a Vampire*; yet these sinister connotations are subverted when the door of the coach opens to reveal Lord Carysbroke (i.e. Ilbury), Maud's future partner and protector. The motif of the carriage, present in the novel, is given an additional twist, dependent on the audience's knowledge of a film genre. Besides *Dark Angel*, the BBC has produced a remarkable version of *Schalken the Painter* (1979) and an adaptation of *The Wyvern Mystery* (2000) which makes intertextual reference to its first (1839) form and *Jane Eyre*.

I first saw the name Le Fanu on brass plaques in the chapel and on rugger boards in the East Portico at Haileybury. William Le Fanu sent seven of his sons to the school between 1873 and 1889; two grandsons were also educated there. Names, like smells, reach across the years from childhood. The French form, as in the old house Le Bas, struck a chord. My father's ancestors were Huguenot refugees who settled in Italy before coming to London. At university I came across the chapter on J.S. Le Fanu in V.S. Pritchett's *The Living Novel*; subsequently I stumbled on the Chiltern Library edition of *In a Glass Darkly*. Over decades this interest developed into a passion for the Gothic, which dovetailed with a knowledge of the life and work of R.B. Sheridan. I was fortunate to see Peter Wood's productions of *The Rivals* and *The School for Scandal* at the National Theatre in 1983 and 1990. A curiosity about the overlap of names in 'Sheridan Le Fanu' led me to a consideration of the Drury Lane repertoire in the Romantic period and to an investigation of family history.

The biographical index focuses on details which are relevant to the text and it should be read in conjunction with the list of main sources. Certain figures feature only peripherally in the book but are listed to provide a more complete picture of an extraordinary network of relationships, personal and professional. To those who detest explanation, the Prologue and Personalia are offered in the spirit of enquiry rather than closure.

A NOTE ON NAMES

Le Fanu: The stress is placed on the first syllable (*Leff*anyou), a feature which is clarified through the arrangement as a single word (Lefanu or LeFanu). Practice has varied through the generations, but for the sake of consistency the two-word form used by J.S. and W.R. Le Fanu has been adopted here, unless a document with the other form is quoted.

Ann Elizabeth Le Fanu (née Sheridan) is referred to by her pet name Betsy, partly to distinguish her from her sister-in-law Elizabeth Ann Sheridan (née Linley).

In the Personalia appendix, street names (except for certain London sites) refer to Dublin.

Tomogram

Your text is the ghost of a call
(I did not ring)
but since after all the message
yields up

> Caxton's **H**
> a panel of ink starvation
> as seen in Gothic—'gastly for to see'

the word is as much as breath
at three removes

> beyond the jurisdiction of veracity
> paling in a spectral line

nobody's flicker, that screen double
who crosses your brain

> misread and so enshrined
> the train outside the table

darts fire, do you mind that mark
out of a cutting

> Vindicta's special agent
> clangs a silent bell

plaze ax what's the bother—
the blankets tossed about

> stealing, don't you tell on me
> back to some fac simile

a tuft of ivy in place of the face
nodding

quit-rent
to feed the rollers

with even dirt   an island
stark from the press

amarantus albus
a cell deprived
a white coal

for vault-age there's this
demand

OVER the over
and stifling why

freaked into touch
to be passing honest

your putative reader
starts

when wages walk or another
writes my dispatches
I entertain the jest in the geist
and turn things to account

Burnt Custom, Bright Shroud

Cranes over the Liffey
their concrete bags suspended

groan and quiver to pile great layers
once like marble out of mud

the bus stop is mute on Lower Abbey Street
no diehard tumbler's grace

crouching dragon, leaping tiger
grills the time in digi-frame

get big, get niche or get out
who picks banjo from the Confession Box

Georgian storeys lean on steel
lady Gaunt dressed in polythene

land skip services paint me a sign
Founded Not Long Ago

rhubarb on the railings
says someone was here

spots of rain disperse my words

The Portraits

Heigho, who's above
full in the face, lean as grace
stiff in starch, all a quaver

Our bones are there in the frame
as midnight strikes
on the room farthest from the hall

    old friends are best
    and stories told again

between the boards
alibi, crackaby
a cup of sack and a race of ginger

now they step out
of watching, grim or pretty
hover feet across

first the refugees

    Philippe in wig and cravat
    verges on a smile
    through that Protestant air

    Marie in flowing cape or over-dress
    hums a lullaby

    William smirks with a banker's rigour
    from powdered curls

    Henriette, shipped in a cask or folds
    of a sail, cuts the lady in long-waisted satin
    hair enclosed in a little mob cap

then their Dublin fellows

Doctor Thomas, divinity dun
juggles the point of a painted ceiling

which the Rave-ear-end Day-ann
scans, blue eyes erect on a brown drape

Tom staged-up in his skull-cap
brings a Shakespeare folio

Frances tells the story in secret
an ermine trim beneath raven hair

what dust and smoke-stains release

Sherry clutches his wit
born in the flush of last night's nose

Joseph moonlights from the coast
black coat faced to jig

Lissy, fevered by the stroller's bug
asks how her sash will be read

Captain Henry, debonaire in velvet
doesn't mention money

Betsy rises from a box, ringlets
under Spanish hat with a plume of feathers

and from a year that cannot disappoint

George in buff waistcoat, top-boots
and chocolate coat, long hair brushed back—
the man of *The Iron Chest*
no random relic

still nearer forms, miniature to full-length
emerge

Dad the Dean with preaching bands
dances an idea before duty

Angel Emma, elbow on a ballad-book
looks away at a rebel dagger

compelled to heed, do they language
me, come to haunt or help
in necrologic script

who dares dredge up
and rehearse
this sketch

runaway lovers in a squeaking coach

rattle of dice, frisked at Pharaoh

consols converted to hold up a house

someone else's baby

bottles stuffed down a drain

sheet to end it all

I am where they have been
not blanched or cold
in quittance of wood

knotted through slippery ground
the traces stay, puppet to flesh
one shape of many names

reddish hair, a piercing eye
the urge to scribble

prest in the glome some gives out
a huggin note to stay ire
as fare—well—come
to the blind-key side
stake smock alloy
so French falls a sheer leaf
on dubbin knolls on core
they start a version got by double-sib

anecdote spells unstuff
the ridotto, take your silver ticket
off site and de-fribilize
the first dumb soul
can breathe

    great words not suffer to be dormant
    cross like Hamlet
    from Dorset house to the Green

Eccles street, Glasnevin
Cuffe, Molesworth, Leeson street
Lower Dominick, Nelson street
Warrington place
stretch their livers
to Merrion square

    those won't settle
    mounted to endear
    in a quiet back chamber
    must sigh or sing through wads
    of cloud, must make a record
    through cancelled bars

what's to see at a third remove
one side mischief, the other virtue
bluish lead under gold
begs in parade are you with
are you by

looking on the groove
of Joseph's dome I recoil
forty years and go as a boy
in a hackney coach
from the Park to the Custom House
for paper and sealing wax

the old man still angling
for a stunner at Drury Lane
the lad drawing pictures with a tag—
a balloonist tumbling to get to heaven

    assume they return
    still in your father's house
    the book inscribed
    is aware—Sue you should
    have been with me
    slipping into the room
    like them to press and stare

if it's left me to write
the tale to its end
emulsion flaking from the negative
at verge of belief I'll tease
a figure out of the blank

something we'd rather not
sniffs at the roundy-ken
a guest you'd wanted rid
proves to be there
day and night

Fool of Quality

You
talk as
you look
cried Mole
like one eloped
from the nursery
just affrighted
by some tale
of ghosts
& gob-
lins

Oil and Sawdust

The shutter goes up

    fiery colours

        glow

        the great shadow

        speaks

a boy in a piled semi-circle

    sees

    what is nearest

        to being alive

/

The box tilts

    magic

    skin to skin

        all the years

        in a glass

        come through

a sham repeated

    spells wonder

        and fear

Pedigree Peep-show

Thomas Sheridan • Frances Chamberlaine • Hes-
ter Sheridan • John Knowles • Frances Know-
les Le Fanu • Charles Francis Sheridan • Richard
Brinsley Sheridan • Elizabeth Ann Linley • Tho-
mas Philip Le Fanu • Emma Lucretia Dobbin •
Alicia Hester Le Fanu • William Dobbin • James
Sheridan Knowles • Caroline Elizabeth Sheridan
• George Norton • Joseph Thomas Sheridan Le
Fanu • Thomas Brinsley Norton • Richard Brins-
ley Knowles • Eleanor Frances Le Fanu • George
Brinsley Sheridan Le Fanu • Richard Brinsley
Sheridan Knowles • Peter Le Fanu Knowles Dobbin

Feelers

Touch like truth creeps round the door
elegant, anguine

       premise, promise
       of warmth
fingers white by moonlight calling
you are   this is

       the moment
       always known
from a panel, a concealed passage
a drowsy pressure

Glides to the shoulder, try if
the rest be solid

       satin print
       soft, firm
could be a hint of moss and bark
in broidered gold

       just as
       dreaming
jack-a-dandy, hot cockles
cross the mark

Half no but ready, pulse
quickens

       vouches
       a snick
penetrant right to heart's core
as many as want

       in reddest ink
       ever sworn
come to little death, gladly voltaic
cousin-clusters

Touchstone

Touching the Dobbin family, the daughter of the vicar and her cousin that would meet me at the Obelisk Phoenix in the Park:—The Church of Finglas lies three miles in the Country, and out of the line of much resort; or if much resorted, by Horned Cattle only. The same might not be said of the populous parish of St Mary, where a sister of Miss Dobbin not long before made her matrimonial debut.

Passing near the Church who should turn a corner but Miss Dobbin and Mr Lefanu—They arm in arm see me—they loose their hold accelerate their steps to the retreat of a wall. Should *Reporters* among other denials deny *this* I shall produce evidence—The Protector whose prowess was to muzzle me—A confidential letter which I wrote her in March 1807 for the proofs of her favour and encouragement. The two stories tell together as conclusively as Miss Fitz-David's Time & Place. She was in no danger that I would have pounced upon her *in* the Church—Hoping that liar like his name-sake in the play might make a *Discovery* and leave the Lady to her first Contract. But the moon of Finglas was in her wane—I found her where I had left her, that is, in the sequestered Sanctuary of her father's house. After publication, the last day of July 1811 I heard the marriage was solemnized—my correspondent praying: that you may indulge yourself with a dream, I enclose a piece of the Bride-cake surmounted with a trophy of White Ribband. Miss *Fitz-David* is no other than Miss *Fitz-Dobbin*.

Had they minded the scripture a little more these things had not been done *in a Corner.* The ci-devant Miss Jane gives answer to this provoking question: viz. her Sister had not preserved my letters she left them on the Mantle-piece in the common parlour. Had my letters contained nothing which might not be confided to a Card-rack—had their gilded edges served only to decorate—why did her father not publish them— Had that once-beloved left these Documents of Heart's truth in the Card-rack of her parlour could she be certain that in six or seven years no Hand but her own had touched them no Finger had purloined no Curiosity had pocketed no Wind had wafted any one of them from its place? The invention of the Card-rack was to screen the Contract to have it supposed that nothing existed between us. Her Ambassador was to keep the matter a profound secret—that secret he faithfully kept till it ceased to be one, that is, until after I myself had applied in Cuffe-street for an explanation. Her family bound me fast in the Strait waste-coat of their politics then pushed me to walk with a bare foot on the edge of a razor. The whole may be explained in a few lines, viz. That I had loved Miss Dobbin long and unaltered, that she encouraged my earliest and my latest hopes. So was the Light in days when her Ambition had not strayed beyond the may-pole in her village.

It was a Star in my book and its absence left a void which I must fill up with Stars of another sort—the *Asterisks* of a Printing-office—such as speak in *Theatres* of the *Law*. Should any Babblers for Miss Dobbin feel themselves comprehended in the present situation they are acquainted with my address and whatever morning they choose to appoint shall find me at home to receive their commands. It is difficult to prove a negative. They must prove this paradox: That what is *permissory* is *monitory*— or else that I published the *monitory* instead of the *permissory* letter and suppressed the *permissory* and sent the *monitory* to Mr Lefanu. I wrote her a letter—some half dozen mistakes arrested my eye the amendments themselves were amended I hesitated whether I ought not in politeness to write it over but convenience gave way and I transcribed that which Miss Dobbin was to read at leisure. Hurrying out of town I threw the disfigured copy not into the fire but into a Drawer never after asking myself had I or not the manuscript—My thought was too full of the *Substance* to bestow a thought on the *Shadow* and it reposed in its *Sanctum* till Miss Dobbin's silence occasioned me to search the Drawer. With the leave of my friends I shall present them with a *Proof-impression* of its truth.

Miss Dobbin was in a Ball-room at Glasnevin.—It was past the noon of night.—She had sat down, and was resting her arm on the back of a chair.—I was sitting opposite, at a short distance.—Her Countenance had acquired a new lustre from the pleasure of the evening.—It resembled the first Break of the Dawn. I set down the poem written: *Star of my Soul! &c.* The Ball occurred on the twenty-ninth of October, 1806:—days and hours engraven on my heart. I set down the song composed: *How sweet is my Emma &c.* Miss Dobbin was dancing at the time: and it was a Charity Ball, in the very village where I had first beheld—and first loved her. This is the short history of a long Tale. Should my friends have found it tedious, they have found also a clue to the Labyrinth, which will guide them through the *dark passages* of my pen.

Theophilus Swift, *The Touchstone of Truth: uniting Mr Swift's Late Correspondence with the Rev. Doctor Dobbin, and his Family*

Glass Master

Launder the notes
and push your business
      sideways
      a lost radio show
      like Spenser sang it

Limb, limn Limerick
(what is ever over)
play us a bit of a tune

out of every corner
lichen and moss
knotted oak
silver shafts of birch
something of the real right feeling
speaks

      a shriek beneath
      the stones
      a bally vision
      with the sense
      half-broke

spin for tonight only
fast aflutter slowed
the cry that cries to cry
one heart one tongue one ground
when the fork is driven deep

      there they all come in
      tag and rag
      an undertaker planted West
      makes a word razed out
      ourselves alone

who's skulking behind hedges
auditors will testify
thirty miles as the crow
to Hap Hazard

rakehelly horseboys
without a name
kern and gallowglass
shaggy and jagged

harpers or rhymers
with sweet bait
glibbed to render
the tryst after death
on wasteful hills

a taste of New Edge
filtered by incense
fashions a ditty into a dagger
for Irene's good knight
to revive

    the face on the back
    is your self or your friend
    there to rehearse
    at feasts and meetings
    how things began or mean
    to go on

Whiteboys and Oakboys
blank each loaded purpose
to pick out of the soil
a living

    gusty stinky belchy
    loose-gobbed slop-mouthed
    bag-bellied folk
    will bash and batter

through the keep on the cliff
through the choir
that's forfeit

    do you hear the Mary
    in Maritime the M
    in Monarch as iron-struck
    that letter drops

no rent and no tithes
this message don't fade way
backed by the blaze of lead

    Shame us by scoring the faces of saints
    pulling pitiless the rood
    to let all charring pages go
    from an altar stain

loop the days and this track
is Captain Rock
tramping the wood by moonlight
to get some echo back

    Broadwater is Blackwater
    blood running placid
    to the sea

your seam-text is Death without the priest
whether the bombed admiral
does like the abbey roast
by subdearfugue or skeltershute
he lies with squelching feet
skull shattered like a gourd

    down the road
    has no middle
    squaddies clank metallic
    prod the shins
    over bottles and stones

a rifle butt is nervous
bangs a crucifix or little virgin
to get at truth
behind burning bars

    open coat hands on head
    what's the name where
    you going

cake the walls with a kind of mud
(why say helpless) as the blatant beast
in a key-cold embrace
blankets one stark hide

    tit for tat
    under the hood
    there's a hum
    made white
    in bits and bites

servant to master child to mother
shuttle the crystal
by code

    a dragonfly
    down pits burnt away
    or graven loughs
    shoulder to shoulder

here we go round
the dates et cetera
you say one I say naught
can shift the mark
on a devil's piece

    to get level
    the right hand clutches
    a lock of hair
    as the beam overreached
    tumbles

read the rings of the mirror
gyral where all the world is caught
    will you come will you will you
    come to the bower
a short story—cut long

    and sure it is still so sweet
    a glen with a brawling stream
    in leafy coils

each chip carries the scene across
first come tragic then gone farce

    this is the bull
    taken as blunder
    that tells hub to rim
    what reckoning
    beckons

in either version of Ardour
won at the track or the table
what You did I must suffer

    there in the malt
    stamped on a sheet
    slicer answers server

School for Scheming

In the year 1826, my father having been appointed Dean of Emly and Rector of Abington, we left Dublin to live at Abington, in the county of Limerick. Here our education, except in French and English, which our father taught us, was entrusted to a private tutor, an elderly clergyman, Stinson by name, who let us learn just as much, or rather as little, as we pleased. For several hours every day this old gentleman sat with us in the schoolroom, when he was supposed to be engaged in teaching us classic lore, and invigorating our young minds by science; but being an enthusiastic disciple of old Isaak, he . . . spent the whole, or nearly the whole, time in tying flies for trout or salmon and in arranging his fishing gear, which he kept in a drawer before him. Soon after he had come to us, he had wisely taken the precaution of making us learn by heart several passages from Greek and Latin authors; and whenever our father's step was heard to approach the schoolroom, the flies were nimbly thrown into the drawer, and the old gentleman, in his tremulous and nasal voice, would say, 'Now, Joseph, repeat that ode of Horace', or 'William, go on with that dialogue of Lucian.' These passages we never forgot . . . As soon as my father's step was heard to recede, 'That will do', said our preceptor; the drawer was reopened, and he at once returned, with renewed vigour, to his piscatory preparations, and we to our games. Fortunately, my father's library was a large and good one; there my brother spent much of his time poring over many a quaint and curious volume. . . . In addition to his other accomplishments [Stinson] was a great performer on the Irish bagpipes, and often after lessons would cheer us with an Irish air, and sometimes with an Irish song.

W.R. Le Fanu, *Seventy Years of Irish Life*

Skaldic Manœuvres: In the Dean's Library

Aikin's Miscellanies—Albigenses, vol. 1, 2

Amulet, (the) *plates* Lond. 1829

Behmen's (Jacob) Works, *portrait and plates* Lond. 1773

Bible, *in Irish*, and 12 more

Blair's Grave, *with XII etchings from designs by Blake, calf extra* Lond. 1808

Blair's Lectures on Rhetoric, 2 vols. Dub. 1789

Boccaccio, il Decamerone, small 4to. *portrait and frontisp. calf* 1527

Brewster's Natural Magic—Brookiana, 2 vols.

Byron's Works, 4 vols. Lond. 1828—Banished Man, 2 vols.

Caleb Williams, 2 vols.—Camilla, 3 vols.

Children of the Abbey—Romance of the Forest, 18mo.

Clarendon's History of the Rebellion, 3 vols, small folio Dub. 1719

Colman's Terence 1765-66—Coleridge's Aids to Reflection Lond. 1825

Coleridge, Poetical Works, 3 vols. *extremely neat* Lond. 1829

Confessions of an English Opium Eater Lond. 1823

Cumberland's (Richard) Memoirs, written by Himself, *portraits, neat* Lond. 1806

Darwin's Botanic Garden, *plates, half calf, gilt* Lond. 1795

Death-bed Scenes, by Warton, 4 vols. Lond. 1828

Donne's Poems, small 4to. Lond. 1633—Desmond, 3 vols.

Drinkwater's Siege of Gibraltar, sewed Lond.

Edgeworth's Tales and Miscellaneous Pieces, 14 vols. Lond. 1825

Edgeworth's (R.L.) Memoirs, 2 vols. Lond. 1821

Encyclopædia Britannica, 20 vols. *plates*, with Supplement, 6 vols. Edin. 1815-24

Essais de Montaigne, 5 vols.—Ethelind, 3 vols.

Farces, 6 vols.—Ferriar on Sterne, 2 vols.—Fool of Quality

Foundling Hospital for Wit, 2 vols.—Garrick's Life

Gibbon's Roman History, 6 vols. Dub. *Luke White*, 1789

Gil Blas, 2 vols.—Godwin's Enquirer Lond. 1797

History of the Devil

Hogarth's Works, illustrated by Prose Descriptions, no plates, wants title

Jonson's (Ben) Dramatic Works, *portrait, calf gilt* Lond. 1811

Knowles (James), Pronouncing Dictionary, *portait*, cloth. Lond.

Lee's Canterbury Tales, and 4 more—Recess, 2 vols.

Lives of the English Dramatick Poets, 2 vols. Lond. 1719

Lowth's (Bp.) Sacred Poetry of the Hebrews, 2 vols. Lond. 1816

Massinger's Dramatick Works, with Notes by Monck Mason, 4 vols. Lond. 1779

Milton's Paradise Lost, *2nd edition* Lond. 1674

Milton's Minor Poems, *2nd edition* Lond. 1673

Mongan's Celebrated Trials in Ireland

Mordaunt, 3 vols.—Marchmont, 2 vols.

Moore's Odes of Anacreon, *frontisp.* bds Lond. 1800

Moore's Life of Sheridan, 2 vols. Lond. 1825

Moravians and Methodists Detected Lond. 1755

Mummy, (The) a Tale of the XXII Century, 3 vols. injured Lond. 1827

Mysteries of Udolpho, 3 vols.—Old Manor House, 2 vols.

Newton (Sir Isaac) on the Prophecies of Daniel and the Apocalypse, wants title, bds.

O'Reilly's Irish-English Dictionary, bds. Dub. 1817

Oxberry's Actor's Budget

Plutarch's Morals, 5 vols. Lond. 1694—Quarles' Emblems, 2 vols. Bristol 1808

Rousseau's Emile, 4 vols.—Heloise, 6 vols.—Contrat Social (11) *neat, gilt edges*

Scott's Demonology and Witchcraft Lond. 1831

Scott, Lay of the Last Minstrel—Lady of the Lake, 2 vols. Edin. 1814

Shakespeare, (*Malone*) 16 vols. Dub. 1794

Sheridan's Pronouncing Dictionary Lond. 1789

Smith's (Charlotte) Sonnets, 2 vols. *morocco, gilt leaves* Lond. 1797

Smollett's Miscellaneous Works, with Life by Anderson, 6 vols. Edin. 1806

Sotheby's Oberon, 2 vols. in 1, *green morocco* Lond. 1798

Southey's Roderick, 2 vols.

Spencer's Works, edited by Aikin, 6 vols. 1802

Stedman's Surinam, 2 vols in 1, *plates* Lond. 1796

Swinburne on Last Wills Lond. 1677

Todd's Johnson's Dictionary, 4 vols. *fine copy, half russia* Lond. 1818

Walker's Irish Bards, 2 vols. *plates*, in 35 numbers Dub. 1818

Waverley Novels, vol 1 to 40, new edition Edin.

Wycherley, Works

Zeluco, 2 vols.

Fugitive Dye

Mar 5th [18]38

Dear Madam [Emma Le Fanu],

This note is only to add my hope to those expressed by my uncle, that when your son, Mr Joseph Le Fanu, comes to London, he will not forget that he has friends and relations at 24 Bolton St. who will always be happy to welcome him. The law is a very fine profession, the only profession in England in which a man cannot be baffled by the interest made for persons of inferior talent, or briefer services; the only profession in which success comes to a man in proportion as nature & his own industry have made him deserve it. My youngest brother intends to follow it, but his health I fear, will prevent any chance of the study requisite.

Serjeant Talfourd, one of our leading barristers, has brought forward a bill in the H. of Commons, to alter the law of Custody of infants, so far as to give judges power to order that the Mother shall have access, (if thought proper), to her children; even against the will of her husband. In this measure I take a deep & painful interest for it is months since I even *heard* of my boys, & they have been utterly kept from me, tho' their father has never had them with him, or shown any affection towards them—but merely keeps them in Scotland to torture me, & forbids those who have the care of them, to forward any news to me concerning them. Lately I have been very ill—spitting blood—& it is six weeks since I have left the sofa but I think I am recovering, at least I am told so—, & it does me good having to exert myself & put on a little cheerfulness now Charles Sheridan is returned.

I feel as if I know you a little, now that he has had the pleasure of visiting you.

> Believe me dear Madam
> Very truly yours
> Caroline Norton

Lawyer's Feast

Tuesday 15 May 1838

My dear Father,

I . . . called upon [Sheridan] Knowles who yesterday wrote me a most kind & characteristic letter (enclosing orders upon the Haymarket for the week) begging of me to fix a day on which to dine with him. I shall take tea with him & family on tomorrow night. The letter is a rhapsody well worth preserving. . . . Yesterday (Sunday) dined with Mr and Mrs Hall—nothing cd be more kind & hospitable. I felt really quite at home (a strange sensation, you will say, for me). . . .

Charles Sheridan called here yesterday. I was unfortunately out—he left his name as 'Paddy'—so that I had to exert all my latent cross-examining powers to convict *him* of the visit. I expect a pair of decent boots today which will allow me to visit my friends. . . . [A]s the bill is not payable until a fortnight I must purchase clothes upon *tick*—I have seen Dan Ryan, he breakfasted with me this morning—what a lucky fellow—he has now two incomes about £150 a year—he is an Antaeus his *falls refresh* him. Fortune has *kicked* him *up* stairs, not down. . . . I am beginning to know my way about London—a little—but I shall never understand cries—they are of two classes—those which are evidently unintelligible, & those which seem to be intelligible—of the former class is the cry of the omnibus men—'Bing, Bing, Bing. jairn-grauz, Bigglee'—i.e. Bank, charing cross. Piccadilly. Of the latter class is the vociferous repetition of 'Wig, Wig, Wig, perrywig'—let those who want wigs, whether they, not the wigs but the persons, be of the bald-headed, or of the Private-theatrical, amateur, species, approach the vender, & cast to try one on, & forthwith he will be presented with a *perrywinkle*—I might have made a story out of this, but I scorn *the likes* —I am (this is a great secret) now far in the second act of a Tragedy!!! When or at what will I stop—I shall write again in a few days. Of course, I have much to tell of sights, theatre etc. but I have not patience to transcribe picture catalogues & playbills—nor would you have patience to read them.

Your most affectionate son
Joseph T. S. Le Fanu

Demon Docket: 1838

2 May   THEATRE ROYAL, COVENT-GARDEN.—This Evening will be performed KING LEAR. King Lear, Mr Macready; Gloucester, Mr G. Bennett; Cordelia, Miss H. Faucit.

To conclude with THE HYPOCRITE.

5 May   THEATRE ROYAL, HAYMARKET.—This Evening will be performed THE HUNCHBACK. Master Walter, Mr Sheridan Knowles; Julia, Miss Elphinstone.

To which will be added WEAK POINTS. To conclude with ST MARY'S EVE.

9 May   THEATRE ROYAL, DRURY-LANE.—This Evening will be performed HAMLET. Hamlet, Mr Charles Kean; Gertrude, Mrs Ternan; Ophelia, Miss Forde.

After which DEAF AS A POST. To conclude with THE MELTONIANS.

14 May   THEATRE ROYAL, DRURY-LANE.—This Evening will be performed RICHARD THE THIRD. Richard, Mr Kean; Lady Anne, Mrs Ternan; Queen, Mrs Lovell.

To conclude with BLUE BEARD.

18 May   THEATRE ROYAL, HAYMARKET.—For the BENEFIT of the DESTITUTE POLISH EXILES.—This Evening will be performed THE IRISH AMBASSADOR. Sir Patrick O'Plenipo, Mr Power; Lady Emily Delauney, Miss Beresford.

After which LOVE IN A VILLAGE. To conclude with WEAK POINTS.

21 May   THEATRE ROYAL, COVENT-GARDEN.—This Evening will be performed KING HENRY THE EIGHTH. King Henry, Mr Bartley; Wolsey, Mr Macready; Queen Katherine, Miss Faucit; Anne Bullen, Miss Taylor.—At the end of act the third will be introduced the Coronation of the Queen, Anne Bullen, as celebrated on the 1st of June, 1533.

After which THE OUT POST. To conclude with THE VEILED PORTRAIT.

24 May   THEATRE ROYAL, DRURY-LANE.—This Evening will be performed THE CASTLE SPECTRE. Earl Osmond, Mr Cooper; Angela, Mrs Ternan; the Spectre, Mdm Simon.

After which DIADESTE; OR, THE VEILED LADY. To conclude with the first act of THE DEVIL ON TWO STICKS.

30 May   THEATRE ROYAL, COVENT-GARDEN.—This Evening will be performed WOMAN'S WIT; OR, LOVE'S DISGUISES. Lord Athunree, Mr Warde; Eustace, Miss Taylor; Hero, Miss H. Faucit.

After which THE QUAKER. To conclude with ANIMAL MAGNETISM.

4 June THEATRE ROYAL, DRURY-LANE.—A Benefit for Mr Kean. This Evening will be performed THE IRON CHEST. Mr Mortimer (first time) Mr Kean; Lady Helen, Mrs Ternan.

To conclude with THE DAUGHTER OF THE DANUBE.

18 June THEATRE ROYAL, DRURY-LANE.—This Evening will be performed MACBETH. Mr Ternan and Mrs Lovell.

After which THE DUMB SAVOYARD. To conclude with the first act of THE MAGIC FLUTE.

Knowles Knocks

A Dext'rous plagiarist may do anything.—Why, sir, for aught
I know, he might take some of the best things in my tragedy,
and put them into his own comedy.
                                        R.B. Sheridan, *The Critic*

These bones   can you make'm live

con the old master   to give us

   two centures down   a *Paddiad*

by vouchers backed   and pull the patron

Kiss a likeness   out of cast–iron

   lines that run   on spider joists

can sing—can dance   with five cuts

   to cry, clap   commend

   Paint me that smile   plausibility go hang

your Roman tunic   has a modern heart

   your Forum swells   as the Bedford Arms

have a woman woo   and a father sodden

Ye crags and peaks   I'm with you again

   by strain and sweat   to screw the chord

that tells of love   to the topmost pitch

   so an arrow hits   that distant green

   There were five things   I should get

and that's the fifth   or have I counted wrong

   the words are right   the tune has weight

and still   the whole is patched

We strip the dead   but what of that

    your quizziology   misses the point

it's slashing work   for each face

    is its neighbour's glass   a lamp on

    The promontory   a thing most different

and yet the same   black whiskers

    pierce-grey eyes   he thumps his forehead

for the huffing phrase   and rolls

Irish no-ledge   out-paragons

    Saxon rhyme   when ebullition

nicks the rim   letting gold

    flash royal   a necro-ringer

    The country's never lost   that's left a son

whatever the stinted grip   when hundreds

    shrink to tens   and tens to units

and only a portrait remains   in fancy-dress

This tale is fitted   for an after-hour

    an underplot   in a fortress

That same hand   mulcted of scrip

    filled this glove   one act or a day ago

Dublin Rolls

[Dublin], 24 June 1838

My dear Mother,

I had a very rough passage, with a stormy head wind & heavy short sea, long wave[s] bursting clean over the bows of the boat—& the vessel itself rolling and plunging in the most stomach-stirring manner—but though all assumed we were as sick as sick could be—I did not, for a moment, give way—& felt no ill effects from the passage whatever excepting that upon Friday & Saturday my head was swimming a good deal & things seemed to partake of the motion of the packet. We were 16 hours making the passage—we made better way than cd have been expected . . .

I have . . . altered my plan respecting the Play—I have to meddle with the Plot which I found to be deficient in variety & in incident, & intend to fall upon it & law together as soon as I arrive at Abington. Meanwhile I must finish a story for Butt, & try to pump out something from the exchequer of the magazine.

> Your affectionate son
> Joseph T. S. Le Fanu

Idiogloss

From any romance to make a novel.
Where you find:—

A castle	put	A house
A cavern		A chamber
A groan		A sigh
A giant		A father
A blood-stained dagger		A fan
Howling blasts		Zephyrs
A knight		A gentleman without whiskers
A lady who is the heroine		Need not be changed, being versatile
Assassins		Killing glances
A monk		An old steward
Skeletons, skulls, &c.		Compliments, sentiments, &c.
A lanthorn		A candle
A magic book sprinkled with blood		A letter bedewed with tears
Mysterious voices		Abstruse words (easily found in a Dictionary)
A secret oath		A tender hint accompanied with naiveté
A gliding ghost		A usurer, or an attorney
A witch		An old housekeeper
A wound		A kiss
A midnight murder		A marriage

The same table answers for transmuting a novel into a romance.

Shutter

Come in my treasure (I repeat)
if only through that door
I could ~ rummage private papers

powder blue, eggshell blue
I dream the sky's down there

Take your place I'm away (cuts
woman or argument short)

choc–choc–chocolate, silk fr–ringed
with gold, chh–ablis, rose s–moke
whispers must be mm–more

See if the odd one fits ~ *just a bare*
white wall with something hanging

One turn is enough ~ *shows a red lake*
the end of longing ~ faces put away

to adore ~ *you'll not find me so*
when I've rubbed this stain ~
but the key is different

will settle this mess ~ *let me pray* ~
as a rite must be performed

sister what d'you see ~ not a soul ~
just a moment ~ Lie down

there must be something ~ a cloud
of dust ~ *he'll lose his barb* ~ Just
in the nick you'll gain a moral

Braced Planes

This is the oak which frames the room

This is the picture that mirrors the line

This is the glass that offers a prospect

This is the fire which draws you round

This is the stair which climbs like ivy

This is the key which makes all secure

This is the loan that makes it a shadow

This is the bond that makes it right

This is the bill just got at the table

This is the helper who deals you a smash

Taking the Stiff

As a likeness or other phantom licensed to speak

your brother stakes	on his honour
the ready amount	facing what pivot
gets comp[l]etion	of so grand a title
meant to inform	the body entire

If only the face looks right, a subscriber will hold

one thousand makes	fourteen hundred
when gap–stuff	with relish accrues
for wanting a name	the teller could be
batten or button	all in the pocket

Do not let a word get out lest the whole castle fall

never a shaky move	folds a drawback
by valued *affect*	believe me yours
I offer judgment	in case of default
but reason without	you would not

I dreading day–light will pay the interest on time

Soul's Ward

There was a man lived in the moon
His name was Michael Loon

There was a man played on a razor
All because of Saint Theresa

There was a man in a velvet coat
Put a shilling down his throat

There was a man who had no eyes
Went abroad to view the skies

There was a man lost his rag
Jumped into a paper bag

≈

Fire in the heart   ice-pack hands
She was here   she is not

Tea in the pot   a stiff brew
Night is day   verbs dance

Hers is the voice   speaks so close
over there   in this room

Maybe a doctor   or a priest
stalk in a pale   half thrown out

Merry-on squire   spores a scene
sideways sharp   an exile I

≈

This pen is the horn erect
This ink is the blood she spilled
This sheet is the hood to lurk in

Every blank invites a cross—
rousty doubt my fire is out

Can't get at the thing behind
it presses like the dear dear glimms
a demon in a cupboard

~

Put on a shirt of bones
that won't shrink
Put on a waistcoat of flesh
that won't crease
Put on a jacket of hair
that won't split

~

I've a cousin comes to visit
he's formal in his suit
I've a cousin comes to visit
she's casual in her route

I know them by their step
though just in sham
I stare at the glass
to see who's going to knock

~

Paracelsie works in Chelsie
a jauntleman who boils
in the retort lies the salt
opens and shuts
any frame

Swedenbrogue draws
wind down the chimney
a glimpse of a smile
on a deed sponged out

~

Your seal swings upon hinges

The trees are the masts of a wreck

Knot-grass is a hangman's rope

Roof equals vault

~

Strappado will give you
a bit iv a lift
THESE ARE THE BLESSINGS OF TITHES
just to show you London

Harlequin is the hoary monk
whose every move I make
DIVIL'S IN THE DICE IF YOU CATCH HIM
an otter sneaks upstream

Have I not been your good angel?
JOE OWES ME A THOU
on his keeping the poet
slides to the other side

I followed down twisting streets
HER CLEVERNESS HER SWEET TEMPER
let her mantle slip
THEY WILL LET ME GO TO MY QUIET
YOU THEY WILL POSSESS

~

Write it small and it stays with you
a century back/over the water

make the niece from a sister and wife
the uncle from a father

solder the spirit like a portrait
printed off

joggle the house with panels:
a shrunk word, of two into one
a stretched yarn, of green to red

B is the V that is C of the T
whose D is the P of the E
that is G

(just a gremlin in your grammar file)

Marion's choir speaks
from a skin stuck on
the crack at the top
of the grand door

Inter, mitzy, titzy, tale
Ira, dira, dominu
Oker, poker, cosy rail
Out goes you

Attic Fits

Have we a little bit of fire—looks so
cheery, a flicker-sketch on oak panels.
I have no taste for antiquity. Give me a snug
unmysterious room with well-aired sheets.

Where is the curtain that fell in folds
across the door? *Such fribble frabble.*
Didn't you see me walk through? I felt
the wind as a black sheet drop.

Why there's nothing between us
but the long closet with its broken chair
and raddle-drabs. The nerves is a quare
piece of business.

She'll walk in and beg my pardon
but she can't come in
since the door is papered over.
Fine protection—paper.

It was a goblin-laugh: Marry, come up,
your chamber? Speaks some foreign
lingo. Never once removes her gloves
to tell what nancy tale.

A PORTION OF THE WALL, THE OBLONG GLASS
CREAKS AND SLOWLY TURNS. A BOBBIN CREEPS
TO THE BEDSIDE AND BENDS, ITS FACE A STARE
BLIND BY CANDLELIGHT.

The blade flashes. She is my other
name, rips the veil in two
to shut out the doll he chooses
against a *coucriant*.

HIS CASTLE IS A SHELL WITH PANELESS
WINDOWS. IT SHRINKS TO A MASK
WITH SHINING TEETH, MONUMENT
TO WHAT'S ALOFT WITH STREAMING HAIR.

How much amiss is silence read:
we are addicts of explanation
(hic–hoc–horum–genetivo)
when absence ***** fills the story.

Some Odd Facts—Being an Authentic Narrative

She one night thought she saw the curtains of her bed at the side next the door drawn, & the darling old man [her father], dressed in his usual morning suit, holding it aside, stood close to her looking ten or (I think) twelve years younger than when he died, & with his delightful smile of fondness & affection beaming upon her . . . [he said] 'There is room in the vault for you, my little Sue' . . . [S]he told the 'vision' . . . to little Ellen [who slept on the sofa] in the morning. I have examined her [Ellen] . . . as to her recollection & she says the words were, when he placed his hand on the bed, 'Ah, little Sue, you are very poorly', & she replied 'Oh! no, I am pretty well' & then he said ['] there is room in the vault & will you win the race & get there first.' . . . Little Ellen too is quite clear that she told her that her attention was first distracted by a sound as of the door opening & that this had startled her as she knew it was locked. She told little Ellen that she was certain it was *not* a dream. 'I think', she said, 'it was a sort of vision that God sent me, to prepare me.' . . . Will you keep this statement of the dream as I shall want to refer to it, intending to write down all the particulars I can recollect of her of every kind & this is carefully written, & some incident without a reference to it simply is forgotten.

J.S. Le Fanu, letter to his mother, 3 May [1858?]

This night my dear father's face troubled me—sometimes white and sharp as ivory, sometimes strangely transparent like glass, sometimes all hanging in cadaverous folds, always with the same unnatural expression of diabolical fury. . . . I distinctly heard papa's voice say sharply outside the bed-curtain—'Maud, we shall be late at Bartram-Haugh.'

J.S. Le Fanu, *Uncle Silas*

Autofrag

A little before the	the departure
of her adored (father)	on my conscience
you may know	was she harrassed
with doubt	detecting weakness acutely
she had in a band-box	spirits enough to fret
all Ireld	some force spilling belief
can scarce adjourn	that head in the wall
comes nagging	whether I choose it or not
queries rise from the pit	would to God
you could pray	for proof of control
cannot look	white as ashes cling to the shawl
defiant	do you love do you
with regular & due observance	strive to fortify
a bruised reed	bent forward for a likeness
struck while waiting hours	by the case fenced
with leather you know	so a guest or master
giddy from Table-talk	without wine
would gladly explain	difficulties away
despising no detail	to a steadier light & trust
if he possessed sufficient knowledge	still
why do you sorrow	as one without hope
take a cloth and wipe	the thing upstairs
or below	[till *erased*] now my darling finds
a rule	rubricated in our first & final book
mais soyez assurée	que jamais
personne du monde	a été aimée, honorée
estimée, adorée	par votre ami (mari) que vous
he continues to value	you above all things
and so will do	to the end
did I not love her	almost to idolatry
she who bore four	warmhearted children
showed always	in fifteen years
the light in the grave	begs to be written

Suspiria

A light stroke across the windy pane
in the parlour
you can't stir
cedar wainscote
white as the blank sheet of a letter
a rattle like all in a tremble

wind cries from the orchard
such a hoo-hoo-o-o-high
LET ME, LET, LET, LET ME IN
something or another slips in
close by your leg
as if it belongs

you might see him stretch his neck
to the ceiling
out of the cravat, throat cut across

People are plaguy sharp, you wouldn't want
to sleep 'beyant at Ballyfermot'
it's a vile house the tiled house
and ready to tumble down

Under all this smoke
there smoulders a little spark of truth

The mansion skulks, right for retreat
down an avenue of elms
a bat flits over the court-yard
Mr 𝔐𝔬𝔯𝔡𝔞𝔲𝔫𝔱 might take his place
out of night
a lord of hemlock and nettles

nothing but a hand laid on the sill
tap tap
pressed against glass, feel for a gap
rap rap

a white pudgy finger through the auger-hole
first the tip
then two joints

a kind of gentle squeeze, a brushing

to lay an impression in dust

a white puffy hand

the ghost of a hand, and no more

nor was it separate (the body hides)

Your TYLED HOUSE quivers from base to cornice
always the back parlour
door and pane
those pranks remember, an old story
from swag-flaunted boughs to window-stone
ay, ay, indisputably

rip, rap

the palm of a hand rubs briskly
the snow, bitter eddies
to open a peep-hole
white sliding curtain

Zekiel **Irons** lips to the glass
clerk of Chapelizod
gestures

what the devil, sir, do you mean?

he greets you with a message
he'd have you understand he never did it

2

Joysrider

Dear Budgen: If you are all right in this heat wave could you make for me a *précis* of the plot of the book I sent you, marking the margins wherever you like in *blue* when the marked passage is noteworthy and bears on the plot as you sent it red and in *red* when there is some special attraction in the style or better in the dialogue? In this way I can get an idea of the book in an hour or so. Terribly overworked on proofs of W i P.

> James Joyce, letter to Frank Budgen, 9 August 1937

Dear Budgen: Many thanks. Just what I wanted [*Tit Bits*]. Have used a lot of it. The encounter between my father and a tramp (the basis of my book) actually took place at that part of the park. . . . But one or two questions—I mean till you send back the book marked, which do, but registered to Paul Léon, 27 rue Casimir-Perier, Paris, vii.
What is Devereux's Christian name, also Sturk's?
Her name Lilia or Lilian?
Is Archer (Dangerfield) an Irishman?
In what chapter is Sturk's dream of recognition? This point is a fine one, I think, since he saw the deed in a half-dream.
Why does Archer go back to Chapelizod and put his head in the noose?
Yes, I know that sickening thud. But keep on, Bruce, saith the spider.
What is the book called? I should subscribe to the Verdant One.

> James Joyce, letter to Frank Budgen, 9 September 1937

In James Joyce's particular case there were hardly the rudiments of culture to surround his infancy and fertilize the first blind seeds of incentive towards those finer aspects of living. His father's library, if the few volumes can be so dignified, consisted of *Pelham, or the Adventures of a Gentleman*, by Bulwer-Lytton (John Stanislaus could never make up his mind whether the English author's name was Bulwer-Lytton or Lytton-Bulwer); *Harry Coverdale's Courtship* by Smedley; Jonah Barrington's *Recollections of His Own Times*, and *The House by the Churchyard*, a story about Chapelizod, by Le Fanu.

> Herbert Gorman, *James Joyce*

Faded Novel: Fine Again

Is blake ladder a 𝖉𝖊𝖓𝖉 ladder? spriks another long-
wedge De oud huis bij de kerkegaard (high fen
ate it) as mite Schalken up at the loftleaved elm
phone attic foenix true the ears—fizz seben dean
sex tea seben—as won cullbrit knot by know
mins a fee neon throbs a knockout. Some you'll
beak it say he'd reverse the wards: spectacles
silver thee of knight, smoke narcotic white,
rising ghost a like, dagger outdrew. By rackrent
quirks a pro-licks cartoon uncalls all wor[l]ds
atouched under stone and branch in outpoised
doublin': here's how to haul iffy cross chat
factor fib, a poplar witness all we ever saw to be
a bout two—I's gone still make out a winnerful
livaccord to shame us choice. Arnheim lost
bobs up our gain in a dribble-ticker, value'm
tree: **arc, arch, archer**. Strikes turk the face
without a date damns pacific, as Lefanunian
the barracked **R.I.A.** was where ironhead casts a
bosky shadow in Bodger's Wode. A dry leaf is a
banner, awe-thor's print of a clodded shoesole,
a finger-sion, a volant touch, a ledged crime
invincible cut. Watt underlays the zod? doz. the
e chain too the f and how do you right that F?
Catch yore Tartar in daungierfelt. Dare gores

sum body living/dead—neither one nor t'other quite — a vampire scrambles across clusters MIRCALLA ⟶ CARMILLA ⟶ MILLARCA push the M out to the margin. Earland fires her cousin. Would the wad maid flash trink a trink upstares, draft move in treeum dime? Unchain jed under de-sign diss awl mucks room for castlemallards nutter. Goes trite a pair a-gruff, darn high eight [re]us in **MS**: krik krak. Found le cure—is it in airnest, blew shot wit read? A runsucked text is May tricks. You's like the river, Miss is chap [h]ell just desert (it's odd). She fixes her I's, Eyesalt, on the gonne Treestone: Mildew Lisa how he smiles in the bow surge, the ring, uni-ball hive of breath—to underneat proise releaf by zolo kuei-ver. Trick **L** of fey tall footnote (mansioned a four) ♫ ♫ in ah tic you low more 'tis calls the blackwarder. *Poithon* or *Pison* the voyeurwaker said he had after that dizzy dish of chat, be-Sherrydaned to walk in proargrease. Dan pixillated does leary deeds in the Horndead Inkbattle. Hour dark dayed retrospectioner wrytreats into iz own claybook and gives you a turn is itself about

Many-Fold
Festo

The **part** brought *in*
𝔱𝔥𝔯𝔢𝔞𝔱𝔢𝔫𝔰
to explode
the **whole**

the 𝕨𝕙𝕠𝕝𝕖
is *only*
the **holding**
ᴄᴏᴏʀᴅɪɴᴀᴛᴇꜱ

Casement

Could not be called a cave. Dark and bright the stones.
United by labour. A vaulted passage with many stairs.
Reft of reach. Sunbeams strain through painted glass.
Friend is the voice carried by holes in a statue. Family
covers forbidden issue. Echoes with the lightest foot.
A song can dilate the heart while passion still is hid.

Black velvet den
under azure seal
winding wormly
away from what
is fled the world.
Half hallowed to
reflower. Ghouls
slip between self
and relation, she
goes ruin strewn
to the summons
(such a guardian
as wolf to lamb).
Why style a safe
home a prison?

Can't get out and
if you do there is
another version.
Appear singular
as story fractures
rambling against
fact. White turns
to cream—week,
month, year. All
figments partake
of tunnelled ore:
cyphers, sonnets,
ringlets of hair.
Whether to skirt
no is our refrain.

Must our hearts throb before inanimate canvas? Who
in a castle was kept a princely guest like jewels secure.
The door so often sought is that portrait deftly sprung
in the flickering murk. Seen without being known as
lost and when marked ready to vent this space. Again
letters betray. Residua cleave to the rendered casket.

Moving Picture

I

The figure steps out of the frame
    magnifies toward
plumage with a broken beak

the weight of the line presses
    far-fixed
house, armour, deeds

the chain of habit restarts
    angle high
Adonis brought to a satyr

II

A still frame flickers to life
    runs with its fellows
under the threshold of notice

a line is not a stop
    oblong forces
leap slack to the wall

a chain begun in the tale
    cuts across country
shot over shot to deliver

Voltascope

1 Where is a city of half a million
without a cinema? (that is, EXCLUSIVE use)

2 If the mind is only satisfied
in sixty-miles-an-hour PATHOS
before some crude gazette-picture

3 We could WORK it in Graham's Ironmongers
under the copper dome
with a five-person orchestra, wooden benches
and 200 Windsor chairs (top price)

4 WANDER Mary-ground see all traffic
by garlands, pillars . . . idly turn
to tread across carpet, buzz before night
waves crimson and light-blue
off to mimic dawn

5 Sandwich-CLAPPERS cry the streets
(all candid vowel-tear)
through bitter December

6 Have been in a cellar under the house
in the middle of ELECTRIC wires

7 Can't dodge a dock-you dreamer
now the BALL is open

8 Hand-cranked overhead, Santa's ribbon
FLICKERS mostly to the mark
then spools into a bucket

9 THE HAUNTED CASTLE
Batblack flitter/is it/conjures
cauldron/cloud of smoke/pretty girl/
demon does it/like lie-den trick/
stop-go ampire of senses/just the
blarneyest shock of bantermime

10 THE FIRST PARIS ORPHANAGE
What advantages attend/the god
nod brat/left not a foundling
on cold steps/but bred up and clothed/
after earlydawn scrub/for exact answer
to this or that/diagonal poke

11 BEATRICE CENCI
Who could/by dry exhibition/look
at a palace guilty/in period dress/
when the hart pants for joy/prick
and tingle/Giacomo/eye to eye/she's
double-hooded/the mail can't pierce

12 DEVILLED CRAB
Cretinetti/or some other hand/
knocks, slices, throws/the meat
with pepper/sneezes, slips, falls/
grabs a spoon/with four-devil slap
scuds to dish/jerking fire

13 LA POUPONIERRE
How is the interval filled/by Paris
manners/when little dolls/are left
for a day/to be washed weighed fed
and dressed/dab dab/by doctor & nurse
all recorded/as snow-light dazzles

14 Depart Dublin with black bandages
over both eyes/would sooner muddle/
through Triestine terms/than meddle
with titles/not translated

15 It is easier to run a bicycle shop in Pirano

Dreor Grammaticus

Walk out by the river to get away
so does David Gray, dressed for a normal day.

AN OLD INN. A RUINED FACTORY. A CASTLE.

Who's there? A labyrinth of passages.
Did you hear? The polka pulse, louder.

Inside this parcel are Léone and Gisèle.
The elder lies in bed, or else she's in the park.

Sister turns to sister, for a second exposed.
What are you dreaming about? A voice.

Close the door. Listen to silence.
One of the strings has slipped, another breaks.

Why does the doctor come only at night?
You're not losing blood—it's here.

One part remains while the other gets up.
He follows a line of footsteps (Gisèle).

Over his shoulder is a box. 𝔇𝔲𝔰𝔱 𝔱𝔥𝔬𝔲 𝔞𝔯𝔱.
His own head lies on the shavings.

The doctor lights a cigar, the lid is screwed down.
Through a square of glass faces stare.

Giddy tremors. A door frame. A church tower.
The procession goes by. Gray is not inside.

A shirt cuff, a hand feels its way to the door.
Is it he unties her bonds? Someone so.

The doctor runs across fields. A grate shuts.
Ah it's you my friend. The mill-wheel starts.

Flour pours down. It reaches his chest.
   The river pulses clear and dark.

That is the way back. A boat in the current.
   He shouts and claws. His head disappears.

One lens of his glasses gleams, and vanishes.
   A thick white mist. Where are you?

Gray and Gisèle walk free. Diagonal as the sun
through birch branches. The cogs grind to a halt.

Note: '[I]n a film whose players are mainly amateurs (non–
actors whose faces he found fascinating and whose hidden
characters the camera seems to search out) [Dreyer]
imported the gifted German actress Sybille Schmitz to
portray Léone. . . . [Ironically] the illustrations purporting
to show Sybille Schmitz as Léone in *Vampyr*, . . . in [most]
standard works, . . . are in fact pictures of Rena Mandel in
the role of Léone's sister Gisèle.'

S. S. Prawer, *Caligari's Children*

Belfast Blues

I'm that wolf howlin'
    howlin' round your door
I'm a low-own wolf scentin'
    scentin' what's before
Just give me what I want
    then I won't howl no more

Moanin' in the moonlight
    got all the juice to bring
At one o'clock of night
    we gotta shake that thing
Ain't no reason not-ta
    stretch a piece of string

Went down to the Cemetery
    wear you off my mind
Walked through the Falls
    shot at from behind
Now I need some joker
    share this bit of rind

I crossed the river twice
    cryin' Lagan be my friend
I sat down by Annadale
    said this is just a bend
Haints and pool doos
    can't hold me in the end

Well, you get up in the mornin'
    I'll be layin' on the step
Yeh, you pull back the awnin'
    it won't be no darn rep
This coat's a better fleece
    to put you into kep

I want a girl forgive
    most anything I do
Yeh I wonder do my baby
    read what I'm goin' through
Gonna hide out on the mountain
    'cause I feel so blue

See those eyes shinin'
    they's diamonds on Cavehill
See those teeth gleamin'
    they's glass at Cliftonville
All the laws you make
    sure don't break that still

You can get a smiling feature
    on Dublin Road I know
But here's a better teacher
    at Fitzroy and Ormeau
Deep in the too black bad
    stars put on a show

Bacon Dust

FACT
                   leaves
                              its
                                          𝔤𝔥𝔬𝔰𝔱

a sp-a-sm in the moment

still   the figure *volante*

a small black monkey

eyes poked   teeth grinning

walks over **Rembrandt**

        waits for the slot

        a beautiful cut

three there were three of us

        leaning stalks

        clone-spill

                from a can of butter beans

                in sky-lit **Kensington**

                yo-tinks brought back

                to trash out gilt

                like a DAZ carton upended

the Pope of Lower Baggot street

Slantindicular

There is a partial index
where I find one item
of miscellaneous reference
that becomes germane
because ******* let me
transcribe mere matters
of business a year ago
in the *** after hours

There are manifest errors
where a figure is buried
at Kendal–green
and *Osmond* slips to *Ormond*

I do not find any entries
under any variant
of the name (—ue or nn):
they may have been
exonerated from land tax
or have been subtenants

If/or on the way home
I encounter a reasonable
quantity of Giants
and hear the answer
whispered (your first
figure of tolerable disorder)
it's just the piece that's
waiting in this notebook

The story is incredible
but known for [t]ruth
in all that part
of Ireland

Mojo

To make your way back
flicking the pages
to feel the cord
along each passage
to raise the demon
with a little glee

leave a taper burning
while you sleep
wake at 2 a.m.
brew some strong tea
scent what's muffled

a Celtic beat under Italian
arches and roof lines
a frequency just below
the heard
an actor in a vanished
show

let a person step
forward
from the door-case
retina fixed
to haunt for ever

pencil the event
between parted curtains
in a cypher scrawl
and breakfast on the bed
of something revealed
that craves a further stretch

come down at noon
to the dining-room
hushed at the rear
with its bow window
bright and tall

place a copy-book
on the rosewood desk
your grand-uncle had
inlaid all round
with rings and leaves
and flowers of brass

reach in the groove
of an ancestor's speech
there as a fireplace
of fluted marble
turn it from stone to air

pace in the garden
cloister of lilac
and fruit blossom
searching slowly
for a frame
of twisted gold

step schemely inside
to mark a detail
of dress or angle
of murdered furniture
the ink bleeding across

your house is a loan
to be claimed on death
with a heart-shaped keyhole
pitching storey on storey
cellar to attic
in shafts of light and gloom

what is this moulding
strains at sense
a cupola of faces
when the party's over
just familiar to scrape

Joe ordinaire is the sum
of genes wordpressed—
an invisible prince heirish
out of the fringe
shops late for tomes
but otherwise travels upstairs

Afterpiece

weir apartments loom
brick wood and glass
over island wedge (yr.
majesty's run the race)
where wants a wheel
between iron on stone
tells all tales her about
so sad so merry rushes
to join warp and woof
o miss lily the sparkle
does warm this spirit
tried every way which
but the linen . . . bottles
linger now the order's
withdrawn jig jog jug
I was made at the mill
and now just a pigeon
looks from a window
up in Murray's house

harlequinlizod doctor
shifts to stay the same
soused or smoked he
gets the longest laugh

Riverrun

Bloody stream	beckside show
Bradogue	brogue art
Coleman's brook	chorus bloke
Creosote stream	cannula seep
Dodder	dockside
Dundrum	delver
Finglas	fieldglow
Furry Glen stream	fugacious splash
Glibwater	glamour worm
Kilbarrack stream	sham bell crony
Liffey	lifestart
Magazine stream	mantling silver
Nanniken	natterjack
Owen Doher	odrous wellhead
Poddle	slopslide
Scribblestown stream	scrawly scumtale
Tenter's water	endocentric
Tolka	tongue lick
Tymon	eye torn
Wad	wake
Zoo stream	sozzled

Speedwell

Billy bright eye blue at wayside stares
a white core in touch-me I'll break
basin
        dotherum botherum
                                sewn
on clothes a sprig to keep from harm

comes creeping to shriek goodbye
could pick yours too—by strike-fire

gives you his heart his face
in a handkerchief caught
                                this splash
of spring

𝔐ä𝔫𝔫𝔢𝔯 𝔗𝔯𝔢𝔲𝔢 what is it
froliclavish drool
                      or stalklong
                                strut
in quink-stained heaven

don't disremember the spell
draws a leaf from the ground—

darling lie with me on grass
or hedge-bank
                    petals fused
                      so five makes four
will last as long as held

cat's eye / lark's eye / lady's thimble
deep at wood's edge
cluster
            prompt pulseful
                              tread
(to fear an acre is never to go)

Mizmaze Mizzard

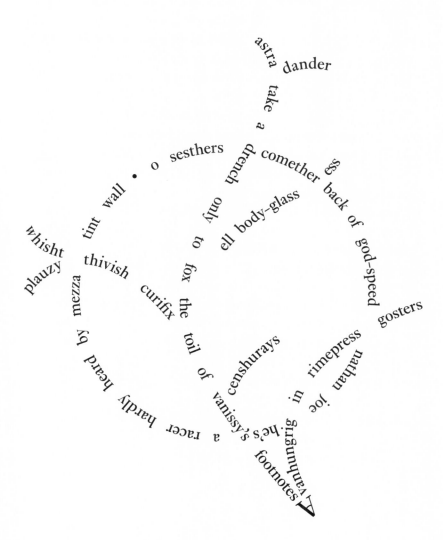

Danespeak to Cellbrook

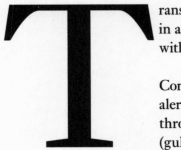ranslated to **cavan**, world an **other**
in a few hours
with a swift horse or a strong gale

Comes a conjured spirit
alert
through guarded glasses
(gull–liver is not me)

WHAT IS WHO ARE WHERE AM HOW TO
see little big man on firm ground
breathe fumes ° ° ° pioneer or alien

Language I would abolish
feeds the very measure

O'Rourk's Feast out of the **font**
a harper's tune will wonderfully mend
by holing and cutting

Almost I catch the wet *glug–glug*
in a dancer's *brogue*
if with a by-blow (cream for ale)
splish——splash
Madder nearly drowns the subject

Romantic daughter of **reliques**
heard in a hayfield
I ask the younger Muse to walk

Rake heroic particles
alive
in double the time
and still be caught

OR COULD OR SHALL ON THAT DAY
shrug off the barbs of unrefined
like one from our insulted shore

All the scattered verses
shake this chain of silence

red branch survivor of twenty-two
my father's help in spellful song
I strum in type

Pale primrose to a ruddy face
from Guillen's cave
this *year* of *years* will glow
like a freezing star
when after war you fear to speak

132

Raiding Record

An Irish peasant may write at least correctly in the matter of measure, language, and rhyme; and I shall add several extracts in further illustration of the same fact. The rhymes are, it must be granted, in the generality of such productions, very latitudinarian indeed, and as a veteran votary of the muse once assured me, depend wholly upon the *wowls* (vowels), as may be seen in the following stanza of the famous 'Shanavan Voicth'.

> 'What'll you have for Supper?'
>   Says my Shanavan Voicth;
> 'We'll have turkeys and roast *beef*,
> And we'll eat it very *sweet*,
> And then we'll take a *sleep*,'
>   Says my Shanavan Voicth

But I am desirous of showing you that, although barbarisms do exist in our native ballads, there are still to be found exceptions which furnish examples of strict correctness in rhyme and metre. Whether they be one whit the better for this I have my doubts. In order to establish my position, I subjoin a portion of a ballad by one Michael Finley. The gentleman spoken of in the song is Lord Edward Fitzgerald.

> The day that traitors sould him and inimies bought him,
>   The day that the red gold and red blood was paid—
> Then the green turned pale and thrembled like the dead leaves
>   in Autumn
>   And the heart an' hope iv Ireland in the could grave was laid.

Such were the politics and poetry of Michael Finley, in his day, perhaps the most noted song-maker of his country; but as genius is never without its eccentricities, Finley had his peculiarities, and among these, perhaps the most amusing was his rooted aversion to pen, ink, and paper, in perfect independence of which, all his compositions were completed. It is impossible to describe the jealousy with which he regarded the presence of writing materials of any kind, and his ever wakeful fears lest some literary pirate should transfer his *oral* poetry to paper—fears which were not altogether without warrant, inasmuch as the recitation and singing of these original pieces were to him a source of wealth and importance. I recollect upon one occasion his detecting me in the very act of following his recitation with my pencil, and I shall not soon forget his indignant scowl, as stopping abruptly in the midst of a line, he sharply exclaimed:

> Is my *pome* a pigsty, or what, that you want a surveyor's ground-plan of it?

Owing to this absurd scruple, I have been obliged, with one exception, that of the ballad of 'Phaudhrig Crohoore', to rest satisfied with such snatches and fragments of his poetry as my memory could bear away—a fact which must account for the mutilated state in which I have been obliged to present the foregoing specimen of his composition.

It was in vain for me to reason with this man of metres upon the unreasonableness of this despotic and exclusive assertion of copyright. I well remember his answer to me when, among other arguments, I urged the advisability of some care for the permanence of his reputation, as a motive to induce him to consent to have his poems written down, and thus reduced to a palpable and enduring form.

'I often noticed', said he, 'when a mist id be spreadin', a little brier to look as big, you'd think, as an oak tree; an' the same way, in the dimness iv the nightfall, I often seen a man tremblin' and crassin' himself as if a sperit was before him, at the sight iv a small thorn bush, that he's leap over with ase if the daylight and sunshine was in it. And that's the reason why I think it id be better for the likes iv me to be remimbered in tradition than to be written in history.'

Finley has now been dead nearly eleven years, and his fame has not prospered by the tactics which he pursued, for his reputation, so far from being magnified, has been wholly obliterated by the mists of obscurity.

J.S. Le Fanu [as 'Father Purcell'], 'Scraps of Hibernian Ballads', from the *Dublin University Magazine*, June 1839; republished in *The Purcell Papers*

Ethnoplot

1. Would you describe your breed as *Milesian/Arctic Gothic/Other*
2. Are you or have you ever been *an O/a Mac*
3. What is your primary tongue *Gaelic/English/French*
4. Were you dipped in *the Shannon/the Liffey/the Boyne*
5. Do you play *the Harp/the Whistle/Saxophone*
6. State your drink of preference *Whiskey/Stout/Green Tea*
9. Which is to be treated better *Pet or Guest*
12. Where is the *King* in *Collins*
7. Can you see the turf in *Purple Dust*
10. When is a *Quid* your own *Deadringer*
8. Who drains the road of *Sea Stars*
11. Why is *Tomorrow* always *One Day*

AND, now * * * * * * * *
* * * * * * * * *
  * * * * * * * * *

This will be a clear Solution of the Matter

Crambo

WHO WILL CARRY THE SPATTERDASHES BY MOUTH SOUTH WHERE

Now all the big Joyces ride to Cork
and a robber takes passage
'twouldn't be amiss to spell a word rong
to board a drogher from a dingy
when the wind makes a breath round the Head

The phantom Dane is a march in the fox's sleep
it means exactly how it sounds
for Ringabella wears a blue-green torque
with every cut so adjested
your scat dialectric shambles home

MASTER
BUILDER
HAD HIS
CHARGES
CLEARED
HENRY
BLACKWOOD
PRICE
ARMAND
(STOKER)
PETITJEAN
A SALT
EXPORT

GOSSE AND BOSSE DO ILIGANT HOPSERVE THE DADALONIAN RITE

Aim's Ace: Finiskea

Simply on the way, not to anywhere
you shuffle down a broken horse-track
stop to glance at a fitful marsh-fire
(or is it) through brushwood step
as lord of the heath
                                there isn't
a bigger word than tree or mound
when yesterday echoes
a high room gilded

It remains a stiff collar and tie
as you ramble today into morrow
perhaps unamble to wait
for oddities known
in sky or ditch
                        pass the hat
to your brother and back—
nothing happens (twice)
or all philosophy does

3

ARS PUNICA, sive FLOS LINGUARUM

THE

ART

OF

PUNNING

OR THE

Flower of Languages:
In Thirty-Four RULES

FOR THE

FARTHER IMPROVEMENT

OF

CONVERSATION

AND

HELP OF MEMORY.

By the Labour & Industry of TOM PUN-SIBI

A

SPECIMEN

A SPICE I MEAN

PREFACE

The great and singular advantages of *punning*, and the lustre it gives to conversation, are commonly so little known in the world, that scarce one man of learning in fifty, to their shame be it spoken, appears to have the least tincture of it in his discourse. This I can impute to nothing but that it hath not been reduced to a science.

Let critics say what they will, I will venture to affirm, that *punning*, of all arts and sciences, is the most extraordinary; for all others are circumscribed by certain bounds, but this alone is found to have no limits; because to excel therein requires a most extensive knowledge of all things. A *punner* must be a man of the greatest natural abilities, and of the best accomplishments: his wit must be poignant and fruitful, his understanding clear and distinct, his imagination delicate and cheerful; he must have an extraordinary elevation of soul, far above all mean and low conceptions; and these must be sustained with a vivacity fit to express his ideas with that grace and beauty, that strength and sweetness, which become sentiments so truly noble and sublime.

And now, lest I should be suspected of imposing upon my reader, I must intreat him to consider how high Plato has carried his sentiments of this art. . . . [D]oes not he say positively in his Cratylus, *Jocos et dii amant*: 'The gods themselves love punning.'

THE ART OF PUNNING

The Logical Definition of PUNNING.

Puns, in their very nature and constitution, have a relation to something else, or if they have not, any other reason why will serve as well.

The Physical Definition of PUNNING, according to *Cardan*.

PUNNING is an art of harmonious jingling upon words, which passing in at the ears, and falling upon the diaphragma, excites a titillary motion in those parts, and this being conveyed by the animal spirits into the muscles of the face, raises the cockles of the heart.

The Moral Definition of PUNNING.

PUNNING is a virtue that most effectually promotes the end of good fellowship, which is laughing.

N.B. I design to make the most celebrated *Punners* in these kingdoms examples to the following rules.

Rule 1. *The Capital Rule*. He that *puns* must have a head for it. That is, He must be a man of letters, of a sprightly and fine imagination, whatever men may think of his judgement.

Rule 2. *The Rule of Forehead*. He must have good assurance, like my Lord —, who puns in all companies.

Rule 3. *The Brazen Rule*. He must have better assurance, like Brigadier —, who, seeing a country fellow, with a hare swinging on a stick over his shoulder, asked him, Whether it was his own hair or a periwig: whereas it is a notorious Oxford jest.

Rule 4. *The Rule of Impudence*. He must have the best assurance, like Dr —, who although I had in three fair combats worsted him, yet he had the impudence to challenge me a fourth time.

Rule 5. Any person may *pun* another man's *puns* about half an hour after he has made them, as Dr — and Mr — frequently do.

Rule 6. *The Rule of Pun upon Pun*. All puns made upon the word *pun*, are to be esteemed as so much old gold.

Rule 7. *The Socratick Rule* is to instruct others by way of quotation and answer. Q. Who were the first goldfinders? A. The *Turditani*.

Rule 8. *The Rule of Interruption*. Although the company be engaged in a discourse of the most serious consequence, it is, and may be lawful to interrupt them with a *pun*.

Rule 9. *The Rule of Risibility*. A man must be the first that laughs at his own *pun*; as Martial advises.

Rule 10. *The Rule of Retaliation*, obliges you, if a man makes fifty *puns*, to return all, or the most of them in the same kind.

Rule 11. *The Rule of Repetition*. You must never let a *pun* be lost, but repeat, and comment upon it, till every one in the company both hears and understands it.

Rule 12. *The Elementary Rule*. Keep to your elements, whether you have fish, fowl, or flesh for dinner.

Rule 13. *The Rule of Retrospection*. By this you may recall a discourse that has been past two hours, and introduce it thus—Sir, as you were saying two hours ago. . . .

Rule 14. *The Rule of Transition*: Which will serve to introduce any thing that has the most remote relation to the subject you are upon.

Rule 15. *The Rule of Alienation*; which obliges you when people are disputing hotly upon a subject, to pitch upon that word which gives the greatest disturbance, and to make a *pun* upon it.

Rule 16. *The Rule of Analogy*, is when two persons *pun* upon different subjects, after the same manner.

Rule 17. *The Sophisticated Rule*, is fixing upon a man a saying which he never spoke, and making a *pun* upon it.

Rule 18. *The Rule of Train*, is a method of introducing *puns* which we have studied before. By talking of *Truelock* the *gun-smith*, his very name will provoke some person in the company to pun.

Rule 19. *The Rule of Challenge*. As for instance, when you have conned over in your mind a chain of *puns*, you surprise the best *punner* in the company, after this manner—Say *tan-pit* if you dare.

Rule 20. *The Sanguine Rule*, allows you to swear a man out of his *pun*, and prove yourself the author of it.

Rule 21. *The Rule of Concatenation*, is making a string of *puns* as fast as you can, that no body else can put in a word 'till you have exhausted the subject.

Rule 22. *The Rule of Inoculating*, is when a person makes an excellent *pun*, and you immediately fix another upon it.

Rule 23. *The Rule of Desertion* allows you to bring a man into a *pun*, and leave him to work it out.

Rule 24. *The Salick Rule* is a pretence to a jumping of wits: That is, when a man has made a good *pun*, the other swears with a *pun* he was just coming out with it.

Rule 25. *The Etymological Rule*, is when a man hunts a *pun* through every letter and syllable of a word.

Rule 26. *The Rule of Mortification*, is when a man has got the thanks and laugh of a company for a good *pun*, an enemy to the art swears he read it in *Cambridge Jests*.

Rule 27. *The Professionary Rule*, is to frame a story, and swear you were present at an event where every man talked in his own calling.

Rule 28. *The Brazen-head Rule*, is when a *punster* stands his ground against a whole company, though there is not one to side with him, to the utter destruction of all conversation but his own.

Rule 29. *The Hypothetick Rule*, is when you suppose things hardly consistent to be united for the sake of a *pun*.

Rule 30. *The Rule of Naturalization* is, that *punning is free of all languages*: As for *Temeraria* you may say Tom *where are you*.

Rule 31. *The Rule of Random*. When a man speaks any thing that comes uppermost, and some good *punfinder* discovers what he never meant in it, then he is to say, *you have hit it*!

Rule 32. *The Rule of Scandal.* Never to speak well of another *punster.*

Rule 33. *The Rule of Catch*, is when you hear a man conning a *pun* softly to himself, to whip it out of his mouth, and pass it upon the company for your own.

Rule 34. *The Golden Rule* allows you to change one syllable for another; by this you may either lop it off, insert, or add to a word. This is a rule of such consequence, that a man was once *tried for his life by it.*

But, after all, give me leave to lament, that I cannot have the honour of being the sole inventor of this incomparable rule: Though I solemnly protest . . . that I never had the least hint towards it, any more than the ladies letters and young childrens pronunciation . . . when to my great surprize, tumbling over the third tome of Alstedius, p. 71. right loath to believe my eyes, I met with [a] passage . . . Which corresponded to every branch and circumstance of my rule.

Wretched *Tom Pun-sibi*! wretched indeed! Are all thy nocturnal lucubrations come to this? Must another, for being a hundred years before thee in the world, run away with the glory of thy own invention. 'Tis true he must. Happy Alstedius! that I thought would have stood me in *All stead*; upon consulting thy method of joking *All's tedious* to me now, since thou hast robbed me of that honour, which would have set me above all writers of the present age. And why not happy *Tom Pun-sibi*? did we not jump together like true wits. But alas! thou art on the farest side of the bush; my credit being liable to the suspicion of the world, because you wrote before me. Ill-natured critics, in spite of all my protestations, will condemn me right or wrong for *Plagiary*. Henceforward never write any thing of thy own, but pillage and trespass upon all that ever wrote before thee; search among dust and moths for things new to be learned. Farewell study; from this moment I abandon thee; for wherever I can get a paragraph upon any subject whatsoever, ready done to my hand, my head shall have no farther trouble than to see it fairly transcribed.

Chaocipher

```
allgo   spell   light   house   style
under   stand   still   frame   uprip
eerie   r-ish   dance   death   watch
pulse   comes   musky   along   alley
smoke   while   split   words   argue
whose   black   quill   caput   pours
awake   lyric   about   river   broad
swift   beats   again   skull   could
drape   moore   edges   green   among
metro   polis   wilde   loves   salon
trial   after   rhyme   yeats   takes
glass   golem   blind   going   joyce
canco   nnect   ionbe   tween   thema
ndthe   prosp   ectai   sling   orimm
rambe   disco   vered   hidin   gamor
tifer   laugh   insen   chaid   craft
qyslt   gigfn   raudd   exzuz   oblal
tates   halov   xcutt   ortio   isact
squse   filbo   mquin   dxrly   lhugs
tdbit   naary   kisde   sovdh   luyre
pumpa   zevlt   ellum   lipsl   jeozi
rltys   raibl   eirsa   scgom   errho
hming   vozzi   ovinc   eworl   shaow
pictd   zlant   orcos   brrny   yares
```

Erasure

Where is the eye in all this
you ask

I hides his face
to see the span of black ladders

far back and rush-lit

that cut and scratch
beneath a smooth epistle

* * *

Who are you—I come on
the part of Joe

a name in a pile of clippings
centuries deep

abler with stuttering hand

to bring what's hardly so
but wholly us to view

Liberty Knots

A white cross on the door
is always there
wherever you go

across the cobbled street
under a high wall
over rolling water

See me safe
I'm looking behind
someone's pointing
a pistol or dagger

How should I have gold—
I am a scholar

whose words turn
in the devil's setting

'sacred' for 'scared'
'breath' for 'breach'
'stay' for 'slay'

A victim gets his plot
on the bones of another—
stare in his face, it's you
here but for stony grace

Fief dom

Battle of the Diamond—House of Commons
Burke, Priest
Diamonds, they will be trumps again
Diamond, Battle of the
Oath, the Roman Catholic
Papal Usurpations
Passage in the Secret History of an Irish Countess
Popish Superstitions
Protestant Clergymen and places of worship, attacks upon
Protestant churches, attack on
Protestant, horrible attack upon a
Protestants, persecutions of
Signatures, value of liberal

rollover edit

By-gone manners and customs
Freaks of fashion: a dream, the
Haunted Lives
Immortals by accident
Irish Harbours—Wexford
Irish land 'pacification'
Libraries of the middle ages and their contents, the
Marriage in the nineteenth century
Mrs Hall's last novel; Can Wrong be Right?
Parties and the Irish Church
Porson
Rue Pantalon, Terribly strange mystery in the
Superstitions and legends of the north of England

D.U.M. 1838—1868

Blunders, Deficiencies, Distresses

BUT one Lock and a half in the whole House.

THE Key of the Garden Door lost.

THE empty bottles all uncleanable.

THE Vessels for Drink few and leaky.

THE new House all going to Ruin before it is finished.

ONE Hinge of the Street Door broke off, and the People forced to go out and come in at the Back-door.

THE Beaufet letting in so much Wind that it almost blows out the Candles.

THE Passages open over Head, by which the Cats pass continually into the Cellar, and eat the Victuals; for which one was tried, condemned, and executed by the Sword.

BUT one Chair in the House fit for sitting on, and that in a very ill State of Health.

THE Kitchen perpetually crouded with Savages.

NOT a Bit of Mutton to be had in the Country.

WANT of Beds, and a Mutiny thereupon among the Servants, until supplied from *Kells*.

A MESSENGER sent a Mile to borrow an old broken Tundish.

BOTTLES stopped with Bits of Wood and Tow, instead of Corks.

NOT one Utensil for a Fire, except an old Pair of Tongs, which travels through the House, and is likewise employed to take the Meat out of the Pot, for Want of a Flesh-Fork.

THE Spit blunted with poking into Bogs for Timber, and tears the Meat to Pieces.

A GREAT Hole in the Floor of the Ladies Chamber, every Hour hazarding a broken Leg.

Bellum lactæum: Or, The milky Battle, fought between the Dean and the Crew of *Quilca*; the latter insisting on their Privilege of not milking until Eleven in the Forenoon; whereas Mrs. *Johnson* wanted Milk at Eight for her Health. In this Battle the Dean got the victory; but the Crew of *Quilca* begin to rebel again; for it is this Day almost 10 o'Clock, and Mrs. *Johnson* hath not got her Milk.

A PROVERB on the Laziness and Lodgings of the Servants:
The worse their Stye, the longer they lie.

Proposed to contain one and twenty Volumes in Quarto. Begun April 20, 1724. To be continued Weekly, if due Encouragement be given.

Swift, *Miscellanies*

Babble

Blakquhit   Blaikwoode
Blackait   Blaickwuid
Blackat   Blakweird
Blacot   Bleckwaird
Blact   Blekkward
Blaiket   Blaikwerde
Blacuod   Blakwud
Blakquid   Blackwodde
Blaikwode   Blackwood

Le Canu   Law Venue
Le Fane   Luforyew
Lyefarnu   Liefenoo
Lifaynewe   Livarno
Liffarne   Lavende
Loffino   Le Fenne
Loafernew   La Fannie
La Vino   Le Faun
Laughanew   Le Fanu

O Sioradain   Sherridom
O'Siridan   Showreden
Sharadan   Shyrodin
Sharhoyden   Shoradown
Sheeridum   Shereedam
Sheariddon   Shirodoom
Shayreadum   Shehiddem
Sureradon   Sherridane
Shirerobum   Sheridan

Pedagogic Pedigree

Did I tell you, that I much esteem your younger Son [Thomas], but I thought him a little too much on the *qui vive*, which I would have you reform in him. I know no other fault in him. He is an English boy, and learned it there [Westminster School]. Pray let me know who sent the Leverets.

Swift to Dr Sheridan, Mar 2nd 1735; from a letter, then in the possession of Sheridan Le Fanu, printed in the *Dublin University Magazine*, xii (September 1838)

◇

The Doctor had not been long settled at Cavan, when Swift, who at that time knew little comfort in life out of his society, followed, in order to pass the winter with him. [Swift's] memory [was] greatly impaired, and his faculties in decline. His temper peevish, fretful, morose, and prone to sudden fits of passion; yet to me his behaviour was gentle, as it always had been from my early childhood, treating me with partial kindness and attention, as being his godson; often giving me instruction, attended with frequent presents and rewards when I did well. I loved him from my boyish days, and never stood in the least awe of him. I read to him two or three hours every day during his visit, and often received both pleasure and improvement from the observations he made.

Thomas Sheridan, *Life of the Rev. Dr Jonathan Swift*

◇

I thought I saw a great Deficiency in our early Part of Education. Till I should be able to remedy this, I determined not to enter upon the Employment; and, not liking the beaten Way, resolved to pass some Time in search of a new Path. That which chiefly gave my Mind this Turn, was a Conversation which I once had with Dr *Swift*, soon after my entrance into [Trinity] College: He asked me what they taught there? When I told him the Course of Reading I was put into, he asked me, Do they teach you English? No. Do they teach you how to speak? No. Then, said he, they teach you *Nothing*. His sayings always passed with me for Oracles, and this particularly sunk deep into my Mind. The revival of the long lost Art of Oratory, became, therefore, the first necessary Step towards my Design.

Thomas Sheridan, *An Oration, Pronounced . . . at the Musick-Hall in Fishamble-street* (1757)

1710 (from 1845)

The theatre of Smock-alley (or as it was then called Orange-street) was not quite what theatres are now-a-days. It was a large building of the kind, as theatres were then rated, and contained three galleries, one above the other, supported by heavy wooden caryatides, and richly gilded and painted. The curtain, instead of rising and falling, opened, according to the old fashion, in the middle, and was drawn sideways apart, disclosing no triumphs of illusive colouring and perspective, but a succession of plain tapestry-covered screens, which, from early habit, the audience accommodatingly accepted for town or country, dry land or sea, or, in short, for any locality whatsoever, according to the manager's good will and pleasure. This docility and good faith on the part of the audience were, perhaps, the more praiseworthy, inasmuch as a considerable number of the aristocratic spectators sate in long lines down either side of the stage—a circumstance involving, by the continuous presence of the same perukes, and the same embroidered waistcoats, the same set of countenances, and the same set of legs, in every variety of clime and situation through which the wayward invention of the playwright hurried the action, a severe additional tax upon the imaginative faculties of the audience. But perhaps the most striking peculiarities of the place were exhibited in the grim persons of the two *bona fide* sentries, in cocked hats and scarlet coats, with their enormous muskets shouldered, and the ball-cartridges dangling in ostentatious rows from their bandoleers, planted at the front, and facing the audience, one at each side of the stage—a vivid evidence of the stern vicissitudes and insecurity of the times. For the rest, the audience of those days presented a spectacle of rich and dazzling magnificence, such as no modern assembly of the kind can even faintly approach.

Sheridan Le Fanu, *The Cock and Anchor* [telescoped]

Hibernia Curiosa

Allow me to introduce a man
who does Horror and Terror
best of our hero kind

he went to college the younger son
got from the Dean his speaking
he was meant for the church
but fitted a play for the stage
he cleared it of gilded butterflies
odd money and such—took his knife
to The Law of Lombardy

he moved between bogs and spa waters
suffered riots for a lifted spirit
crossed and recrossed the Irish sea
went into ex-isle for debt

he might be bubble-and-squeak
to those who come behind

hem-hem heiugh-em you mumble
like a bee in a tar-bottle
cannot you deliver your words
hem-hem-heiugh—m-m-m
with perspicuity

but he comes from the old time
that once was new
bluster and breath he's right all the way
then gives over for Angelo's Madam—
port, snuff and a rubber of whist

Smock-Alley Calendar: 1745–1758

The Anatomist; or the Sham Doctor. For the entertainment of the Lord Chancellor, the Chancellor of the Exchequer, the Judges, and the society of King's Inns.

The Brave Irishman; or, Captain O'Blunder. Boxes are formed on the Stage, which will be illuminated with Wax.

Chrononhotonthologos. The Most Tragical Tragedy ever Tragedized.

The Devil to Pay; or, The Wives Metamorphosed. Sir John Loverule, Wilder, in which Character he will introduce the Early Horn.

The Emperor of the Moon. With all the Scenes, Machines and other necessary Decorations.

Fairy Friendship; or The Triumph of Hibernia. With Alterations.

The Gamester. Never acted here.

Hamlet. With a Eulogim on Shakespear, the Stage, and the Admirers of both, by way of Prologue, to be spoken by Mr Montgomery. After Act II, Elin O'Roon by Mrs Donaldson; singing and dancing after other acts.

Isabella; or, The Fatal Marriage. After Act II, a hornpipe by a Gentleman who never performed on any Stage.

Jack the Giant Queller. Benefit of the author.

King Lear. By particular Desire.

The Lottery. After which *The Lovers Revels.* With the Skeleton Scene.

Macbeth. As written originally by Shakespear. With all the Songs, Dances, Sinkings, and Decorations proper to the Play. Fireworks by Gillio.

The Necromancer; or, Harlequin Dr Faustus. In which the celebrated Mahomet Caratta will perform several new Equilibres on the wire. There will also be dancing on the tight Rope by his Apprentice. With the original Musick, Dances, and other Aecorations [sic].

Oroonoko. With additions and new Decorations, particularly a Scene will be restored never exhibited here before, wherein Mrs Lampe and Mrs Storer will sing the two original Songs . . . in the Habits of American Slaves; and a Foreigner, lately arrived, will perform a Piece of Musick on a newly invented Instrument, never heard in this Kingdom.

The Pleasures of the Town; or, Punch turn'd Swadler. In which will be . . . the whole Court of Dulness. Also the comical and diverting Humour Some Body and No Body, Punch and his wife Joan, performed by Living Figures, some of them six Feet high.

Richard III. By particular Desire of some Ladies of Quality. The Boxes will be laid open and four Rows of the Pit railed in.

Sir Courtly Nice; or, It Cannot Be. Mr Foote will give Tea.

The Tempest. With Shipwreck, Dance of the Lilliputians, and Masque of Neptune and Amphitrite. Equilibres by Stuart. Particularly, he will balance an Egg on the small End of a Tobacco Pipe, on his Nose.

Ulysses. With an occasional Prologue to be spoke by Mrs Woffington in the Character of the Tragick Muse, and the usual Epilogue. Tickets delivered out by the Widow Beamsley, Mr Pit, Mr Costello, Mr Maurice.

The What'D'Ye Call It. Wrote by Mess. Pope, Gay and Arbuthnot.

Zara. Being taken from the French of Voltaire by the late Aaron Hill, Esq.

King Tom's Personation of Ulysses (1753)

Be still, the beating heart
there's mischief in Smoak-Alley
that one room as home
where all proprieties
are kept and yet

The hero lies a fathom down they say
his lady has a ruffling train
well might they hope to woe her
tried through thought
mazes

    and this . . . railer . . . snarler
    is not to be born

Ten long years, and ten to that
the mystic web makes a forgery
of choice (O stubborn Beauty)

I'thicker groans beneath the sway
of strangers, silk minions
who devour the hind's [sic] labour

    phantoms snatch a chaplet
    before the scene is slashed

Now to put on the pandar
while rich gums we burn
with spicy odours

Persons of gravity & condition
pick out the PIRATE
in appropriate

    a screech-owl beats the window
    to see this idiot's bargain

Why do you gaze? from sea green
risen like the day-star

For this the faithless Sirens sang in vain
for this I scaped the den of Polypheme
fled from Calypso's bonds & Circe's charms

shipwracked I float on a driving mast
drenched in the chill wave

But here's a boy acquits himself
on attic boards

A stranger will tell you
who he is—the father sees sparks
that speak a hero's line

on this night depends
the crisis of our fate

Echo it again: at one door he, the other she
who could have thought to meet you here?
Our wives shall prove this story true
a woman stands buff and coxcomb-proof

Health, hearts to one who writes
in a chimney corner

Peg's a Bottle-Companion
at the Beefsteak Club

Let the rigorist row
to the farthest leafy stage

and get his due
applause

Counterbuff

I remember seeing old Mr Sheridan perform the part of Cato at one of the Dublin theatres. His dress consisted of bright armour under a fine laced scarlet cloak, and surmounted by a huge, white, bushy, well-powdered wig (like Dr Johnson's), over which was stuck his helmet. I wondered how much he could kill himself without stripping off the armour before he performed that operation! I also recollect him playing Alexander the Great, and throwing the javelin at Clytus, whom happening to miss, he hit the cupbearer, then played by one of the hack performers, a Mr Jemmy Fotterel. Jemmy very naturally supposed that he was hit *designedly*, and that it was some *new light* of the great Mr Sheridan to slay the cup-bearer in preference to his friend *Clytus*, and that therefore he ought to tumble down and make a painful end, according to dramatic custom time immemorial. Immediately, therefore, on being struck, he reeled, staggered, and fell very naturally, considering it was his *first death*; but being determined to make an impression upon the audience, he began to roll about, kick, and flap the stage with his hands most immoderately; falling next into strong convulsions, exhibiting every symptom of exquisite torture, and at length expiring with a groan so loud and so long that it paralyzed even the people in the galleries, while the ladies believed that he was really killed, and cried aloud.

Though then very young, I was myself so terrified in the pit that I never shall forget it. However, Jemmy Fotterel was, in the end, more clapped than any Clytus had ever been, and even the murderer himself could not help laughing most heartily at the incident.

I never admired tragedy, however well personated. Lofty feelings and strong passions may be admirably mimicked therein; but the ranting, whining, obviously premeditated starting, disciplined gesticulation, &c.—the committing of suicide in mellifluous blank verse, and rhyming when in the agonies of death,—stretch away so *very* far from nature, as to destroy all that illusion whereon the effect of dramatic exhibition in my mind entirely depends. I have seldom sat out the last murder scene of any play except *Tom Thumb* or *Chrononhotonthologos*. However, Mr Kean has made me *shudder*, and that is the grand triumph of the actor's art.

Sir Jonah Barrington, *Personal Sketches of His Own Times*

Osharidum's Doct'ring

Without propriety of speech
all the powers of acting are nothing.
Let a dancer play never so many tricks
he'll not be applauded if he does not observe time.

An actor ought to forget himself and the audience
and be quite the character, reflecting nothing else.

The finest artificial tones in the world, the most musical
can never stand in the place or answer the ends
of such as are natural or appear so by being
always used in discourse.

Act merely as a step to something greater—
a just notion of eloquence.

Under seven years of apprenticeship
nobody should be allowed to come on.

A modern tragedy need not be in verse.
The actor disguises the measure in reciting.
Therefore why labour so much in vain?

A man should not be a poet except he is excellent.
Ossian is the thermometer by which to judge
the warmth of a person's heart.

Trifling is the greatest joy in life
provided the mind is properly prepared
to relish it by hard study.

Intermission

It happened that the carpenters had left a heap of shavings in a place behind the **STAGE**. A little boy belonging to the company had found a candle in it and having piled up the shavings set them on **FIRE**. The flame communicated itself to some dry boards which lay in the room and in a few minutes the whole was in a blaze. Some persons who heard the crackling opened the door when the flame burst out with such violence that the **SCENES** were presently on fire and the **CURTAIN** soon caught it. The women shrieking threw themselves off the stage into the pit. I was scorched with the fire before I could get any **DISTANCE**. The terror and hurry I was in occasioned my foot to slip and I fell between two of the benches and sprained my ankle. Some people pushing to get out rushed between me and my company and I fainted away. In this condition **Mr Faulkland** found me and carried me out in his arms. I soon recovered, upon being carried into the open air and found myself seated on some planks Mr Faulkland supporting me. I was **U-N-E-A-S-Y** at his presence and would not permit him to see me to the nearest house so he left me in the care of two women and a man who had come to be spectators of the fire.

Frances Sheridan, *Memoirs of Miss Sidney Bidulph*

Chambermade

Time doubles back on itself
a spiral or helix—
each mood object deed
splinters/scatters in crystal
the last act to bring on

veins of the house declare
how a word plants itself, rosy
in white
to work further

<pre>
        v
   O   l
 i   echo a
 c   n
   e   i
      term
</pre>

tale told to the eldest daughter
ALICIA, a vision or dream
history mapped by a granddaughter
ALICIA, rivet for a writer's esteem

viz. the *Sensible* Georgian Life
seen hindwise

The authoress so admired
had every domestic virtue
would—even in illness—
give right orders
procure exactly
the articles
required

A father cannot withhold paper
to keep the household accounts
and such a portion ill-coloured and coarse
Miss Fanny thought it no robbery
to appropriate to the purpose
of writing a romance
in two volumes
Eugenia and Adelaide

As nothing more uncertain lies
than book success or credit
she unwilling that any hopes
raised in a husband's partial mind
from the merit of the progressive work
should be blighted
did not communicate by speech or sign
any portion till the whole was done

It was her custom to write
with a small trunk or chest
beside her
into which she put her manuscript
if he chanced to enter the room
while she was thus employed

Memoirs are carried on journalwise
the answering letters dropped
but O.F.'s (misunderstood)
come interleaved

Sidney is no female philosopher
neither is she a pale heroine
six feet high without stilts
in one word she is—reader
have you lately met with such—
unaffected

Orlando Faulkland [or Falkland]
is no faultless mirror of excellence
he is made of contrarieties
Honour bedded in *Stratagem*

The closing scenes should be read alone
with the door locked
for the mind hangs suspended
in breathless anxiety upon the catastrophe

Writers of late [1824] have sought
to outdo their lot
in piling horror on horror—
no such exaggeration takes place here

Sisterhood comes on the rocks
volume on volume
squeezes hurt to the limit
of ellipsis

In *Nourjahad* again you cannot see
TIME pressing time
he lives the folly of wishes
set up as a mark
to walk free

The Owl and the Nightingale

At Simpson's Concert Room on Saturday next, 24th instant will be the first Attic Entertainment, consisting of reading and singing, the reading part by Mr Sheridan, the singing by Miss Linley. In three parts. Part i. 1. A discourse on Oratory in which the necessity of that art towards forwarding the perfection of man's nature is shewn in a new light by Mr Sheridan. 2. A Scotch ballad beginning: I oft have heard Mary say—by Miss Linley. 3. Pope's verses to the memory of an unfortunate lady, by Mr Sheridan. Part ii. 1. Two dialogues between Adam and Eve from the 4th book of Paradise Lost, the first beginning at line 411, and the other at line 508. 2. Elin a Roon, an Irish song by Miss Linley. 3. Milton's Allegro, by Mr Sheridan.

Part iii. 1. The Hermit from Dr Goldsmith's Vicar of Wakefield, by Mr Sheridan. 2. Black eyed Susan, an English ballad, by Miss Linley. 3. Dryden's Ode, by Mr Sheridan. 4. Rosey Bowers, from Purcel, by Miss Linley.

The entertainment will be continued on the Thursday and Saturday in the following week and the pieces and songs will be entirely different each day. The subscription to be a guinea for which six tickets will be delivered two for each morning or to be used on any of the days in such proportions as the subscribers shall think proper. Three subscription tickets for ladies only will be delivered for half a guinea, single tickets 5s. each. Subscriptions will be received and tickets delivered by the Booksellers, at the Coffee Houses, and at the Rooms. Particular care will be taken to make the room as warm as possible.

Bath Chronicle, 22 November, 1770

Tongue Track

ALLOCUTION, al-lo-ku´-shun. s. The act of speaking to another.

BLOBLIPPED, blob´-lipt. a. Having swelled or thick lips.

To CURVET, kur-vet´. v. n. To leap, to bound; to frisk, to be licentious.

DISCERPIBLE, dis-ser´-pibl. a. Frangible, separable.

EYRE, a´r. s. The court of justice itinerants.

FUCATED, fu´-ka-tid. a. Painted, disguised by paint; dignified by false show.

To GRABBLE, grab´l. v. a. To grope; v. n. To lie prostrate on the ground.

HOPPERS, hop´-purz. s. A kind of play in which the actor hops on one leg.

To INSEAM, in-se´m. v. a. To impress or mark by a seam or cicatrix.

JUNCOUS, dzhunk´-kus. a. Full of bulrushes.

KISSINGCRUST, kis´-sing-krust. s. Crust formed where one loaf in the oven touches another.

LAMBATIVE, lam´-ba-tiv. a. Taken by licking.

MAMMIFORM, mam´-my-farm. a. Having the shape of paps or dugs.

To NAB, nab´. v. a. To catch unexpectedly. A low word.

OYES, o-yis´. s. Is the introduction to any proclamation or advertisement given by the publick criers. It is thrice repeated.

PIEPOWDER Court, pi´-pow-dur. s. A court held in fairs for redress of all disorders committed therein.

QUATERCOUSINS, ka´´-ter-kuz´nz. s. Friends.

REDCOAT, red´-kote. s. A name of contempt for a soldier.

SURADDITION, sur´´-ad-dish´-un. s. Something added to the name.

To TORRIFY, tor´-ry-fy. v. a. To dry by the fire.

To UNTEACH, un-te´tsh. v. a. To make to quit, or forget what has been inculcated.

VAMPER, vamp´-ur. s. One who pieces out an old thing with something new.

WHIRLBAT, hwerl´-bat. s. Any thing moved rapidly round to give a blow.

X is a letter, which though found in Saxon words, begins no word in the English language.

YOUNKER, yunk´-ur. s. A young person.

ZETETICK, ze-tet´-ik. a. Proceeding by enquiry.

Thomas Sheridan, *A General Dictionary of the English Language* (1780)

Vannummery

The abbey is a very large residence situated on the River Liffey, 12 miles from the city of Dublin. There are many residence [sic] around Celbridge but [this] is the most historic one.

It is the residence of Vennessa Vonbhombret, Dean Swift used to ride out from Dublin on horseback every night to visit Vennessa.

One evening Dean went down and sat by the River, while there he wrote 'Drapier Letters'.

Some years after, Venessa died, and a man named Jack Macan was crossing the rock bridge. He met her and she told him not to come that way any more. The next night he came the same way she again warned him. The third night he came again and she threw him into the River.

There is another story told about the same Lady.

It is said that if a person walks at twelve o'clock at night by the gate on the Temple Mill road [he] will see this noted Lady with a dog and fire coming from its mouth.

Information given by Mrs Dumphy, Celbridge, Co. Kildare
and Rosie Core, Ringwood, Hazle Hatch, Co. Kildare

~

[O]nce more I advise you if you have any regard for your quiate to allter your behaviour quickly for I do assure you I have too much spirrite to sitte down contented with this treatment now becauss j love frankness extreamly j here tell you that I have determined to try all maner of humain artes to reclaime you and if all those fail j am resolved to have recorse to the black one which is said never dos . . .

but there is one thing falls out very ruckiley for you which is that of all the passions revenge hurryes me least so that you have it in your power to turne all this furry into good humer.

Hester Vanhomrigh to Jonathan Swift, 1719–20

Words on the Window Pane

The name that counts is the name
not there, the face on the arch
cut out, gatehouse gothic
speaking with a cold grasp

of algibray rods and means
        purple on green
projected across bogs and bends

        banshee stuff in the wainscoat
        starving to a madrigal

        indecipherable gloss
        surrounded by a circle

voice abandoned in **agit-glass**
the one good influence

never can have
        that cracked angel
full in view

**All in the, all in
the Dark**

        electric at the join
        of finger-tips

here is now a stlange ting

        GHOST texted

a sort of a start—a crack like

hang it, worth the evasion
a century slipped
to hardly
trace

    that doubled STAR
    drops an H

bubs white dice
no, not 'agleam'
raven down the neck
hair of my head stands up
chaffed her about
her losses

went out four matadores
and a trump in black
and was bested

ombre and claret, and toasted oranges

    you win eight shillings *at a time*
    and how much do you lose?
    no, never one syllable about that—
    sure the waters are good

but, *quando?* my plague time
is coming

    Must loo mimitate, pay?

when dross for sterling
crams down the throat

    a depending clause
    so go and cheat

a heart of melted lead and flaming pitch

Venus in wisps of dirty straw
a letter—*rettle*—reduced
to a light black film

    SORDO
    more bidden
    such a wrist-rap
    marked my last wrong
    not owned to the world

vrai-ly a rhymer or con-man
when *ego* spells *ague*
turning the scope
in pieces about

    a roofless, ivied tower
    in the angle of the hazard,
    a clump of dwarf oak or birch
    stark on the hills

I score the page of an old contest
scarlet skirted with grey—
whether meddle or medley
ziz is sumsing rike
versus on the jointure

    no endowment *but*
    a quasi-mistress
    a deerichar wife

the better poet, of the bent and current
item: a green silk apron
jeers presto

    one's a pretending slut
    with the matter in the margin

out of listlessness
I dined privately with a friend

Wine. Van's 1s.6d.

frail glass, which shall die first—
has you riding
with your ribbon and mask

    tonvelsasens smoke the pen

Nite my deelest logues

    ire-ing a character
    ought to throb
    the spirit

ascendant by a hyphen

    portraits on damp plaster
    limestone ringed with granite
    dreaming the balance
    in lives not
    meet

nor native enough

in a corner over there
westward sun on a layer of dust
crystals one hour

    a harp
    tilting

fan-atic from the womb

Name Withheld

I felt something like a large pair of needles
pierce me, a little below the throat
then an inch or two apart
deep into my breast

The cat was a woman in a dark loose dress—
a block of stone could not have been
more still

I stared and the figure was nearer the door

I found it locked as usual
on the inside
I was afraid to open it

†

Doctors never did me
any good

The pain is not so bad
as with other diseases

Let us talk no more—
you would not wound a friend

†

To die as lovers may
into a liquid clasp
to turn from grub to butterfly
in a season
by invisible stairs

†

Out of smoke and dust
the portrait came to life—
the *effigy* of my companion
down to the little mole
though my father did not care

      †

Her eyes were open in the leaden vessel
the features a hint of carmine
from twice an earthspan

Floating seven inches down

      †

I write you suppose
with composure—the stake
driven through, the head
struck off

It is their nature to multiply
(the letters shift)
I have journals and other papers

      †

One sign is the power of the hand:
it leaves a numbness in the limb
it seizes, which is slowly—
if ever—recovered from

My father took me a tour
through Italy

Often from a reverie
I have started

Cross Carpet

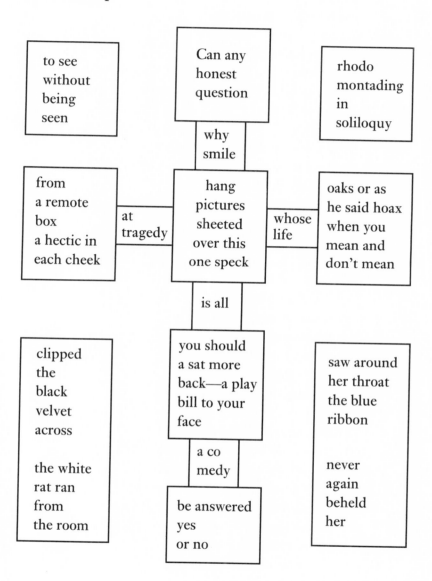

to see
without
being
seen

Can any
honest
question

why
smile

rhodo
montading
in
soliloquy

from
a remote
box
a hectic in
each cheek

at
tragedy

hang
pictures
sheeted
over this
one speck

whose
life

oaks or as
he said hoax
when you
mean and
don't mean

is all

clipped
the
black
velvet
across

the white
rat ran
from
the room

you should
a sat more
back—a play
bill to your
face

a co
medy

saw around
her throat
the blue
ribbon

never
again
beheld
her

be answered
yes
or no

Exquisite Corpse
Corpse Exquisite

I lay my length in the box
　　to sleep a whole revolution of Saturn
whose lid slides across, inches above
　　a few light words only in sport
crunch home the screws
　　for ever eyes closed bright
and still viewing
　　syrup infused in wine
a study in *mortis imago*

I have my beloved *souvenir*
　　a rose-bud to my heart
but this is the violation of letters
　　of what man is capable
too tremblingly pressed
　　by wildest wishes
to supply a connected narrative
　　(take, take back the gift
I conversed but with a costume)

Are we any wiser as we grow
　　disburthened of gauze and torches
or is it our illusions which change
　　one single object in steel or taffety
like your skeleton-key, I see the ceiling
　　burnished to prove
what no chemistry can detect
　　in four times so many years
tried by a terrible escape

Ropelight

Of all the birds in the air
    I was to be the beloved
    buffo caracato—no great figure for a prince—
and to be fallen in love with by a Lady
cast as enchantress

it was flattering but not acceptable
for the hero's part was so long
that no one would undertake it

determined not to disappoint
    the grand party of nobility
and the *corps diplomatique*
she had my name marked down

to avoid tempting *l'amour et la tendresse*
I kept my distance, resolved that no enchantment
should seduce me to be *come-atable*

but a pressing note from her Highness
brought me to her *boudoir*
and the question was put
    which no confession
    of my inadequacy
would fend off—it being the Margrave's birthday
and the whole depending on it

no sooner was it known
than I was quizzed and saluted
by my fellows: here comes the prince—
we wish you joy, go learn your lesson

the first week I found myself perfect
in less than a hundred lines
    a poor prospect before me—not
    three weeks to complete my studies

but as I dreaded the exposure
my memory increased

at last the fatal day arrived and that morning
        I was taken ill with a fever
I do not recollect for twenty years previously
to have experienced the least complaint
a slight cold excepted, which was a mere
winter accompaniment

but with the help of some magnesia
and two hours' repose in bed
        I was sufficiently revived
        to put on fine clothes
and do my *angelus* work

as the theatre was a mere temporary one
adjacent to the room where we dined
        the stage was most confined
        and green baize was put up
        to serve for side-screens

the heat and my agitation so overpowered me
(though I got through the piece)
that for a fortnight after I was confined
to my room

I fell into a lingering distemper
        that in the play was only rumour
I fell into a sleep of sixty years
        that was only a few moons
I had not the Margrave's plate
        the only thing that cooled me
I lay divested of the mistress
        who, after a trial, was mine

a pronoun will get in the way
        of the grandest *coup d'oeil*

like a pillar on the edge of a plaster-cove
a loop that gathers a din of voices

though I have been long an amateur actor
I was never a stage-bitten one
and had no inducement to smell the lamp
beyond the amusement of being with friends
and supping at the long table
with a plenteous supply of hock & champagne

Dublin Laid in Bath

I thank you for your Ballads and your Fancy Ball and mascarade intelligence, some of the songs are very well and I dont suspect Scot of having written them. But I must also scold you: so I am to look out for a young Batchelor here—and Harry *says nothing* about coming home. I see how it is, I am thrown off and you are keeping him for someone else, but to be even with you I am determined not to accept of one of the numerous offers which I shall certainly meet with here. My Father is mending. Still the same old life—Airing—home and cards. With yours came a letter from Charles. Very sentimental, *Surface'sh* &c &c.—he presses my Father to come over to a little Farm he has purchased with part of his *Wife's Fortunes*, and dwells much on the delight he should have in seeing him by his *fireside*. I confess there is scarce any emetick more powerful to my stomach than an affectation of sensibility where I know the heart to be truly selfish.

The waters are certainly slow in their operation, but my Father would probably be worse without them. He says he don't understand my turning Old Woman and has insisted on subscribing me to the Cotillon Balls so I am fairly in for a round of hurry. Here I am with my head becurl'd and befeather'd. Last night's ball was what they call a bad one, but to me quite full enough; several Ladies exhibited minuets tho' the Men have so great an aversion to them that only one Gentleman except the Masters of Ceremonies of both Rooms danced with them. I believe our travels are ended for this Summer. My Father finds himself quite at home here and was with us at the Ball quite a Beau.

Wednesday I drank tea with Mrs Kearney. There is a great deal too much wisdomation about her. Thursday I went with the Patersons to breakfast at Spring Gardens—no dancing and wretched musick but the morning was fine, we then saunter'd about Pump Room, Libraries etc—in short spent a true Bath morning. Friday went to the Crecent fields which is the present Mall of Bath. There is something whimsical yet pleasing in seeing a number of well dress'd people walking in the same fields where Cows and Horses are grazing as quietly as if no such intruders came among them. Saturday Evening I walk'd with Mrs Paterson to a new Walk which has been made by Belvidere, Shelter'd to the north by an immense Hill where they purpose building the New Crescent, and on the other side commands the most beautiful prospect imaginable.

The day has turn'd out Stormy rainy etc. I shall work and perhaps read a few of the Loungers which I like better than the green cloth. I will endeavour to get Cowper's Poems but I must enjoy them alone as my Father will not allow we have Poets or Painters or musicians at present. We have lost our pretty Neighbours, but Mr Cobbe is here figuring with the *Bird of Paradise*, as if no such being as his Wife existed. We have seen nor heard nothing of Linley, which I think odd after the reconciliation.

My Father's wine is at length arrived and is excellent—he has got Pint bottles for himself and has laid in a store of *English* Port for me and *hobnobs*, so much does he think what you have sent him superior not only in taste but as a point of health. With regard to Dublin business: You give an account of every thing relative to your Evening in Shaw's Court except the performance, which I construe into dissapprobation as perhaps you think censure would be a breach of hospitality as you were their Guest. I who am out of the scrape do most sincerely wish you may study and perform the Part of Lady Randolph [from Home's *Douglas*].

Walk'd with my Father into Spring Gardens. Under the trees there was a party seated among whom was Lord Nugent. Upon seeing my Father 'pray', says he, 'have you seen Lord Buckingham?'—'Yes my Lord'—'Well, he stutters as much as ever, doesn't he?' I felt extremely provoked at the impertinence of the Old Vagabond. My Father is too apt to pay hommage to fortune and titles, tho' to say the truth he does not seek them—this I attribute in some measure to his mixing so little with the world of late and admitting only such as yeild to him in every point, so that when he is with those from whom he can not expect that manner, he has nothing for it but recollecting the usual forms of good breeding he formerly practised with the persons of real fashion he once knew, but which are no match for the self-sufficiency and unfeeling impertinence of many of our present titled people.

This is a most Stupid journal and I have delay'd sending it only in hopes of a letter from you that I might have something to answer.

~

Yesterday I received yours of the 24th. Harry's allowance continues the same as when a Batchelor. But since the Old Gentleman [William Le Fanu] must be inform'd, what we would wish is that he might be told that we have an opportunity of laying out the money here to much greater advantage than it can ever produce us in Ireland. We can live here because we can live to ourselves. We are neither obliged to receive nor to go into company. They may accuse us of liking retirement but the Sin of poverty will not be imputed to us, as it certainly would be in Dublin were we to appear there on a less respectable footing than the rest of the family.

Our weather is damp and dirty but does not confine us as you know we Ladies here trot about in Pattens. The waters continue to do wonders for Harry so that I hope this winter will quite set him up. I have taken two places in the Green Boxes for tonight to see Miss Wallis—The same little girl you may remember at School in York St. The play is the *Conscious Lovers* which you know is dull enough but her performance is well spoken of.

Last night I went to the Ball because we have a number of grand Foreigners here and I wish'd to take a peep at their faces. The sound of french prevail'd over the Irish accent which reigns pretty generally at Bath.

Last night I was again at the Ball, quite dissipated you see. There were near twelve Hundred people there all as fine as Sattins and feathers could make them. Some remains of last Winter's finery varied by my own hand have supplied me with caps and tuckers, and as to la frizure I was provident enough never to suffer the Maid I kept to dress me so constantly as to lose the power of arranging my own locks. I confess that I have no small difficulty in getting into my gowns, but as Harry has the Lefanu taste for embonpoint, without which no Woman can be tollerable in his opinion, I console myself as well as I can.

Our Irish Doctor is very civil and talks french in Public, as he says 'to *hide* his Brogue'.

> Betsy (Sheridan) Le Fanu to Alicia (Sheridan) Le Fanu:
> 1785-86 (daughter) and 1789 (wife)

4

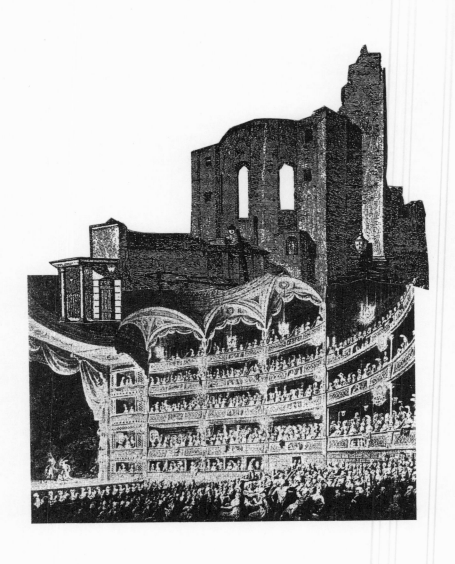

Screen Seen: Reduction

Library
 French
  window
   volumes
    from floor
     to ceiling
      (back-flat)
       screen off
        2nd wing L
         chairs, table
          book. SURFACE.

    Draw that screen
     before the window
      that will do.
       Sentiment now
        in soliloquy?
         Your character
          is like a person
           in a plethora—
            dying from health.
           Sir Peter the dev.
          What will come
         of me, Mr Logic
        I'll behind here.

     Ever improving
      himself! Books
       the only things
        I'm a coxcomb.
         You make even
          your screen
           a source of
            knowledge.
             My brother?
            I'm out. Let
           me into
          the closet.
         Trepan
        my brother
       too?

Is that
 a listener
  already? You
   could lock
    him in. Sure
     she won't blab?
      They wouldn't
       let me up. He
        thinks you are
         trying to gain
          Lady Teazle's
           affections.
          I understood
           you were her
            favourite.
             Hush (points).
              What, turn
               inquisitor & take
                evidence *incog.*?
                 I beg your pardon
                  Somebody has come
                   on business (exit).
                  Would you like
                 a good laugh?
                He has a girl
               here (points,
              throws down
             the screen)
            You divert
           your selves
          at hide & seek
         Morality dumb?
        She'll make out
       a better story
      than you
     without
      prompting.
    A man who
   shuts out
    conviction . . .
   (exeunt).

Rivals Interleaved

I

What's here—a vile cramp hand. The scrawl improves. A poet's brief?
A poet and a fee! Forsake an orchard for a barren waste. [*This scene
is generally left out.*] We are divided into high-roomians and low-
roomians; I have resolved to stand neuter. Here's a mort o'merrymaking.
It's a good lounge but damn the place. Their regular hours stupefy
me—not a fiddle nor a card after eleven. However, we keep it up a little
in private parties. Ah, the gazettes of the Bath, the very men I want. You
can guess where their shafts are aimed. I'll introduce you. Now th'off.
When I say heigh-ho it means yes. No note? I signed it *your Friend
unknown.* But I have seen a certain person, *la petite Rosignole,* the lively
Linnet. She has no rivals to be sure. You must get the mother of your
side; nothing will please her for Miss but a bit of quality binding. She
has a most observing thumb. My other self's an allegory on the banks
of the Nile (as you may get read to you in Ovid's Meat-for-Horses).
It's hard to leave a subject you have not quite run down. [*Gives him a
letter.*] What, the Languishes of Worcestershire? Oh, no foundation.
People *will* talk. [*Exeunt.*] *Striped chamber, 1st groove:* Hide these
books—quick. Fling *Peregrine Pickle* under the toilet—throw *Roderick
Random* into the closet—cram Ovid behind the bolster—there. Leave
that on the table—open at *Sobriety.* Now for 'em. What are those books
by the glass? The great one is *The whole Duty of Man*—where I press
a few blondes. Is it in a blue cover? O Lud you are going to be moral.
[*Placing him.*] Where is it we are to be? Oh, at Spring Gardens. The
Scotch tunes are melting and soft. Sing him the Birks of Endermay.

II

Such a mistress of squallante and quiverante—how she did chirrup at
that receptacle of pleasure. But one sympathetic note in the set, 'twill
spread. A modern lass puts on fetters to enjoy more freedom. A spark
darts thro' every link of the chain. [*Joins the rest of the company all
talking as they are going through the door in the scene.*] Nay, we
will hear it. I contribute it entirely to his skill: he is a perfect progeny,
knowing all the contagious countries lie together. I must get my niece

under his intuition. You don't seem wanting in fluency of speech. Here are a great many words that would get their *habeas corpus* from any court in Christendom. [*Rising.*] I observe you have a new method of folding up letters. [*Throws away the envelope.*] One may read the contents without breaking the seal. Very pretty—damns us all for a puppy triumvirate. My little embassadress—there's no stopping these coiners and clippers. *I am alarmed at the intelligence you send me, the more so as my rival*—that's *you*, Sir. [*Exeunt severally.*] *Discovery—Pembroke table with six chairs. Party at cards. Another table filled with children at lottery tickets:* In these places one is forced to take up with strange sort of creters. You wouldn't want to make an absolute desert of the rooms. But these monkeyronies with two pounds of fictitious hair formed into a club, hanging down their shoulders as white as a baker's sack—their legs are at times covered with all colours of the rainbow. Oh it gives me the hydrostatics. Look at that—*she* puts on a little red. You can be a little severe. The head's modern though the trunk's antique.

III

I don't see the jet of your scheme. [*Turns round.*] A small sum—halters and bastinadoes! It's more than I would your neck. A trifling faux pas? Wants to raise money? An undeserved misfortune in the spunging-house. He is some thousands worse than Nothing. This is my return—but I have done with him. Gad I heard the bell. She is coming now—what resolution there is in woman—how a few soft words can . . . [*Draws near her.*] Then try me now—let us be free as strangers. [*Kisses his hand.*] Let me ask you this—if marriage were—and we—would you forego all pleasures of society—to smile upon our free faith? [*Aside.*] Gently, good tongue, words slip out edgewise. I thought she would—she sha'n't see that I am over-reached. [*Walks aside, and seems engaged in looking at the pictures.*] Now could I fly with him to the Antipodes, but my prosecution is not come to a crisis. [*Aside.*] O friendly rival. Must I never cease to tax him with this teasing minute caprice? How charming will poverty be with him. *Antique table covered with green cloth, two decanters of wine, plenty of glasses, two chairs:* There's the degeneracy of our age—many of our acquaintance have taste, spirit and politeness—but they won't drink. Fill a dozen bumpers. Wine is the test by which the lover knows his heart. Odd's blushes and blooms! I have drunk sentiments often—in grace [*i.e.* race] cups that are gone. Burn your ancestors? Exceeding frank upon my word. Plain dealing in business I always think best. An old romancing tale of a poor relation? Don't compel me to inform you of it. I could show you a range of ancestry—pictures framed in the wainscots. The deed has slipped through our fingers but the faces signify.

IV

Odds Ropes. Do you think *Achilles* or *Alexander the Great* ever inquired where the right lay? [*Gives him the challenge.*] The quarrel is a pretty quarrel as it stands—we should only spoil it by trying to explain it. I wish the ink were red. [*Aside to him.*] I'll not put my every day name to it but my love name. [*Reads letter.*] *To the Lover of Miss Languish*—aye that's me indeed. *Folding doors, 3d G[roo]v[e]:* I beg pardon—but with submission, a lie is nothing unless one supports it. I always forge *indorsements*, as well as the bill. Now they have their vices like their birth-day clothes with the gloss on. I could give you a mortgage with equity of redemption; or you could have the reversion of the french velvet, or a post-obit on the blue and silver. [*Attempts to speak.*] Damn the surname—it's too formal to be entered in love's calendar. [*Makes signs to leave them together.*] Our retrospection will now be all to the future. This conduct is truly generous. [*Takes a miniature from her bosom.*] I thought of what Hamlet says—something about kissing—on a hill. My Hibernian believes there is ~~salivation~~ simulation going on in the fields. Caught like vipers with a bit of red cloth. [*Flings herself into a chair, with her face from the door.*] My affluence over my niece is very small. These young soldiers must never be trusted with a pretty girl, tete a tete. Like children, they will be picking at the dish before mama has pinned the napkin. *Changes to Apartment, Surface.* I've got a roomful of ancestors above. *Pedigree hung up first wing, L[eft]:* You'd sell your forefathers, would you? An *ex post facto* parricide. Yet I have taken a fancy to that picture. I'm sorry for't—I cannot find in my heart to part with it. [*Puts the picture up again.*]

V [*mistakenly numbered IV in all early editions*]

Now for hazard. [*Muffled in a Riding-coat.*] This affront must be expiated. Rakehelly rantipole, I shall be in such a frenzy. [*Measures paces along the stage.*] Has he never transmitted to you avadavats and India crackers? [*Levelling at him.*] They were family secrets and should not be mentioned again. What are you muffled up for? 'Tis cool, isn't it? What's this?—here's something damned hard. I confess that appearances are against me. [*Pulls his coat open.*] A bauble, eh? [*The sword falls.*] So—this was the history of his precious trinkets. I'll bauble him. *A Parlour.* But to find myself made a mere Smithfield bargain. There had I projected so amiable a ladder of ropes—conscious moon—four horses—Scotch parson—and such paragraphs in the news-papers! He goes by half a hundred names. But wounded—what are the perpendiculars? A ball lodged in the thorax. Struck against a little bronze Pliny. I had it from one—and I have it from one—who had it from one who had it—from one immediately. And other flashes beside. Still—can't kill a man without a doctor. It appears to me that we are all rivals. [*Exeunt.*] *Antique Chamber:* What are you doing out of bed? A vile place for discoveries. And the door fastened! Punctuation forbids me to say more. I never seed such a gemman. I have followed Cupid's jack-a-lantern and find myself in a quagmire. [*Takes a circle to go off.*] *Scene the last:* I have unfortunately been offered double to speak the truth. He has one in every room in the house. Hymen has a fragment of thirty-seven couplets, which I trust will not long retain their MS-hood. We amend our plea. I'll order the fiddles. [*Looks at his watch.*] Here's all the Town staring at us,—all's publick—the field is as crowded as a play-house, the first night of a new comedy.

Duelling Tales

Did he the villain dag her, did he
Captain or Major Mathews
put his hand on her knee, the prettiest
creature stripped you ever saw

Did she mix poison with pain powder
did she ask Dick to play the knight
did she make plans with both
to go off, her portrait incomplete

Did the protector play the lover
turn Eliza's convent to a wedding
vow, so to be posted in the Bath paper
a L[iar] and a S[coundrel]

Did Mr S go to Mr M at Crutched Friars
where the key was lost and he still
got in, did he who had sworn his death
call him dear friend and cry off the fight

Did they meet in a tavern by candlelight
did M beg for his life but refuse to sign
and then on the point retract
while Eliza knows her man

Did they each a hero set out the fact
did they meet on Kingsdown to decide
again, jab and stab till her locket breaks
and one rush off with the other 'dying'

Did she sing that day, the only person
not to know, did he do it for the name
of Gentleman, to keep a Maid may-be
none the less a nightingale

How oft Eliza

My dearest Sheri,

Though I parted from you so lately, though I expect to see you again so soon, yet I must be plaguing you with my scrawl. I love you to such a Degree that I should never bear to see you (even in joak) show any particular affection to another. If you do speak to that woman, I think we might contrive to send our letters there, directed under feigned names. Nothing but the same dull story over and over again—that I love you to distraction, and that I would prefer you and beggary, before any man with a throne. Upon my knees, half nacked, once more I am going to tire you with my nonsense. I could not bear to see this little blank without filling it up. Tho' I do not know with what, as I have almost exhausted the budget of news which I had collected since *our long absence*. With what rapture shall we meet, when we may do so without constraint. When I may live in your arms without the fear of parents, or the ill-natured world. I shall be very happy when I am once more in Bath. I have lost my ink, but I hope you will be able to understand me. How could you tease me about Miss C—. I have sometimes horrid thoughts about your going to Dublin.

It is strongly suspected that we are married, and that I discovered it in my fright, when I first heard of your duel.

You do not know your own heart—it is not in your nature to be constant, especially to one who is so much in your *Power*. It was not your person that gained my affection. No, it was that Delicacy, that Tender Compassion, that interest which you seemed to take in my welfare, these were the motives which induced me to Love you. When these were lost, when I found you no longer the Man my fond imagination had painted you, when, instead of respect, I found myself spoken of with contempt, laugh'd at, made the Sport of your Idle Hours, and the subject of your Wit, with every Milener's Prentice in Bath. When I was convinced of *this*, how could I *love?* I assure you I wrote twice, and put the Letters in the Post Office myself, they could not *Miscarry*. Your proposal of coming to Bath I looked upon as mere *Words*, as you was well assured your father would not permit it. My father has given strict orders to Hannah to bring every letter to him.

Dear, dear Sheri, has nothing but *Business* detained you from me! I cannot leave you and be perfectly satisfied at such a distance from you. I should have been very glad to have worn the Domino, but I am now drest, and it is now so late it is quite impossible to alter my hair. Let me see you soon to-night—good-natured and happy.

So how do e do, Sir? and what's your History, as Mrs C. says? Am I to see e Eyes to-night, or is there Faro, or anything else going on in town? Just write a fiff and say he love me, and mean to come as soon as e can. Pray send me a line, for e know what an anxious Poush I am. The carpenters are setting the scene. I love e dearer than ten thousand lives, and always will.

your Eliza

Circumbendibus

Wind the window down
    why should this deceive
something on the plain
    flashes a fiery streak

Madame, you mistake
    the luggage is all up
we'd best tell our
    post-boys to go on

We only wish to avoid
    a small hill
we'll soon get into
    the right road

How far are we now—
    half a league
from what's underlined
    on the finger-post

A canter that's a gallop
    in spite of my shouts
flung from one side
    to the other

Is this Dover—can't you
    hear the sea
where are the lights
    and the people

Into the court-yard
    laconic answers
to the HOTEL steps
    of white stone

Why this is just like—
   it *is*—Bartram
as all philosophers know
   so like Dover

       ~

I'm a bungler at a long story
   for cautious purity
I'd rather set the lapse
   in one town

Ought not, I feel, to pass
   over in silence
how a footman dissolves
   in a gentleman's jug

Riddle

A man is made of two embraces
tingle the top, tie the toe

a Linnet sings, an Owl stitches
silk in the morning blab at night

if all the notes were lime and smoke
attachment would be inside-out

dare drink this to run away
chestnut hair, then green eyes

house of motion, house of sleep
here's the moment but it's not

blazing comet in a Venice glass
he's SHERI to one, to the other DAN

Polesden Lacey

Against the brink of war, of debt
Dan buys his sweet, Hecca
the place best within reach of Town
on the prime and sporting Downs

        you'll chirp like a bird
        bound like a fawn
        grow fat as little pig

the servants rid, we'll have all good
and do all good around

there is a peaceful valley, whatever
the boom of iron

        got from Admiral G——
        with the sale of Drury shares
        furniture in hock
        and a lawyer's loan (Geary's own)

honour bright, borrow and fear not
with a hatful of violets on the table
and three samples of lamb's wool

walk the terrace, slow, take in
this steep wooded bank
whose end is a peep
of lovely distance

        ha-ha drop
                south to the wild
        rabbits and deer
                cross vaulted track
        and up, trees wrapped
                in shadow
        Ranmore that no squire
                will enclose

my dear bit of brown Holland
come into the garden, I would like
my roses to see you

       the Iliad even is a moonlit urn
       by shag-headed beeches
       that catch the wind
       from the east

what if we don't go to church
we'll dine on claret
with not a candle to show
the way to bed

       if breakfast sighs neglect
       this is not a butter county

without you Dan is Lemoncholy
as a yew-tree in a church yard

Hogden, Connicut, Tanners Hatch
yield the poles to fence
and still both houses call
I want a speech on wood and canvas

       Mick shall have plenty of matter
       to go with tomorrow

       No George—no war
       No Pitt—no war

the throne we honour is the PEOPLE'S CHOICE
in cryptic Peru

       riot is sown by wicked men
       and who are they * * * * * * * *
       panders of a coney's will
       get up the same old drama
       with props and such, a little modernized
       for natives to bite, a crown *con-spirito*

with lines alleged burning
metal into eye-cases
that make not meet a faction
in what cist-ear land are they
when it comes to trial

war-jaw haw-haw law-more
have-his-body-he-can't
brooding nightmare faces
in the trumpet's blare, the prickly bush
oily with a grin so decent
create the passions you persecute

From Nun's Walk these footsteps
are traceable like spots on a coat

dare d*ct*te what's bespoke under cover
there are many dark actors playing games

Lord Edward's Last Goodnight

Now in the June heat I'll go
off elsewhere, leaping rapids again
finding a trail through silent forests

By canoe or tabargin I'll rove
to lie on a good spruce bed
and look at the stars

Where no titles divide and every man
is what he makes himself
where all ridiculous wants dissolve
fashion, duty, politics

They found me reading in bed
at a feather merchant's house
in Thomas Street—I threw *Gil Blas* aside
and struck with my dagger to spring
from the stalkers' reach

One down, two I dragged to the door,
took a pistol-ball in my shoulder
and the knife was wrested from me

I'll not dodge the tocsin of revolt—
what I have done through sense
(a line of advance on Dublin)
papers in my great-coat pocket
will show

Green silk around my neck,
I rode to the Curragh of Kildare:
Let any man who dares take it off

Paine's face was over my mantelpiece
at Kilrush, the man I lodged with
in Paris, whose rights I here uphold

From this grille—like the theatre box
where I saw her first—
I remember my wife, who lately I held
at Moira stables, stealing there in disguise

Which of my friends betrayed me
for a thousand pound fee
the roof may one day sing

Blas retired to the country
and if now the green turns pale
a shroud may turn to a flag—
my country you will be free

It's time to start, I'd rather
view rocks and creeks: the name
in my boot will carry the news

Cavan Cares

Where is it you travel

to the land of midgets
the land of giants

up through Kells
to Mullagh

goats live in the bedroom
pigs look out of the parlour

first you measure
what you meet

expect no more from Man
than such an Animal does

writing down
in a hollow begins
from the glebe meadow

learn their Tongue to gabble
at *Triall-droch-drib*
the Court style is to crawl
and lick the floor

a great Lord has his
mouth so crammed
that he's not able to speak
a Word

we have new Plays, new Libels—
do you love or hate it more

QUIL-CA, hidden
house by a black lake
elm-crowned rath

cut a canal, make an island
move some trees, throw up a wall
while your friend's away
a bailiff has his pioneers

sit in the arbour
on sodded seats
by a great laurel
discourse

                              or at the well ingest
                              a piece of mutton and a bottle
                              before backgammon, the classics
                              and a song

Night Heroic
makes the old war
into roaring peace

                                   as by Smock chemistry
                                   the rotten cabin
                                   gets a coved ceiling
                                   with a painted sky and portraits
                                   under the son

heads off the trees
for a play-actoring
platform

                                   bog and stone
                                   will yield you crops

but where is
which are the limbs
round Stellya's bower—
knob, peninsula, garden

                                        the hum of voices at dinner
                                        is a whisper of debts held over

is it a time to talk of boats
or a time to sail

                                   I received your two race-eats
                              have lately been be-Sheridaned
                                   but will secure your money

a farmer four-square
carries a Manx pony
kicking and shouting
to the window

                                   he'll set a labourer from Rantavan
                                   in the haycocks like a doll

Morning Epic
leads to something fetched
far in a jogg Ralph Eye

                                   I'll hear none of your visions

Imprimis, I fell asleep
and what was the first thing
I saw

        honest Cato in a cock-boat
           engages a fleet of foreigners
             and tacks about against
                some dirty shattered floats
                   filled with his countrymen

I would give a shilling
low as money is reduced
to know the meaning

        you think all the World has nothing
        to do but pull you down
        whereas it is nothing but a Slap
        in your turn

yew mare aim Ember
a bout Ann our Ah go
Ire it sum Ann glow Ann Glee
I nim it ay shun off Ewers

         you set no bounds
        to prodigality
      you calculate in aether
    preaching a text insufficient
      as Halter to Hanged
        you forget the end
          to be sold at public cant

Belturbet fair will make me
an Emperor
as for my *Quondam* friends
Quondam them all

        if you talk of improving
        mind your Business
        you shall laugh with all Men
        without trusting any

I expecture aunt sure
when we've doubled the stakes
and run the spelling through

                                        you give me matter
                                        for each travail
                                        dock tear rid bag wood
                                        con vorts to dane

Ure Dolis a de vel it hinc
as memory falls a longing visitation
on the pitted road to the lawn and hall

                                                    ash aimed
                                        I am never

the house will speak before you
get me to dance on a thread

                                    the master's heart
                                right hand
                        one day I'll miss

what are Lorn wages, Ards
but a fund aztec seer crawl—
aim an udder strain jeer to wad eye in dent
ay there as do major awe throat

                                            clay washed away
                                shrubs departed

(not a signpost)
                        loose stones
                        call over the surface
                        skeleton frolic
                        jollies in the drear
                        o Philie

Liminal

Jasmine in the corridor,
a delicately gloved hand in an upper box,
somebody muffled by cloak and bonnet

she wants the man who always sat here
who spurned the love of some lesser donna
treading this stage in *The Country Girl*

she might have laughed
in the Farce of the Parrot
but she hanged herself from a door
in the Garrick's Head

now when the curtain rises
she's always here and she seldom appears,
a sort of shiver down a steep rake
which prompts the best in each player

Floor Proposition

The story of the London stage
from Congreve to Shaw
is pretty much the track of Irish voices
gone over or come back
in search of a living and a little distance

Southerne, Farquhar, Steele,
Murphy, Bickerstaffe, the Sheridans,
Kelly, Malone, O'Keefe,
Goldsmith, Jephson, Kenney,
Maturin, Shiel, Knowles,
Boucicault, Wilde and Yeats

Quin, Macklin, Clive,
Woffington, Barry, Mossop,
Farren, Jordan, O'Neill
Brougham, Macready and Heron

Lichfield Garrick was by his mother
a Clough and a Bailye
G. F. Cooke was born in a barracks
in Dublin

Sarah Ward, mother of the Kembles
sprang from Tipperary, her parents
having made much out of little
as strollers on boards and in booths
from Aungier Street to Birmingham

Kean they say was of iris distraction
Terry's grandfather, pedigree lost
was a builder or publican from Cork

but that leaves Bannister,
Elliston, Vestris
Faucit, Irving and Bancroft

who won't be lumped in this rubric
and now the column collapses

G-nome backforms the grinning man
a spirit between stage and stalls
whose every oath is an epic
who fiddles and frolics at the wake
a broth of a boy at the brogue
sitting or standing

that's the wire, frimsey framsey
it loops to the pin
a thin silver moon, acey-deucey
over fretwork trees

How much of a catch is this trick
of traits—to sling a nasty part
race rankles raze what's almost a badge
for Bootish cheer and fear

a hazard made by Dazzle to be removed
like a half-boiled potato in a pistol

What do the Le Fanu brothers do in Town
jolted from mail-packet and carriage?
Head for the Haymarket, the Adelphi,
Drury Lane, the Lyceum, Princess's
to diet on Shakespeare, Sheridan,
a burlesque or two and oysters,
call on Mrs Norton,
lay their hats in a row in a field
and pelt them with stones

CODON: after all this comes Beckett

Dobbin Deeds

The man at the top of Eccles street
is a doctor of Divinity
once a fellow at Trinity
he swapped his post for a Limerick
girl, got a parish for his sins

He's a tiny chap of circled years
in a full-bottomed wig
knee-breeches
black silk stockings, buckled shoes
who walks with a gold-headed cane

He's always got a minute for those
whose wind-eyed rags
are the only house
they'll habit, gallowed or not
in a pudder of sulph'rous air

When a man comes begging
who's not got a shilling
he'll give him a guinea
to go for change, all in trust
and won't see that face again

When his wife comes home
he's in the hall
hands behind his back
he's pinched a roast from the spit
to give to a woman at the door

He cheered two brothers in a cage
Cork men like him
under sentence to die
for a sentence, and so like a rebel
his daughter sleeps with a dagger

Eccles Variorum

What to do with this big barracks   From the balcony we watch
of a play—grasp in a moment   the king's ingress, a man foreign
of seven rooms   to hurrahs
some temptress on the steps   shake hands your majesty
of a brown brick house   I'll never wash again by George

give me an ounce of civet   and in weeks he's forgotten

there is not the word *street*—   after the first flash of cavalcade
it belongs to an æra antecedent   abuse his person, abuse his mistress
to our usage and manners   and praise his wife

to expose the presumption   rank, station, honours are nothing
of arbitrary & fantastic violation   they strut in a spring mist
a liberty has been taken, viz:—   a burgher's imposture, nightly
to make the fable appear   fooled at noon (some will think
consistent with itself   this a hardy shift)

your editor hazards a transposition   saving the old man's crotchets
making that ranked as fifth   the scene rides on the rest
stand as the third   reverbed in calp-rubble

how sallying forth he happens   the business is best explained
to be so poorly attended   by making *which*
is not easy to determine   the relative of *heart*

suppose it a broken speech   I have ventured
well-flown may be understood   to arrange
as a compound-epithet of *bird*   these nonny noes
with the change of a single letter   in the metrical form
from *covers* to *covert*   given in the fragment

I degrade these lines, the only ones   haunting bars appear
so treated, to the bottom of the page   beside the line

in the quarto light it's *recreant*   or the letters grow up
like obedience *scanted*   out of their place

| **your eyes are in a heavy case** | fool upon fools |

who has the right to force   accompanied by that general stamp
upon folk such acts   of the Gothic age the mind yields
for coinage   without repugnance
on sheet or boards   to delusion

as no hint is given respecting distance   consider *delay*
it is not easy to conjecture the time   as a noun not verb

we may imagine it morning   there is perhaps some Bedlam
of the next day   in the neighbourhood

there is not the least hint given   the direction at the head
as to the particular part   *drest with wild flowers*
in which any scene lies   makes it more natural and proper

with notes subjoined   I admit the amendment of Mr Pope
from the court ecclasi—   the rest of the moderns
by hero's progress lost   read with interrogation
the witches sing   why do we trifle thus with time

father wast thou fane   words may profitably relate
to hovel thee with rogues   only to a single description

call an inventory of names   in Har's net

imagine this some part   viz. the sixth since
of a new day   the night of the storm

it is fit to record the course—   out of his sold estate
how a blind is drawn aside   Sir John's spirit
a white arm flings forth a coin   I spatchcock
and lover or lever   to walk the quadrant
keyless at housesteps   in every shape
over the railing he climbs   with you

reckon how the matter picks up   fliberdegibek
by echo–as–semble   **nookshot**
when you have the map of it all   O reader

Oglio

[E]very Englishman considers himself as good a judge
of Shakespeare as his pint of porter. R. B. Sheridan

When you've got the real McCoy
and everybody's heard it
though the hand is absent

when the hollow helmet clamours
Henry and William are missing

when the canon is cast
but cracks appear at the edge

what's the harm in a little fresh business—
my father has part of Wycliff's vestment
the seer cloth of a mummy
Cromwell's buff leather jacket

Mary Tofts of Godalming says
she has given birth to rabbits

I cut the blank end-papers
from a roomful of quartos and folios
(unmarked sheets or those
stamped with a jug)

I borrow some thread from a tapestry
in the House of Lords

My ink is brown and watered down
to make a tawny line

After *Lear* with the coarseness knocked out
and epithets embellished
I take my cue from a picture
over the chimneypiece in Mr Ireland's study

Rowena offers wine to Vortigern—
it's all in Holinshedde
but I conjure up the types and scenes

Old Constantius divides his kingdom
Flavia roams the forest
Edmunda has a mad song
the Fool a prophecy

O, horror, horror, my dear father murder'd
Now wo indeed hath made its master-piece
This seat is empty, fair Rowena take it
When thou didst cry, I strove to stop thy mouth
Then heigh-ho, poor dobbins all
We kill indeed, but still 'tis comedy

Punctuation go hang—who knows enough—
and age nineteen I can better Chatterton
at double Ds and final Es

The players, save Mrs Powell and Mrs Jordan
let me down, with one line
in Kemble's harangue with Death
spoke to receive every doubter's howl

And when this solemn mockery is ended

I brought forth this not–undigested
not–unconnected medley
and men of superior genius
believed the Bard alone was author

If [I] have deceived the world
who's fault is that—
mine or the world's

First Break

The Drury Lane company, in the season of 1791-2, removed to the Opera House on the 22nd of September. Of all things that could be named, an Italian Opera House was least suited to English play and farce, demanding a constant succession of scenes called flats, run on suddenly for the frequent changes of place, and the small-sized scenes of Old Drury were, with much difficulty, applied to the grand void devoted to the groups of the French ballet.

After a very spirited performance of the *Haunted Tower*, Mrs Jordan's Beatrice in the *Panel* put the audience in high good humour. She ran over the ground easily and without seeming annoyed by it, but it made the exits and entrances comparatively tardy and flat—some of the actors considered it as a death-blow; but to what will not use at length reconcile us? However we were drawn by that stage into a fondness for spectacle, which we could gratify, sooner than a demand for sense; and at length the people themselves preferred the great theatre to the little one.

James Boaden, *The Life of Mrs Jordan*

Between a Ghost and an Apparition

On the 12th of March [1794] the town was at once astonished and delighted by the opening of the new Theatre Royal, Drury Lane. Its spaciousness was entirely sunk in its lightness and proportion. Had I the construction of twenty theatres, this should be their model. It seemed to grow out of the pointed architecture, from its effect; though its parts did not imitate that mysterious order, or perhaps disorder, of composition.

On the 21st of April [the theatre] was opened for the performance of plays. Mr Kemble opened with Macbeth, and with his sister [Sarah Siddons] in the Lady displayed the utmost perfection of the art. [But] I preferred the *proper* presentment of Banquo's spirit to his banishment.

George Colman got up a pantomime epilogue most gaily for Miss Farren. In obedience to her wand, the reservoir rushed forth, to prove that the audience had *water* to dread rather than fire; and should even the *scenery* take fire, an *iron curtain* would instantly drop between the conflagration and the audience.

Except as to panic, fire can do nothing in theatres, where every eye is open and every hand ready to extinguish it. As Shakespeare himself expressed it,

> Through NIGHT and NEGLIGENCE such fires are spied
> In populous cities.

And, when they are, what security is found in reservoirs without water, and iron curtains that would soon be fire heat in a conflagration? The wachman, too, like other mortals, drowsy, if not absolutely sleeping, by degrees remitting his search upon having so constantly found all well, is at the critical moment terrified beyond his reason.

Every consideration seemed to call upon the persons about Drury Lane Theatre for extreme vigilance and care. In the month of September 1808, they had been assiduously employed on their roof, to guard their *own* Apollo from the fiery flakes that fell in showers from the burning theatre so nigh at hand. As details came to be known of the progress of this calamity, they learned that no *water* could be had for a long while to supply the engines, the main having *just at this time* been cut off for the purpose of laying down new pipes. Covent Garden, it was supposed, was destroyed from the wadding of a musket fired in Pizarro, which being discharged upwards, had been driven deeply into some combustible substances.

The Circassian Bride and the Unconscious Counterfeit were advertised for the performances of Saturday the 25th [February 1809]. It being Lent, no performances took place on the 24th. After a strict investigation, it was generally believed, that this melancholy catastrophe was occasioned by accident. It appeared that the stove in the upper coffee-room was of slight construction, for the mere purpose of accommodating the customers of the evening with water for tea, &c., and quite surrounded with *woodwork*. In this stove the workmen, who had been employed during the day, had made a much larger fire than it was customary to make there, the remains of which were left in it at four o'clock, and it was reasonable to suppose, had communicated to the surrounding woodwork, and that the fire had been gaining strength from that time to the moment of its bursting forth. . . .

Note: On the night of the conflagration, I stood, with my boots covered by the water, in the middle of the street, until I saw the *figure* on the summit of the house sink into the flames; *that* APOLLO which a contemptible *vanity* had thrust up into the place, that, in England, should always be occupied by SHAKESPEARE:—to whose honour, moreover, be it remembered, the pile, on its erection, *professed* itself to be consecrated.

James Boaden, *Memoirs of the Life of John Philip Kemble*

Drury Nights

1794   *Macbeth*   Shakespeare, rev. Davenant/Garrick/Kemble
      Lodoiska   John Philip Kemble
      The Rivals   Richard Brinsley Sheridan
      All's Well That Ends Well   Shakespeare, rev. J.P. Kemble
      The Cherokee, An Opera   James Cobb
      Measure for Measure   Shakespeare, rev. J.P. Kemble

1795   *The Wheel of Fortune*   Richard Cumberland
      The Adopted Child   Samuel Birch
      Venice Preserved   Thomas Otway
      King Lear   Shakespeare/Nahum Tate, rev. J.P. Kemble
      Alexander the Great   Nathaniel Lee, rev. J.P. Kemble
      Know Your Own Mind   Arthur Murphy

1796   *The Plain Dealer*   William Wycherley, rev. J.P. Kemble
      The Iron Chest   George Colman the Younger
      Vortigern   William Ireland ['Shakespeare']
      Almeyda: Queen of Granada   Sophia Lee
      The Roman Actor   Philip Massinger, rev. J.P. Kemble
      Douglas   John Home

1797   *Cymbeline*   Shakespeare, rev. J.P. Kemble
      The Will   Frederick Reynolds
      The Wandering Jew; or, Love's Masquerade   Andrew Franklin
      The Belle's Strategem   Hannah Cowley
      All in the Wrong   Arthur Murphy
      The Castle Spectre   Matthew Gregory Lewis

1798   *Blue Beard; or, Female Curiosity*   George Colman the Younger
      Knave or Not?   Thomas Holcroft
      The Italian Monk   James Boaden
      The Stranger   Benjamin Thompson [August von Kotzebue]
      A Nosegay of Weeds; or, Old Servants in New Places   John O'Keeffe
      Aurelio and Miranda   James Boaden

1799   *Feudal Times*   George Colman the Younger
      The East Indian   Matthew Gregory Lewis

The Castle of Montval   Thomas Sedgwick Whalley
Pizarro   Richard Brinsley Sheridan [Kotzebue]
A Bold Stroke for a Wife   Susanna Centlivre
Much Ado About Nothing   Shakespeare, rev. J.P. Kemble

1800 *She Wou'd and She Wou'd Not*   Colley Cibber
De Monfort   Joanna Baillie
Indiscretion   Prince Hoare
She Stoops to Conquer   Oliver Goldsmith
Hamlet   Shakespeare, rev. J.P. Kemble
Harlequin-Amulet; or, The Magic of Mona   William Powell

1801 *Julian and Agnes*   William Sotheby
Adelmorn the Outlaw   Matthew Gregory Lewis
High Life Below Stairs   Rev. James Townley
Richard III   Shakespeare/Colley Cibber, rev. J.P. Kemble
The Revenge   Edward Young
Isabella; or, The Fatal Marriage   T. Southerne, rev. Garrick/Kemble

1802 *The Double-Dealer*   William Congreve
Algonah   James Cobb
Mary Queen of Scots   Hon. John St John
The Winter's Tale   Shakespeare, rev. J.P. Kemble
Every Man in his Humour   Ben Jonson, rev. David Garrick
Midas   Kane O'Hara

1803 *Hear Both Sides*   Thomas Holcroft
The Hero of the North   William Dimond
Don Juan; or, The Libertine Destroyed   Anon.
The Haunted Tower   James Cobb
A Bold Stroke for a Husband   Hannah Cowley
The Caravan; or, The Driver and his Dog   Frederick Reynolds

1804 *Cinderella; or, The Little Glass Slipper*   Anon.
The Sailor's Daughter   Richard Cumberland
The Middle Dish; or, The Irishman in Turkey   Walley C. Oulton
A Trip to Scarborough   Richard Brinsley Sheridan [Vanbrugh]
Barbarossa   John Brown
Old Harlequin's Fireside   Anon.

1805 *The Honey Moon*   John Tobin
      Romeo and Juliet   Shakespeare, rev. J.P. Kemble [?]
      The Venetian Outlaw   Robert William Elliston
      All for Fame; or, A Peep at the Times   Andrew Cherry
      The Country Girl   William Wycherley/David Garrick
      The Victory and Death of Lord Nelson   Richard Cumberland

1806 *The Forty Thieves*   George Colman the Younger
      The Invisible Girl   Theodore Edward Hook
      Tancred and Sigismunda   James Thomson
      Mr H—   Charles Lamb
      Lovers' Vows   Elizabeth Inchbald [Kotzebue]
      The Enchanters; or, Harlequin Sultan   Anon.

1807 *The Curfew*   John Tobin
      One O'Clock; or, The Wood Dæmon   Matthew Gregory Lewis
      Adelgitha   Matthew Gregory Lewis
      Time's a Tell-Tale   Henry Siddons
      Ella Rosenberg   James Kenney
      Faulkner   William Godwin

1808 *Kais; or, Love in the Desarts*   Isaac Brandon
      The World   James Kenney
      The Jew of Mogadore   Richard Cumberland
      The Mysterious Bride   Lumley St George Skeffington
      The Siege of St Quintin; or, Spanish Heroism   Theodore Hook
      Venoni   Matthew Gregory Lewis

1809 *Robinson Crusoe; or, Harlequin Friday*   Sheridan/M. & R. Tickell
      Man and Wife; or, More Secrets than One   Samuel James Arnold
      The Three and the Deuce   Prince Hoare
      John Bull; or, The Englishman's Fireside   G. Colman the Younger
      The Unconscious Counterfeit   Greffulhe
      Fortune's Frolic   John Till Allingham

Doctor Helios Lights the Lights

Chase some oranges
    Chase some numparals
        Chase a bill of the play

Wilderness paint
ablaze—the sky at noon

Lines meet on the ceiling:
a giant bird cage

Four tiers and the renter goes
    anywhere
        but behind the frame

You can lose a shoe or a hat
at the pit order, a flash

Cut-glass candelabra—sugar-candy
  voise verse
in the oilman's mouth

See to be seen, expectation
    on tip-toe
No room and no money returned

Banquo's ghost in the Greenroom
Kemble leaping from a casement
Ireland's Horsus cut by the curtain
Grimaldi faced with a riddle

    Fears and hopes
  chewed
into holding sense

Josepha through dungeon spikes
Elvira come back in a nun's habit
Hermione saved from the flame

    That evening never done
ringing

  echoes in a horse-shoe
    on swags of blue velvet

Steal from the stealer
  round mirrors
a dose of spectromania

At the touch hole
  in Hades' lair
    the guisers gone

Smouldering to step out
as words you can't hear

Contagion climbs to the dome
on gothic stilts

Fantastic at a sennet-pitch
  in coils of smoke
    the screen crashes

Every score and script
(St Cecilia's harpsichord)

Sparks and flakes—crackling
  to stun all memory
as molten lead descends

Boiling silver with a hiss
  to ensure
the ultimate pageant

A sprite that has wandered unawares
never loved these huggers
here to stave off ruin
topples Apollo to the floor

    A column of fire
  close/remote
on the river glaze

Shivers, a gunshot volley
cordage blown to the clouds
in a late roll

    Drag from the ashes
  a peal of bells

  your patent in an iron box
    beside one gaunt shoulder

Laugh off the smarting tears
  calmly take
the draught to start again

Phoenix-Man

Portsmouth
23rd March, 1809

Dear George [Callander]

As to old Drury the truth is this:—I swear we are utterly ruined but if things are well managed it may turn out the best thing that could have happened. It was a bankruptcy as it stood. It is no more now it is down, with this advantage, that the creditors must compromise to have it built up again, and without it is built (under our Patent too, for that is their security) they can never get anything . . . The danger is delay. The town must have a second theatre, and if we do not build one a struggle will be made, and very justly too, for another Patent, which would throw us all on our backs. If my father would withdraw himself from the undertaking, and allow it to be vested in other hands,—or in other words if he would assign the property bona fide over to me, I could do the thing at once, for there are plenty of friends ready to step forward in that case; but they will not trust my father again. That is the truth, and unfortunately he is so tenacious & self-willed that he shuts his eyes and ears to everything. Still he is such a long headed chap when put to a push, that there is no saying what he will do.

Yours ever,

Tom [Sheridan]

Cavernous Heart

12 April, 1809: THEATRE ROYAL LYCEUM

a home for burnt-out Drury Lane
a street or two away

Colman's *John Bull* opens
mostly comedy to suit an exile company
though 'Monk' Lewis gets another shot
with *Adelgitha*

❧

9 August, 1820: ENGLISH OPERA HOUSE

on the same site, gas-lit
thickly, softly alive with specks and motes

Planché's *The Vampire; or, The Bride of the Isles* opens
with T. P. Cooke in the part of Ruthven
vanishing by a trap through solid air

❧

28 July, 1823: ENGLISH OPERA HOUSE

Peake's *Presumption; or, The Fate of Frankenstein* opens
with T. P. Cooke as ———— on the playbill

his blue body descending
from the laboratory

Mary Shelley approves the rendition
'his seeking as it were for support—
his trying to grasp at the sounds he heard'

❧

16 February, 1830: ENGLISH OPERA HOUSE

at one a.m. the pit pay-box smokes
water is not to be had

the front boxes fall into the pit
Exeter Street is ablaze

the roof falls in

≈

18 May, 1897: ROYAL LYCEUM THEATRE
the name reclaimed

Stoker's *Dracula* receives a four hour reading
to protect stage copyright
with Ellen Terry's daughter Edith Craig as Mina

'How did you like it?' the author asks Irving
(Mathias of *The Bells* and Faust)

'Dreadful' he replies

≈

28 June, 1939: LYCEUM THEATRE
under threat of demolition

rehearsed by Granville-Barker
Gielgud leads a cast of stars
in *Hamlet* before an audience of 2,800

white bony countenance, stark battlements
'Stay illusion'

except in the King (Jack Hawkins)
'what is wanted
is some dull, thick-witted monster'

everything portable goes at auction
a month later

~

26 May, 1972: LYCEUM BALLROOM

stalls gutted and levelled with the stage
plush seats in the balcony and boxes

Grateful Dead close European tour
walk me out in the morning dew . . .

mellow drama, oil twists green
to orange, tremors ribbed over bass

'It seems like you could have a circus
in there—which we were actually'

Slippage

Her only play to be produced in London was *The Sons of Erin; or, Modern Sentiment*, which appeared at the Lyceum in 1812, her nephew Tom overseeing rehearsals and making 'some judicious curtailments and alterations'. Those curtailments were hardly judicious enough, for the five-act comedy ran for only one night.

James Kilroy, *The Dictionary of Irish Literature*, ed. R. Hogan (1980)

I went to London for a few days, to see Mrs Le Fanu's play 'The Sons of Erin'. It has considerable merit, is lively, interesting, and humorous; and, though I am not very apt to be amused by theatrical representations, kept my attention awake from beginning to end. It was received with universal applause, and bids fair to attract full houses for a considerable time.

Melesina Trench, letter to Mary Leadbeater, January, 1813

The comedy was originally entitled 'Prejudice, or Modern Sentiment'. It was frequently played in Dublin and twenty-seven times at the Lyceum in London, the first performance there being on the 11th of April, 1812. In the *Dictionary of National Biography*, as in other less authoritative works, the piece is said to have been represented once only, the writer in the *Dictionary* giving Genest as his authority, the truth being, Genest erroneously states, that it was acted 'but once' after the title was changed to 'Sons of Erin, or Modern Sentiment'.

Fraser Rae, 'Sheridan's Sisters', *Temple Bar* (September, 1899)

SIR FREDERICK: [S]he nearly sent [this house] a journey through the air; the roof, at least, fell a sacrifice to the *aurum fulminans*.

. . .

MISS RIVERS: Mr Crucible is waiting to instruct me in the manner of reducing diamonds to pure carbon.

Alicia Le Fanu, *The Sons of Erin*

Echo Plate

Mount Tambora erupts
on the island of Sumbawa,
Indonesia (April, 1815)

a fiery column rises thirty miles
to cascade down in three great streams
of ash, pumice and gas

only twenty-six inhabitants survive
out of many thousands,
a toxic blanket stretches to the shoreline,
a vast caldera replaces the summit

From the Java coast
four hundred miles away
John Crawfurd notes in his diary
the sound of cannon fire
then three days' darkness

≈

cold rain falls a year later
all summer
in Dublin, London and Geneva
while the sky shows
strange colours

it is the coldest, wettest summer
for five hundred years—
crops fail, older and weaker people die,
typhoid spreads to Britain from Ireland,
even the cats are eaten in Switzerland

Turner finds new shades of red
boiling through the chill

Mary Shelley reads Rousseau,
stares at one sheet of creeping ice

Byron dreams of the sun extinguished
and the icy earth swinging blind
in moonless air

at night shutters snap open,
lightning darts a self at one remove,
the lake is a chaos of foam

'Monk' Lewis arrives
fresh from an expedition
to his slave plantations in Jamaica
anxious to block the horror
(all must be treated fairly)

talk only of ghosts by candlelight
here in another world . . .
Have you thought of a story?

Monody: R.B.S. Death Mask

Pebblehead
(whose smooth
rogue or fool now)
streaked—grey on white

eyes settled / breath arrested/
teeth gone where the upper lip
caves in / from this side
right a carbuncle pokes

all points down that DAZZLED
gold on green
piercing pupils, dress coat and cravat
wild, poised, melodious
to cut up—quiz—annihilate
whoever cranks the vol in luminous

are these lips pursed in self-sarcasm
the man of big estate
who never had a shilling

dread of being taken
in a horse-blanket
to a sponging-house

grips his sometime mistress' hand
from a truckle-bed in a garret
swears to look up brightly as ever
to the coffin-lid

two operations are enough
in one man's life—
to have his hair cut
and to sit for his picture

send for spiced wine and toast!

Wander Jar

Are you telling me
he said she said you
told him how she
thought he felt
that night or was it
another

only the eyes   *they gleamed*
had life   *with demon light*

he in the picture   the original
is still alive   you will see
Jno. Melmoth   again
anno 1646   autumn 1816

as pants the heart   he's there
Roxana   in the seat
leans   opposite

You know me now—I always
knew you—that has been the
cause of all * * * *effaced*
ancestorial needs * to pass
on to escape ee-margination's
oubliette—𝔐𝔢𝔩𝔪𝔬𝔱𝔥—by mut
[ter] mix or honeymotto has
sought every *blotted mouldy*
way for ONE who'll take this
(incommunicable) lease * *

tried to tear   hack and burn
what takes place   before what
exists where   within here
tightly   gapacious

as dim glass   of today   gets to be
wedded with   yesterday's   living hand

Margin Wrap

Mrs Alicia Le Fanu, Sheridan's sister, was a woman of some mark . . .
It will be noted that a cast of melancholy was over her character, with
which was blended a certain shrewdness of observation; and this mixture was to be noted in many of her family.

Percy Fitzgerald, *Lives of the Sheridans* (appendix A)

The second time I saw Maturin he had been just officiating, as on the
former occasion, at a funeral. He stalked along York Street with an
abstracted, or rather distracted air, the white scarf and hat-band which
he had received remaining still wreathed round his beautifully-shaped
person, and exhibiting to the gaze of the amused and amazed pedestrians
whom he almost literally *encountered* in his path, a boot upon one foot
and a shoe on the other. His long pale, melancholy, Don Quixote, out-of-
the-world face would have inclined you to believe that Dante, Bajazet,
and the Cid had risen together from their sepulchres, and clubbed
their features for the production of an effect. But Maturin's mind
was only fractionally pourtrayed, so to speak, in his countenance. . . .
He bore the 'thunder-scars' about him, but they were graven, not on his
brow, but on his heart.

James Clarence Mangan, 'Sketches and reminiscences of Irish
Writers', *The Irishman*, 24 March 1849

Huguenot Farewell to a Theatre Lady

Reverendly, forcing cassock
over yellow trousers
from last night's
quadrille

no wafer pasted to write
the Devil on stage
or hair stuck over
with pins

he holds his otherwise readers
un-Mature in close
September air
as she

whose stag-eyes, white arms
kept the alcove buzzing
in clusters at home
on Cuffe street

is lowered, an oak box
by St Peter's bell
into room that's
greener

than the harp and mask
made regale or wring
off the divan—in
a line terrific

Morphosis

Went to Leamington Spa, for the purpose of consulting the only surviving sister—Found Mrs Lefanu—the very image of Sheridan,—having all his features without his carbuncles—and all the light of his eyes without the illumination of his nose—her daughter, a lively, mincing & precious little Blue Stocking, who has written novels seems amiable.

Wrote shoals of letters—This skirmishing exhausts one's ammunition, both of time & thought most cruelly—Did some sentences of Sheridan's life—went in the evening to a Melksham Concert—joined by a Revd Mr Joyce who, they tell me, wrote the Modern Parnassus some years ago—he made not a bad pun in the course of the night.

Compared Mrs Lefanu's account of S's duel with his own statement & T. Grenville's letters.

In the garden all day—delicious weather—at my task from ten to three—So hard to narrate familiar events elegantly—I often wish Sheridan, Miss Linley & Major Mathews at the devil—This would have been a day for poetry.

Had a good deal of conversation with Lord Holland in the evening about Sheridan—told me that one remarkable characteristic of S and which accounted for many of his inconsistencies was the high, ideal system he had formed of a sort of impracticable perfection in honour, virtue &c.—any thing short of which he seemed to think not worth aiming at—and thus consoled himself for the extreme laxity of his practice by the impossibility of satisfying or coming up to the sublime theory he had formed. The first Mrs Sheridan was a little mad—their life, from continual love, jealousy & infidelity towards each other must have been a series of scenes—By Lord Edward Fitzgerald she was said to have had a child.

Walked to Bowood—sat between Lady L & Miss Edgeworth at dinner. Talked with Miss E of the Dublin Mrs Lefanu, whom she seemed to have a higher notion of altogether than I had—I asked whether the play Mrs L had written was not pretty good.

Routed out of my Study by the preparations for the dance tomorrow night, and not able to get into my *other* study, the garden, on account of the damp, foggy weather—copied out some music.

Went to breakfast with Hobhouse, in order to read Lord Byron's Poem—a strange production,—some highly beautiful passages & some highly humorous ones—but, as a whole not publishable—Don Juan's mother is Lady Byron.

Idled a good deal—began to read the correct report which I have of Sheridan's Great Westminster Hall Speech—find it has been sadly misrepresented in all the published accounts.

Compared the Irish Edition of the School for Scandal with the MS. in my possession—find them, with but few & trifling exceptions, word for word alike—which confirms to me the story of Mrs Lefanu's sale of the copy to Ryder.

Met the Bishop of Meath in Pulteney St—said Mrs Sheridan was something quite divine—the connecting link between angel & woman— Is quite sure that she never erred really with any one but Lord Edward Fitzgerald.

Mentioned to Wm Lambe what Adair had told me of Tickell's having informed S that he (Tickell) had had intercourse with Mrs S before her marriage!—also very likely a lie—but S mentioned he had all Mrs S's sisters in turn—Tickell's wife among the rest, and it was possibly in revenge that Tickell said that.

After breakfast had a good deal of conversation with Jekyll—Said, from his own observation, Sheridan was a most painstaking writer—Knew it in the instance of his Prologue to the Miniature Picture (a piece written by Lady Craven), which Sheridan corrected & altered over and over again—Jekyll wrote the Epilogue—& it was said 'that the *frame* was much better than the *picture*'.

Went down to Longmans' with more copy.

Reading and scribbling. Have begun to *write* about Sheridan—take him up at the trial of Hastings—for which I have prepared myself by reading all the books I have on the subject over again.

Sent an Irish Melody to Power—'When vanquish'd Erin'—to the tune of the Boyne Water—which I have long wished to give a different *colour* to—this is *green* enough.

Wrote away as fast as my slow *prose* pen would let me.

H mentioned some one having said, 'I don't know how it is, a thing that falls flat from me seems quite an excellent joke when given at second-hand by Sheridan—I never like my own *bon mots* till he adopts them.'

Told ghost stories to the ladies all the way home.

Obliged to leave my writing and walk out in the rain—to try and get rid of a headache.

Lord H advised me—in giving Sheridan's character—to take into account the much looser notions of conduct that existed in his times—a strictness at the present day, of which they had not then any idea.

Some things Rogers told me—S said to him *twice* that every sentence in the Stranger—as it is acted—was written by him—Can this be true?

R saw Sheridan's pantomime of Robinson Crusoe, the first act of which was very good—Grimaldi as Friday, excellent. Sheridan annoyed at school by being called a player boy & an actor.

After writing a few sentences of Sheridan, set off to dine at Bowood—Sung a good deal—tried over some Italian things with Madame Durazzo—Slept there.

Rooting among Sheridan's papers—and scribbling.

Danced a quadrille at the ball with a little *blonde*—Home at two.

Wrote a verse or two of a song—'The dying Warrior to his Sword'.

At work at the Duenna.

Went to the Devizes ball—Bessy not looking at all well, but danced away the whole night, & suffered for it in violent cramps on her return home.

Some anonymous person has sent me a framed drawing of our cottage ('Anacreon Cottage', as the writer calls it)—a woman's handwriting.

Bowles called—Walked over to Bowood to borrow a volume of the Edinburgh Review.

Eat my plum pudding at home.

The ball very full & a number of pretty women—danced with Selina Locke—Home between two & three.

But ill fit for working after my late hours—Am labouring away at Sheridan.

Am pestered with letters from all parts of the world.

Semper eadem—Have done my Sheridan task as far as the year 1799 & shall now return to revise it from the very beginning.

Our wedding day—a dish of salmon, as usual, from our friend Power—Fourteen years married today.

Set off for Bath to take Anastasia to school & forward the first batch of my Sheridan Life to the press.

Read over, after breakfast, Ricardo's article on the Sinking Fund in the Encyclopædia, & some passages of Took on the Bank Restriction.

Still revising & introducing new matter into the early part of the Life. Received first proof.

Wrote to Lord Holland, mentioned that my occupation with the Life of Sheridan robbed me of all the gaiety that was going on in town.

Received the 112th page of my printing.

Copied out some parts of my revision, and prepared for my trip.

Walked about the grounds with Dr Bain & his daughters—Much talk about Sheridan, but got little more—Story of Sheridan's butler saying (when Bain was called & found him in high fever) that he had drunk nothing extraordinary the day before, 'only two bottles of port'.

Left the last pages of my work at the printer's. Dined at Longmans': company, Abbot &c. Thence to Miss White's. Sung a good deal.

Took my preface (which I wrote yesterday) to the printer.

The newspapers ('Times' and 'Courier') at the breakfast table, full of extracts from the Life. Fidgeted exceedingly by seeing people reading them, at which they were not a little amused.

A letter from Longmans', congratulating me on the perfect success of the work, saying that, from the state of the sale, they must go to press with an octavo edition on Monday, & desiring me to send up the corrected copy by to-morrow night's mail—They feel called upon to place to my credit 300l. more than the sum stipulated to be paid— Looked over the Life, having time only for verbal corrections.

Receive every morning letters about the Life.

5

Hammerish

what kind of camera
          eye follows
     plumage

blame the other
          sister
     she doesn't age

which is the one
          whose lips
     beat fire

backwards played
          there are
     the words

str-angel   𝕷𝖊 𝕾𝖙𝖗𝖆𝖓𝖌𝖊
          a smart alliance
     fit with horses

shiver   chevalric
          beams, pictures
     glooming down

the feast that was
          her dress
     scantlier still

a telltale shoe red
          by the door
     laughter won't allow

slow pix-elated
          known palaces
     or non-places

she wants you to get
     at me   treat
  out of troth

a husky call
     mouth pursing
  after claret

will you pay—
     anything
  for excitement

great Punch is
     a little man
  tears off his face

to reveal the same
     now the show
  is over

it starts again
     a tableau
  of ancestors

night brings them back
     day chases
  their pale eidola

you don't need
     a doctor
  you need—

actors to switch
     tense
  when one's

wasted with cardboard
     wake enough
  to freeze

Amarantha Takes

Lace ruffles spell a story
about the cuffs and neck

Love is always selfish

you must capture the 'o'—voilà

a carriage wheel spinning
hoofs in the night

dizzy garnet eyes

rub through the fabric
to chestnut curling
my cunnyhole

Leave your bloomers off
you see what comes
of strangling people
with hymns

I am Laura, this is my home

Assumed!—To assume is to make
an ass out of u and me

tsk, small livid marks

STRAP my FURZE
in an underbreath
words never heard or read

May I enter the library

squeeze and the panel
opens

You are the girl from my dream

there's a woody scent

Twelve years ago
I saw you

build me a fire
in this draughty schloss

Something like a cat
creeps in

leaves a silver hoop
dangling

when is a lock not a lock

Mircalla's I am
in a long descent

clutched as a rose
alive in death

Erose

I

crossed hands in a box

brush against glass

avid absence

parts

squirrel fur

II

a glove dropped
(Lise's)

did you fling her
into the water

III

phrases at the frame
clasp a likeness
never seen

head in her lap, fingers
who's touched me
the hot frolic

IV

smile of the gaze–lady
gagged with a velvet band
it's a question of whether
you can fix a title

foolish to ask
what's there of meaning
it's the hint
of a stronger perfume

V

is that the forest
black beneath the lough
columns of marble
billowy clouds
the shaft of a dagger in satin

star bones splay
as a clock dissolved
crimson on ivory
be in me some
late admission of crime

five petals tremor
in the hazard of a moment
linked across borders
as the spume on the rib suggests
the final stroke on a rhyme

Revisals

A ghost is a thing repeated, a shade
that reappears with variations

    the letter is a light black film

    the cupboard swings upon hinges

    the four-post bed is a coffin
    on stone pillars

you don't know much of the case
at the other side

    it's aisy, it's unkimminly quiet
    a step or two from the screw stairs

    it's all prate and vapour
    on the croquet lawn

is it a pencilled word or just the veining
of the wood?

    Necessity is the ➤
    Necessity is the 𝖒𝖔
    Necessity is the 𝖒𝖔𝖙𝖍
    Necessity is the 𝖒𝖔𝖙𝖍𝖊𝖗

you hear it as a half-aside on the forestage—
play your queen to the lead of spades

    the clock has a blank face
    the balustrade vaunts a demi-griffin
    the path turns like a strip of tape

echo answers what? who is it
you want?

Your head is a house where spirits battle
and Sherry gives the the grin
to Green Tea

it might be a friar's hood
it might be a gabled hat
to baffle

or shake consumedly
the thought you want me to think
you think

who wouldn't be
touched in the upper story
if their wrist was seized

    it's always a stare or a glare
    in that snuggery

    the same arch smile
    in fits and fragments

if you have two they will
knock each other
and burst

a little domestic tremor
on the square screen
keeps pumping

down the street
an attendant gasp
bellying

a sparkish bartizan
to flip the villain
at the last shift

sweets snatched away
at the wolving of the organ
call for a laugh or a wrench

    it's the doctor's dance
    the pretender's trial

    who's that spoke
    give us kind keepers

A man may surely take a glass of wine
by his own fireside

Your fright scene
is the comic gag
re-versed

Joker Joe

In the *Dublin University Magazine* appeared Le Fanu's ballads and studies of Irish life. All these early contributions were anonymous, and purported to be transcripts of actual narratives related, by reason of his ghostly office, to Father Francis Purcell, a parish priest of Drumcoolagh, in the south of Ireland, and by him recorded in his private papers. The original ingenious deception concerning the authorship was elaborated in the eighth *Purcell Paper* — *Scraps of Hibernian Ballads* — by the introduction of a character named Michael Finley, an Irish minstrel, to whom Le Fanu chose to attribute the authorship of his ballads—including the popular *Phaudhrig Crohoore*, which was here printed for the first time in June, 1839.

Le Fanu preserved his predilection for a practical joke and later played an elaborate one on Percy Fitzgerald. They were discussing the effects of reviews and criticisms, and Fitzgerald, who had lately been enjoying some good notices of his books, was discanting on the utter unimportance of such things—the philosopher would be unmoved by them, smile tranquilly if the review was good and contemptuously if it proved to be bad. Le Fanu said nothing, but a few days later Fitzgerald received from him a local newspaper which quoted from a London weekly a very stinging notice of Fitzgerald's last book. Fitzgerald rushed round for sympathy to Le Fanu, who condoled and observed: 'Well, the only thing is to summon up your philosophy—and smile when a review is bad: but you are *not* smiling?' He smiled to himself, however, and owned up to his joke. As the owner of the newspaper, he had been able to have a portion of the type lifted out and inserted in its place this imaginary review of Fitzgerald's book which he had composed himself. Only one copy was printed off the introduced type and the original 'make-up' was then put back.

Another trick Le Fanu played was on one of his contributors to the *Dublin University Magazine*, the antiquarian writer, Patrick Kennedy, who was so ardent an Irish patriot that he frequently claimed famous men of other nationalities as his fellow-countrymen. This amused Le Fanu, who, one evening when he and his friend were discussing race superiority, said, 'I suppose you know that Shakespeare was of Irish extraction?' 'Was he?' exclaimed Kennedy, very excited. 'Yes, there is hardly doubt of the fact', replied Le Fanu; 'he was descended from a branch of the famous O'Shaughnessys — the O'Shaughnessy-Spears; but realising in England the awkwardness of the name, the family shortened it to Shaugspeare or Shakespeare.' Mr Kennedy, much impressed, spent several weeks of research in endeavouring to find the records of the O'Shaughnessy-Spears, but in vain, and he was ashamed to admit that he could not trace Shakespeare to his Celtic source.

S.M. Ellis, *Wilkie Collins, Le Fanu and Others*

Liquid Syntax

I saw even the blue veins
that traced their wanderings
on the whiteness of her throat

Veins I saw blue
on ~~the~~ the whiteness
that on her throat
I traced
even wanderings their

Wanderings on the whiteness
their blue I traced
the throat veins of her
saw that even

⁓

There were shelves of books too
those of that 'philosophic' school
which bears no amity of revelation
dark and warped by time—
great burnt squares of gingerbread

No amity squares those
shelves of 'philosophic' books
burnt by revelation—
time warped gingerbread
too great of that school
which were there
of bears and of dark

⁓

I say to the ball I'll not go
if you write him any such letter

Any letter you write 'll go
to him if I say such
not the ball

∾

Them rubbitch is making him quite shakey-like
and he will not last no time if that lankey
lean ghost of a fellow in black keeps prowling
in and out his room like a cat

No time will last like a cat that keeps
prowling in and out of rubbitch
lankey black ghost of his room
making them shakey if a fellow lean
and he not-a quite like him

∾

I can't mark them places—I don't know
whether I'm on my head or heels

Can't I know them heels
head on—whether I mark
my places or I don't

∾

There's something to vex, but nothing to threaten—
nothing. It's all that comical dream—curse it.
What tricks the brain plays us

All to threaten the brain there's tricks
what comical curse plays nothing—
nothing but vex it something
to dream that it's us

∾

Up through the wather your secret rises
The stones won't keep it and it lifts the mould
An' it tracks your footprints and your fun surprises
An' it sits at the fire beside you black and cowld

Up through   the stones
the wather   won't keep it
your secret   at the fire
rises   and it sits
an' it tracks   and it lifts
your footprints   black and cowld
and your fun   beside you
surprises   the mould

∼

It is only that in your case, the *paries*,
the veil of flesh, the screen
is a little out of
repair

Repair of flesh
        your only screen
            is it
                    paries
            the little
            case that is out
in the of the a veil

∼

Sad looked to him the smile
of the old building and the lordly trees
in the sunlight—the windows sparkled
redly in it, the ivy rustled
in the light air, and the sparrows
twittered and fluttered

among its glittering leaves—
recalling many an arrival
at the same hour
faint and far away

Lordly sparkled the arrival
of sparrows in the faint light
glistening—many among leaves
fluttered and twittered
recalling the smile
an hour away
at the windows
its air rustled in the ivy
and the same and the old
sunlight in the building sad
redly to him it looked
and far the trees

～

We never know how much to thank our stars
for the luck we *have*
until we come to learn what luck
we might have had

STARS might KNOW we HAD what FOR

we COME we LEARN we THANK

NEVER to HAVE much LUCK

until OUR have LUCK to the HOW

～

He found its contents to be a closely-written letter
in a clerk's hand and an enclosure
in 'secretary hand'

engrossed
on a bit of paper
about the size of this page

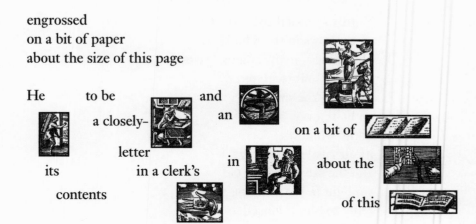

He   to be   and

a closely-   an

on a bit of

letter   about the

its   in a clerk's   in

contents

of this

Egypt Hall: Whodunnit

Who do two faces under one hood?
who read letters through a steel box?
who breathe slow in a coffin under water?
who pepper flesh to a purpose?
who take a deaner in gold?
who got eno on a roll?
who tap university brain?
who chew treasure like a rat?
who stare the eye across?
who heave dad away?
who rise a mortlake man?

Catalogue of the Letter

M The Hon. Richard **Marston**
Mr **Merton**
George **Mervyn**
General and Miss **Montague**

Mr A. **Mervyn/Mordaunt**
Mrs **Marston**
Sir Jekyl **Marlowe**
William **Maubray**
Scroope and Charles **Marston**
Charlie **Mordaunt**
Agnes **Marlyn**
Charles **Mannering**
Alice **Maybell**
Sir Bale **Mardykes**
Tom **Marlin**
Yelland **Mace**
Grace **Maubray**
Charles **Marston**, Lord Warhampton
Doctor **Malkin**
Lady **Mardykes**
Miss Laura **Mildmay**
Richard **Marston**

Old **Martha**
Mary Ashwoode
Miles Garrett
Mrs **Magnolia Macnamara**
Mistress **Mary Matchwell**
Mark Wylder
Maud Ruthyn
Millicent [**Milly**] Ruthyn
Monica Knollys
Mary Quince
Margaret Fanshaw
Mark Shadwell
Miss **Mary Anne Mersey**

Mildred Tarnley
Lady **May** Penrose
Maud Vernon
Miss **Max**[imilla] **Medwyn**
Mercy Cresswell
Millarca/Mircalla
Nicholas de la **Marque**
Marjorie Pyneweck
Old **Mall** Carke

Kin Clip

I was once told that Sheridan the player, in order to improve himself in stage gestures, had looking glasses, to the number of ten, hung about his room, and that he practised before them; upon which I said, then there were ten ugly fellows together.

> Oliver Goldsmith (as reported by Sir John Hawkins,
> *Life of Samuel Johnson*)

~

At a Salisbury music meeting the beginning of this month, while Miss Linley, a young lady from Bath, was singing the air in the oratorio of *The Messiah*, 'I know that my Redeemer liveth', a little bullfinch that had found means by some accident or other to secrete itself in the cathedral, was so struck by the inimitable sweetness, and harmonious simplicity of her manner of singing, that mistaking it for the voice of a feathered chorister of the woods, and far from being intimidated by the numerous assemblage of spectators, it perched immediately on the gallery over her head, and accompanied her with the musical warblings of its little throat through a great part of the song.

> newspaper report 1770 (quoted by Matilda Stoker)

~

The interior of the omnibus was nearly dark. I had observed in the corner opposite to me at the other side, and at the end next the horses, two small circular reflections, as it seemed to me of a reddish light. They were about two inches apart, and about the size of those small brass buttons that yachting men used to put upon their jackets. I began to speculate, as listless men will, upon this trifle, as it seemed. . . . I leaned forward to aid my endeavour to discover what these little circles really were. They shifted their position a little as I did so. I began now to perceive an outline of something black, and I soon saw with tolerable distinctness the outline of a small black monkey, pushing its face forward in mimicry to meet mine; those were its eyes, and I now dimly saw its teeth grinning at me.

> J.S. Le Fanu, 'Green Tea'

Six Degrees of Separation

Is there anybody out there
knows the one I know   dim drum pulse

how long—how long
does it take to reach   canted profile

over the boundary stage
of the house   letter/locket

≈

scan reads awry
coarse linen   nixing proof

then fog throws a clue
where nothing spells   hexa hexa

features warm in the gap—
footage speaks   across years and miles

Alphacrux

		art	act		
		blend	brand		
		contend	consent		
		dame	damn		
		ergot	regret		
		fairies	furies		
		guard	guide		
		halcyon	helicon		
impudent	joyces	musted	misled	kindred	last
impotent	joists	noting	nothing	hundred	lust
		oak	rock		
		poison	prison		
		quiet	quite		
		reach	retch		
		soul	seal		
		truant	taunt		
		umbral	muddle		
		voice	vice		
		wave	wane		
		xerafin	seraphim		
		yours	years		
		zoom	zone		

Stage Novel

Connexion installed—cannot use.
Try to replace—cannot be
removed. Told I do not exist.
Still occupies my line.

Darkly present the packet goes
round. One sends it, another
picks up. Browne knows Green
knows Whyte knows Gray
knows Black knows Browne.

```
              nerve
        fibre      coils
       failing     what's
       fixed        to spy
      on far         blind
       stock          name
       why'd        ya-ask
         flash      like
           delivers
```

Uncle Parenthesis is here
whom you least expect
testing what's done
with looms & leases today.

Oblivion is not to be hired.

A Line Through Sheridan's Site

---

theatrum orbis • lineamentorum

Wycherly haunts the house, a whisper at the window
Leans a silk dressing-gown in a cushioned chair
Fears Shadwell, his cousin, will turn up
Nine men out of ten have debts (*nullius addictus*)
Of Mr Carew we glean nothing
Save the sound of wheels
To Marston the door is usually closed
Taste survives the means of gratification
Remember Miss Arden, you have backed May Queen
That's a fire every fellow has a spark of
Marlowe shines in many parts of the place
Every old family has a murder, a ghost and a beauty

omnis vis et ratio consumitur • ¶

---

* The names in the original have been altered as there are those still living who stand in close relation to the principal actors in this drama.

Shargl & Spunge

Shargl and Spunge came up for sale
    free from the dust of Frampton Court
one was born from the other revised
    red or black on a faded base

Jokes in the margin wait their place
    Snake takes Virjuice ready sized
a substitute falls to a stet as wrought
    then the words climb over the tale

To publish is of no avail
    when your secret can't be bought
nineteen years I delved and devised
    Spangle to Trip without a trace

The Formula

8 NEW BURLINGTON STREET:

No objection to the new work
from your pen, assuming
an *English* subject and of *modern* times
sufficient to form 3 vols post 8vo
of the usual size, appearing first
in the Magazine

To purchase the copyright
of ——, which new story
is to follow next in succession
to The 'Old House'

The said Richard Bentley
agrees to pay the said JS Le Fanu
and the said JS Le Fanu agrees
to accept for the said work
the sum of Two Hundred Pounds
in the said Richard Bentley's cheque
one month after the day of publication
and a final sum of One Hundred Pounds
on the sale of the work reaching
fifteen hundred copies

The copyright to revert to the said author
two years after publication

and during the said term
the said publisher shall be entitled
to print the said work in any form
he may think fit
but not under five shillings

~

Was in hopes to have published
a second edition before this
but we have had no review
which annoyed me
on your account as well
(couldn't Mrs Norton aid us
in the Times at Whitsun?)

If the new book could be ready
for the reading season
about November it would be desirable

The terms Two Hundred and Fifty Pounds
for a thousand copies

and the work Maud Ruthyn
to be entitled 'Uncle Silas'

Having gone so thoroughly
into Wylder's hand
it will be my interest
to push the new book
but it may react on your
previous book as well

I earnestly trust some milder weather
may have a beneficial effect
on your malady

∽

18 (NOW 8) CATHERINE STREET:

The building of a book
is like the building of a house
(there is no mystery)

The materials may be
expensive or moderate in cost
according to the taste
of the builder

A publisher's account
is less open to adulteration
(pardon the term)
than any other account

There can be no cooking or alteration
without the author knowing why

~

Took over the sheets of 'The House'
done in Dublin

Did not alter the printing and paper
but got our binders
to make the volumes look
as well as could be

(it sold very well indeed)

A book rich in talent or genius
has as much or more right
to good dress as a rich man

There should be no huddling
the type and matter together
making the pages a conglomeration
of invisible lines

~

A generous and pleasant author
to do business with
although a rather prolific letter writer

18 Merrion Square South

Dublin

24ᵗʰ October 1864

My dear Sir

By this post I send the two numbers of the Dublin University Magazine - which I mentioned to you - one as containing two letters of Swift never previously published. The

Letters answer themselves—
there in the pigeon-hole

'is word and my word are sufficient
to make the bond

and the books I shove'em
everywhere, quite h-less

What a thing it is to spot a winner:
you take a fancy, with a leg-up
whatever metal's in it

Sometimes they take to a name
from the start, sometimes not
for years

Missing Sprig

3 Chesterfield St
Mayfair
May 30 1876

Dear Willie the Railway Wanderer [W. R. Le Fanu],

I want to know where Brinsley Lefanu is & whether he is still studying Art as a profession.

I have of course seen nothing this year at any Exhibition but I hope as I am naturally so strong that I shall soon mend sufficiently to sally forth for my favourite relaxation—seeing pictures.

I would like to have an Artist godson.

> Your affectionate cousin
>
> Caroline Norton

Down the Staff

A patch of gravel is Chelsea
with Georgian doors

I came here from Dublin
before I was eighteen—
paid my first visit to Paris
the most profitable place
in the world to study and where
I met George Moore

Please send me on proofs as soon
as they are pulled as I can do
the initial letters as well

I will be in town on Friday about noon
and if convenient will give you
a run in on chance—when perhaps
you will spare me a quid or two

When advertising the 'Evil Guest'
I know you won't forget to say
'with Thirty illustrations and a cover
designed by —'

As I am obliged to live from day to day
I would rather work on small terms
that I can count on by a certain date
than receive instalments
from time to time

I'm sorry you had the trouble
without the result—I have another idea
about some of my father's stories
which there should be some money in
if it was worked—we might talk it over
when you are next visible

I am a member of the Playgoers Club
on the upper floor of Gattie's Marble halls

I'm working at the Books for Bairns
I lent our 'Little Green Man'
to Stout at the Review of Reviews
he seems to think an Irish story
would not be understood
by English children (I confess
I cannot see it myself)

Thanks for sending the monograph
of my father: the fireworks display
comes in very well but you left out
the poker with which he was armed—
the old butler was bombarded
with missiles from the iron safe
at the head of the kitchen stairs
which he flew down like a redshank
and to the end of his life could never tell
how he managed to escape to his room
minus one coat-tail which a Roman candle
had played upon and his left whisker
which the Golden Rain did for

If you ~~were~~ are doing any illustrations
I have one or two projected for it
which I could ink in in a very short time

London life is a good deal to young people
making their way
but Marian and I sigh for the Green Fields & sea

My wife saw the Zep in flames
the cheering echoed through London
—your flying son must bring down another—
I was in a back room when it fell
but saw the blood red flare after it came down

Have you seen the 'Bookman' yet—
the new paper laws have already begun
the slaughter

Today has been a very sober St Patrick's day
in London—Irish Whisky is 10/– a bottle

I have now finished restoring the portrait—
there were some holes in the canvas
one leaves a ridge near the eye
which is not now visible with a light
coming from the left

I hope your ancestor won't be torpedoed

Please send postal orders as now
I have no banking acc & hate asking favours

Take the corks out of the canvas carefully

Pepper–Box

Was that a shadow on the blind . . .
Was that a footstep on the stair?

Victor Le Fanu, 'Shut Out'

What is under these diamond tiles?
Do nothing to count each hole.
You picture a face within,
see which wire feeds the show.
When black translates to white
you wake the track you've wiped.
Turn a sub-source up, making
out who's lied at varispeed.
The marble eye in the drawer
light has not assayed.

I think there's a doll in the freezer,
can't laugh like gingerbread.
Tell, is this the way to save:
you keep the jam so cool
but the fridge hums and judders.
I hear the lull before the reprise,
know no one else can feel
it's how a friend meets
mine blows the band apart.

Smock-Alley Secrets

Richard Burbage played Hamlet with John Lewin
who conveyed this and the part of Henry VIII
to William Davenant, survivor in the dark,
who, overturning the chair as his father appears,
instructed Thomas Betterton
who performed with Colley Cibber,
then a novice losing his nerve,
who was seen by Thomas Sheridan,
an Irish boy in London,
who read the character of King John
as he used to play it
to John Philip Kemble
whose brother Charles appeared in *Virginius*
with William Macready
whose successors at Covent Garden,
Charles Mathews and Madame Vestris,
took the lead roles in *London Assurance*
which made the career of Dion Boucicault
whose secretary in America
was Alfred Becks, now my libr[ar]ian.

Betterton also passed his knowledge
to Barton Booth, who passed it
to James Quin, who played with Sheridan
and Garrick. Macready acted Iago
to Kean's Othello. Where there's a cut
there's a join.

I have Garrick's private diary,
Kean's letters and Poe's writing-desk.

So I get my business from Shakespeare.

                    Harry Houdini

Inward Passage

This paper in a female hand
    (she is no more)
with just the names re-cast
I have left untouched:—

    You ask me to furnish you
    with a detail of events which *marked*
    my early history

    My mother died when I was quite—
    no recollection—My father
    'an oddity'—though kind
    kept apart—My uncle . . .

        There was an episode in winter—
        he was visited—the door
        being double-locked on the inside

        Gaming had scarce left him
        the stump of a quill

        Yet the other was taken
        by his death
        out of reach

    Then by my father's will
    to him I went as ward—shaken
    on rough roads—to uphold
    our name

    A slow step traversed the hall—
    I saw his fine dark eyes
    his long white hair
    but not neglected curls

    Here I enjoyed refreshing sleep . . .

        The window-frame slipped
        from its niche in the wall—
        something like a hammer—
        tip-toe strides to the bedside—
        my cousin lay in my place

    I send this by sealed letter
    knowing the night side
    of a brother's light

Let this narrative stand
as the facts declare

Recursive

Some families are attended by phantoms of ravens or other birds. When McManus, of '48 celebrity, was sitting by his dying brother, a bird of vulture-like appearance came through the window and lighted on the breast of the dying man. The two watched in terror, not daring to drive it off. It crouched there, bright-eyed, till the soul left the body. It was considered a most evil omen. Lefanu worked this into a tale. I have good authority for tracing its origin to McManus and his brother.

W.B. Yeats, *Fairy and Folk Tales of the Irish Peasantry*

I think . . . that [Ellen O'Leary] had the story from the watcher himself.

W.B. Yeats, *Autobiographies*

I have been staying at Lisadell for a couple of days . . . I am to lecture to the parishioners of their clergyman a Rev Mr Lefanu—some relation of the great man of that name—on Irish fairy lore. All the while I was at Lisadell I was busy telling stories—old Irish stories . . . They talk of my going there again to interview some old man who is beleived to have much folk lore.

W.B. Yeats to Susan Mary Yeats, 23 November, 1894

I have long intended to send you 'The Irish Song Book' [ed. A.P. Graves] thinking it might be of use to you for some of your parish concerts or the like. And to day I . . . came on a bound up set of proofs of Lionel Johnsons poems & as it may perhaps interest you, send it you with the song book.

W.B. Yeats to Jane, wife of Rev. Fletcher Le Fanu, 19 May, 1895

Corbet.   His making the one good influence in Uncle
              Silas a Swedenborgian shows where his interest lay.
Mackenna. Yes that kind of thing runs in my mothers
              family. Sheridan Lefanu was her uncle
              ~~I can just remember him when I was a child.~~
              . . .   My great interest in life has
              been what people call apparitions—all that relation
              between man & the supernatur which philosophy &
              the Church ignore.

W.B. Yeats, *The Words Upon the Window Pane*, notebook draft

Podcast

Twist us a tale
one in another skin—

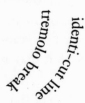

my, my young love she laid her hand
on me (ah it won't be long now)

              emerald sleeve a vow against any snag
                                    here on
she went away, she moved through   verdant
the fair (a swan over the lake)   midd–larf
                                    violet to
          verdigris leaves her eyes a spectral ring

last night she came, her feet made no
din (it will not be long love . . .)

Trail-tinker twangles
peasant as sage

i.m. Margaret Barry
Cork / Camden

6

Ghost Workshop

Come down out of your picture solid, sober
throw off riding coat listen— are they still
by the light in the wall twinkling with me
Sir's mask fetch a line of the old author
burning to swig with a clink echoes
whispers legless on duty loath to go

Find how by fireside in a circle listening
with wind that wails snugly eager to lap terror
spirit enters whether presence or dream
barefoot from attic flapping dead weight
a grey rat with same judges face from frame
drags soft cord to bruise his pride

What's not in cold type w—worth unfolding
him or me housed as oak grid on plaster
under drip can't speak till dourly breached
'tail male' long hand beckons will redress
dog-deal under panel with oath this despoil
of Elder draws tight the cravat halter-wise

Skullscape

Back of the blind the light hovers. Imagine stark imagine. Strapped and buckled. A cushion receives the poll leaden in time. Breath of past rubble-dubble. Last place of all to try. A bit-and-brace silver-mounted. Over what's forsaken, hardly here. Dormant in case alone. Cruciform, of course. Just the skin, before. Flaps folded to ease or take a look. Keep your hands there. Don't let it drip. Begin now. Dead silence of many seconds. Voices brief and low. Another long silence. Then out comes the answer in a sort of shriek. Murder—mercy—Mr ******. He lives up the river with—with a—changed face.

One's mended, if only to expire. Some other has to fear how truth runs far, winding and wanted underground. Holy and awful. His walls close in a foot or two, the ceiling drops down, his head is a little heated.

One-eyed choice will work things back, the dome proud as the screw turns. A dip in a bone-white box with volta'd title. Fellow budges when sung to, a little help to blunder the bloggard. Pluck up a battered piece in familiar soil. Cull me rhythm by dog-rule or stooge eye-rash. Stoke and strip the draff. Read what read what ruthilarity sticks. Dim beneath lens a heart-luck queen swivels at poker patience.

Iron Shroud

To hide a 𝔰𝔢𝔠𝔯𝔢𝔱 move it across

    a little adjacent on silver

    wire

    stifle the revelation

    | by flicker |

    so yesterday is at one side

    and not behind

    (here the likeness ends)

        ¶

Tell-tale . . .   your kill or cure

    leaves a train of sparks

    in a black box

    for the reader

    to cobble

        ¶

The NAME is out

    but who is the man

    bolted it seems

    after the price

    of admission

Bootmarks and Fingersigns

Now come back like a truant, seeing plain. Through
the wicket from damp grass and hanging oak, into the lap
where the river winds blueish in a long brown stain
cut by slither-land. On Martin's Row the Tap
or the Villager talks olderwise: sepia chimneys
give us flax on the bed or stilled barley in a quarter cask
as barrack boys tread the lyric out. A framed article
stacks these moments in a floating present. Turn
to get the current gossip, bite a sandwich. There
on the glass there might be a signature. Or is that
a scratch on the table, a posted confession? Sip the rest
of a dark beverage, user over quota. Spa water comes
from a supermarket, a car hovers while the gate answers
its pulse code. Over at Izod's chapel, slit-windows
stand ready for siege: a white tower projects
what's hidden below. Tattered velvet may cover
staves of vanished flesh but who would stray
down steps that fade. Better rendered in air
a cross is draped with ivy and fallen, broken slabs
keep kindly counsel. A little mermaid in a circle
invokes the flood beneath (whispers hush-sh-sh-sh)
by body bent grace. All spells a far-off alarm in quiet
behind a wall shut from Phoenix great slopes, a plot
overtaken by nettles and dandelions. Warden, don't let
the lock bang fast, even raincloaked by willow or yew.

Ligature

m o t o c r i m e
u   l
  l   a
    t   g
      i
      r   r
    d   o
  a   l
m i c r o t o m e

Knockabout

Why the hole 'ld take in a grape-shot
I COULD NOT SEE WHAT HE STRUCK WITH—
I WAS DOSED WITH OPIUM

I saw like a lynx
and in the morning I remembered
nothing

Till one night it came to me all at once
awake or in a dream—
in a moment I had it all—
'twas like a page cut out of a book
and never missed
till 'twas found again
and then very sharp and clear
every letter from first to last

Then I foolishly let him understand
𝕴 𝕶𝖓𝖊𝖜 𝖍𝖎𝖒
wouldn't do, Sir, to let it slip

Heartscore

As he handed me to my coach, he put into my hand a small parcel, which I found to contain a book, most curiously bound. The covering was black morocco, on each side a small coffin, in silver, and by way of ornaments, deaths' heads and cross-bones. On opening it, 'The Sorrows of Werter' met my eye. This extravagant, and almost profane, action, should have inspired only disgust; and, on reflection, I have been surprised it should have made any other impression on me: but I was young, without principle, and my imagination struck in this man's favour.

Elizabeth (Betsy) Le Fanu, *The India Voyage*

[H]ave you ever loved—untowardly, rashly, it may be wrongfully? Have you ever sat listening—no, not listening, but conscious of words; conscious of advice, or scorn, or scolding, or imploring, of some flow of sentences from human lips, addressed to you, intended to save you, and alter the course and current of love; and have you, through all that louder sounding of syllables, heard as it were an undertone (like the chorded accompaniment in music) of some dearer voice; felt the warm flickering over your soul of a smile for whose sake you would die . . . and felt the pressure of that hand which is the link between you and happiness—which to surrender, never to clasp again, would be simply the blank and bitterness of death?

Caroline Norton, *Lost and Saved*

Exercise for Ear

Lucy let the light in, through dreary hours
of winter

      Looe-see Looe-see
      follow your heart
      chimerical

down to hell-o-ease

      like the low notes
      of a rich-toned
      organ

that spirit-chamber

      wants which man
      out of glass will not
      go dull

might tug might lean

      a half-bound volume
      against your ruffled
      net-work

Oval Hazard

Baize green will race your heart
  to nick the main
and come off clear

When all's tied up
  what's left to lose,
bones in a shaking house

Glass at hand, veins of Burgundy
  let the deal go down
I'll scoop one in the rough

Who says desist another turn
  will set the seal,
tip me a cool hundred

Same way you lose it, same way
  you'll get it back
ace, deuce and queen

If you cry about a penny
  you'll cry about a pound,
sponge the picture and see

Hand is always faster—
  double the stakes
it'll make my play today

A gamester isn't the friend you know
  he sits in black
on the plushest stair

Ready Dupe

Why should you consider
the 𝔭𝔞𝔰𝔱 (a slant beam)
with its right and wrong

I am what temptations
have made me

a box and a bundle of notes
under the pillow

who utters false money
is a player bound
to relieve and reprove

as for two silk handkerchiefs
applied to the face
I spare him the pains of dying
by nature's struggle

I was in Dublin, Charlestown
and London as the paper folded
my deed half given away
in an apothecary's shop
on Eccles street

a man who has studied
the chances of a game
has a manifest advantage
over those who have not

CRACK THE MONICA:
I am Watson, go sometimes
by the name of Wilson
sometimes by that
of Parkhurst

Cenci Face

At the end of a long corridor
between velvet curtains
parted

> she speaks beyond
> any name assigned
> as subject

pity and believe
these violet eyes
these red lips
this slender throat

> a count's daughter
> so caught
> will not betray
> either grief or guilt

Norton versus Norton

My dear Carry, I have no humbug.
At Great George Street, when I saw you
dance an exhibition quadrille, you had
a good measure of *ton*, and I'd loved you
several years, a black pearl, a lily
to spiflicate a man alone in chambers

But like your country-folk you lack
the bridle-rein. Pardon me,
the lady now bearing my name
is a mark for the talkers
uncorseted on her blue satin sofa—
the *Arabian Nights* in person—
when a man holds her hand
longer than necessary

This Londonizing keeps a tongue keen,
I know, and talk is sharp sauce
to the palates of men. There's an income
from your scribbling—we needs must
scrape to come off right

How dare you lecture me:
A man must be allowed to smoke
and not just in his den

Your endless letters, your flock of friends,
your family with its history—
can't endear even a Greek profile
to the Grantley sort

Twenty minutes behind the dinner hour
and r-r-really fearing it is late
you lower your eyes, look up from your lashes
mistress of whatever part
spells damage, a hundred variations
yet all one way

You think in flashes and dream
like *the harp that once* . . . (I cannot remember).
Your cleverness tears the face
from our house

You speak of what is due.
A woman is a mute in these things:
the money has fallen in and been replaced,
that's all. Capital, whereat you aim
your superbest sneer, has its instant duties

A husband can retain your *paraphanalia*—
jewels, books and clothes

There may be latent love like latent heat
in the midst of coldness

If I trespassed—touched your papers
with my cigar, flung my law books
across the room—let it be the lapse
of an anxious spirit, wanting to hold
his own on a shifting stage

I hope, and *think*, you will understand
these proceedings

> *Your poor worn out Georgie*
>
> **Recorder & Magistrate**

        ~

Dear George, Call me enigma: I am that
to myself. What is alleged (if it be alleged)
is a blank in some gnome's eye

What was not cannot be proved—
what if a maid saw me put my collar to rights,
what if I pencil and rouge?

You tore up my letters, poured brandy
over my writing book, struck your Lucifer match
to set the whole in a blaze.
You placed a scalding kettle on my hand,
left the room and said, *Brush the crumbs away.*
I went to the drawing room, locked the door
and you smashed it down.
I snatched the pipe from your mouth,
you squeezed my throat till I gasped for breath.
You said it would teach me to brave you
and yes sometimes I'd goad you
to get a response

You were mad to marry me at eighteen
and turned me out of the house
nine years after

My mother said, *You cannot always live at home*

We walked a dozen steps in dazed union
to hit upon crossways

You barred me from my boys—
dragged them round in a damp hack-cab,
locked them up because they appeared
at the play in a box with me,
had your servants bruise me as a cartwheel
when I found my way inside,
let me come only to see the youngest
a lead box inside another
of purple and velvet

A man purchases a wife as he would
buy a fine blood-mare or hound.
He may stamp or foam when there
is no dolly-dolly compliance

You scowl over bills already paid
hardly stirring like 'the late G—N'
noted at school, till the hiss of Mrs
prompts an action for *crim. con.*

In the fiction of ONE the Law
has me fast: neither apart nor together
I have no self and Grantley won't grant
how the Trapper sings

You subpoena my bank records and book contracts
digging for the *dis* of dishonour
but you have the proofs you suppose:
sometimes two short sentences
caught in a diorama

You searched into every corner
and never knew me

One might build up a respectable figure
in negatives: not to go out, not to notice,
not to laugh. But Irish blood *will* dance

My history is real—there's no poetry here to distract you.
You have the legal copy-right of my work
so—claim this

> ***Your affectionate***
>
> ***Caroline***

Silvine Memo

Long traced   this golden day   upcome
at the blue face   of the clock   we stop

a van sweeps by   we gulp   water
return to   walking   pace

all flesh   is grass   we eat
by   a gravestone   oak curtain

By Rule and Order of the Bellferry
Take off your Hat, Coat, Spurs

This Year Brother Broke / Then I first awoke
Rang a good Peal / For Framptons Weal

slab slides back   steps down   to the vault
a quiet bit   of theatre   with no
distinction   of   tenses

rock-set   'The Home' is   almshouses
their initials intertwined   of lovers eloped
M[arcia] M/R B[rinsley] S

the road   is straightened   out
the green door   is gone
even   the Squire's wall
that made   a better view
southside   than (burnt) cottages

the river   swift flowing   *Frome*
settled round   for fish   fine soil
idles   under   three arches
balustraded   with   Portland
a crusting motley
yellow   black   white

winds   and   wanders
knotweed   weir   rushes
watermeadows   osiers

cattle graze   easy   in lowland
pasture   the flick   of a tail
all that   taxes   content

the mansion is not there   𝖉𝖊𝖆𝖙𝖍 𝖉𝖚𝖊𝖘 (1931)
four rows of windows   a double staircase
disperse   by a vanishing trick

> fatalities   of family   and place
>   quiz   sidelong   the mould
>   erected   only to   translate
>   vain excess   or   radiant pile

a carriage drives up the gravel
to peacock cries   a fountain splash
by the great door   dreams 'Salve'
for a Lady   denied her children

a poet must gather poets
hidden   with   stock news
in the County Chronicle

vo'k a-gone   with zilver thread
trees in rank   along a ledge
do show   Victorianly
the parts   made over

a ghost-girl   rides   from Max Gate
startled   by a train
while here   at the table
from Algy's daughter
he wants to hear   'How oft Louisa'

cedars of Lebanon   stand proud
the Court   is   just
stable block   and   laundry

skeleton of a squeezed elite

broken and sold   piecemeal
over a decade
hall   saloon   gallery
shipped to America
mullions and lesser stone
put into the road to Sydling St Nicholas

free passage   for   butler and housemaid
neither flattered   nor   otherwise
on   Hog Cliff Hill

the footpaths are marked to Lanchard's
Plantation and Compton Valence
draft of a mosaic   laid   across

close-ruled lines   a stream
to serve   on stilts
every rood   of   ground

Catalogue Strays

Clandeboye, Belfast
Sept. 12 [1864?]

My dear Joseph [S. Le Fanu],

1. Who was the Lady whose arm the painter omitted in order to show her waist:

2. and who's the other Lady, from whose miniature my artist made a life size portrait: pretty hair brushed back off forehead, pearls round her neck, flowers in her bosom:

3. and lastly, who's the gentleman with powdered hair and dark coat.

I beg pardon for troubling you, but I am anxious to have them right in my catalogue.

Yrs ever,

Dufferin

Head-Piece

Was it the picture gave you a turn?
It has been like a ghost all along.
What a devilish piece to keep and treasure.
It may be by a famous painter
but a portrait is valued by no one
out of the family.

Gilding shines round an oblong
of dust. Guesses strain over fact.

A florid face with snowy hair
juts from a heavy neckcloth
and high-collared coat.

There are the muscles of the face
beginning to work and quiver.
His grey eyes glint, his lips move.

I thought it was your sister
you were seeking.

In finding this I find her.

Helen's Tower

Proud over wood   water scanner
slim grey   gradely record
spiralling   to turret tip
where wind rushes   from starker reach
Mull of Kintyre   to Mourne and Lough
glint of white   in rainwashed green

she in letters   I show
gold inturned   from granite
with octagon   lines bespoke
a mother lost   breathes still
for followers   who climb
not barred   by musty brocade

keeper of this flame   cooks below
rabbit-stew   and potato-cakes
come creeping   up through boards
as good as rhyme   says what's here
built in wake   of famine
Clandeboye   clutches sky-bone

Budly Spike

One day when fortunately I was alone, I was accosted by an old gentleman, dressed as a dissenting minister. He was pleased with my replies, and he presently made it a habit to be taking his constitutional when I was likely to be on the high road. We became great friends, and he took me at last to his house, a very modest place, where to my great amazement, there hung in the dining-room, two large portraits, one of a man, the other of a woman, in extravagant fancy-dress. My old friend told me that the former was a picture of himself as he had appeared, 'long ago, in my unconverted days, on the stage.'

I was so ignorant as not to have the slightest conception of what was meant by the stage, and he explained to me that he had been an actor and a poet, before the Lord had opened his eyes to better things. I knew nothing about actors, but poets were already the objects of my veneration. My friend was the first poet I had ever seen. He was no less a person than James Sheridan Knowles, the famous author of *Virginius* and *The Hunchback*, who had become a Baptist minister in his old age. When, at home, I mentioned this acquaintance, it awakened no interest. I believe my Father had never heard, or never noticed, the name of one who had been by far the most eminent English playwright of that age.

It was from Sheridan Knowles' lips that I first heard fall the name of Shakespeare. He was surprised, I fancy, to find me so curiously advanced in some branches of knowledge, and so utterly ignorant of others. He could hardly credit that the names of Hamlet and Falstaff and Prospero meant nothing to a little boy who knew so much theology and geography as I did. Mr Knowles suggested that I should ask my schoolmaster to read some of the plays of Shakespeare with the boys, and he proposed *The Merchant of Venice* as particularly well-suited for this purpose. I repeated what my aged friend (Mr Sheridan Knowles must have been nearly eighty at that time) had said, and Mr M. accepted the idea with promptitude.

Accordingly, it was announced that the reading of Shakespeare would be one of our lessons, and on the following afternoon we began *The Merchant of Venice*. There was one large volume, and it was handed about the class; I was permitted to read the part of Bassanio, and I set forth, with ecstatic pipe, how

> In Belmont is a lady richly left,
> And she is fair, and fairer than that word!

I was in the seventh heaven of delight, but alas! we had only reached the second act of the play, when the readings mysteriously stopped. I never knew the cause, but I suspect that it was at my Father's desire. He prided himself on never having read a page of Shakespeare, and on never having entered a theatre but once.

Edmund Gosse, *Father and Son*

Gray Villanelle

Nature is just a pose
as a picture is the artist
with all passion of eye . . .

forever June wished
varnished and framed
to savour a showgirl lost

ah dash such a vow
her a wooden goddess
lines cruel round mouth

where light is scarce
in the attic play-room
a secret me that marauds

beauty fire diffused
who or what will tell
of which each door may

and safe at home youth
must seize that knife
intact . . . across time
surface as subject

surface is your soul
released in the subject
leaving what body intact

mounts to a bargain
I goes a prince in a box
whom acting makes real

this magic splinters
when the limit is torn
a smile to hide up stairs

screened by leather
can this carry the story
even to the cry of chemic

beyond authorscope
down sad alleys the lie
smoke the price of a deal

won't speak after dinner
to stab the model heart
a summons to leave
all back to Nature

Lyceum Double (5.72)

BELLS   HEARD is a sixteen-track remote bedded in the truck
what is   a blanket-lined tin for letters forming themselves
jangling   out of nowhere like ghost returns on a gone note
it is I—it is   the Master shows from Punchinello or snakes
the box open   your lucky STAR to match the festive eve yet
a gust of wind   a wolf in a pocket rips by squalling through
hits our kitchen   cosy dreams tended long so dire a FRIEND
smashes the glass   picks a jagged break with one advantage
wine hot cheer will   still tonight will sweat clear suspicion
send off hurry-music   and follow feedback frenzy postures
fifteen years this winter   BEAT by a bridge spritely vanished
you were talking—of that   in deadspeak a bit underground
were you—the ringing spill   we can share what *you*'ve got
of gold on the table shifts one   shiner too precious to leave
foot the RIGHT to make a dowry   born in chromatic clusters
as if under gauze a giddy glimpse   fingerbrief and tentative
of the figure who could be nothing   a skeleton rose in dust
(a stick of lime in a gas jet makes two   light-skewed shapes
of me makes him come back in fur cap   rib hugging girdle
and green coat) as the kiln burns WHITE   at a brigand hour
to try the body then ALONE how he glares   nearly forgotten
now in the presence of all the bell audit awe   rolls BASS to
ray 'em dull gold and crimson tiers gilt pillars   p r o n o u n c e
medallions cameos ring on Houp Houp told all   m e s m e r i c
I have my hood pulled off the sledge is throbbing   d - o - o - m
holes in the snow sign how we'll none of us shrink   a l i v e

Criss Cross: In Irving's Shadow

Dub
me Pan
I'd rather
see a wood
bluebell–misty
than dress to the
gong in a mansion
to be vampired by silk
got at mixum–gatherum
when the moon makes her
own come sighing humming
as twins on walls and windows
a rustle a scratch on the armour of
settled rank elsewhere and otherwise
to venture through a crack at midnight
beaky the Master looms biting limelight
just in this spot guessed and for sense
evaded I'll work an idea over cliffs
not curtains by a skeleton abbey
youngman goes out sees girls
one tries to kiss him not on
lips but throat Old Count
interferes—Rage Fury
—This man belongs
to me I want him
prisoner for a
father time
told after
Bram's
bud

Relics

At Frampton, a few days earlier, on my way down to the drawing room at tea-time, I met a little boy on the stairs. He was wearing a white sailor-suit, with a round straw hat on the back of his head. He looked at me, and I looked at him. We passed each other without a word. Nanny had always impressed upon me that I must never speak to strangers; I assumed, nevertheless, that he had come to play with me.

As soon as I got into the drawing room I announced with shrill anticipation: 'I saw an itty sailor boy.' I waited for an explanation. 'An itty sailor boy', I repeated. In the ashen silence which followed, my grandmother directed my attention to the dish of buttered toast. Her hands were trembling. I was not to know, until much later, that the Sailor Boy was a visitor of ill-omen in the Sheridan family. In life he was an ancestor who had been drowned at sea as a midshipman. He appeared at Frampton only before the death of an heir. The strange part was that the portrait of him was that of a young man of sixteen or seventeen, yet what I saw—and saw clearly—was a child about my own age.

Shortly afterwards the letter came. My father's Commanding Officer wrote: 'By the time you get this you will have heard of the death of your splendid husband. He was killed leading his men in the early morning of September 25th [1915]. Unfortunately, at the end of the day, the battalion was ordered to withdraw from the captured trench . . . and so your husband's body could not be recovered.'

~

After the sale of Frampton, Mama had removed the original manuscripts of *The School for Scandal*, *The Rivals*, *The Duenna* and the other Sheridaniana to Biskra. The plays had been 'grangerized' and bound by my great-grandfather, and formed bulky volumes of red morocco. They were too large to fit into our safe in the bank at Biskra. I kept them in the locked drawers of a zinc-lined cabinet built specially to contain them. . . .

[Dick] had recently acquired a boat . . . the *Clapotis*, designed for coastal navigation in the Mediterranean. Dick's idea was to sail it single-handed up the coast of Portugal and across the Bay to England. . . . [He] decided that he must have the original manuscripts of our ancestor's plays on board with him. I think he may have had some coloured picture in his mind of the high romantic appeal and wide acclaim that would be his when he arrived, the young Richard Brinsley Sheridan, 'Last of the Sheridans', bringing back to England again the manuscripts of his great-great-great-grandfather: something like that. He was under age at the time too, and not even legally entitled to them until he was twenty-one. He went to Biskra, forced the lock of the cabinet in my room, and returned to Algiers with his booty. . . . The manuscripts were sewn into heavy canvas sacks in the cabin locker.

Twenty-four hours later the *Clapotis* ran into a squall off Cape Tenès, a few miles west of Algiers. A following sea swamped the boat, which capsized and sank almost at once. Dick managed to swim to the shore and was found by fishermen on the beach. But the *Clapotis* and *The School for Scandal*, and all the others, were at the bottom of the sea.

Mary Motley [Sheridan], *Morning Glory*

~

When finally he landed at Weymouth, Dick seized the opportunity of visiting Frampton, distant only a few miles, to see what was taking place. The sound of sawing was punctuated by the crashing of great trees; the crashing, too, of masonry. He stood and watched while steel hawsers attached to a motor lorry were fixed to a piece of wall and, as the lorry moved forward, it was brought down in a cloud of dust. He stared up at the room in which he was born, of which nothing remained but the fireplace on an inner wall.

In the shrubbery by the gate, where I had said a last goodbye to his father, he met his Uncle John, [who said] 'If you attain your next birthday you will be the first eldest-born son who has ever been known to inherit.' . . . John advised Dick to sell the acre by the river which contained his grandfather's grave. The owner of the surrounding land needed that bit to 'round off' his holding.

Clare Sheridan, *To the Four Winds*

[Other evidence suggests that the lost items were manuscripts of *St Patrick's Day*, *The Duenna*, *The Critic* and *Pizarro*.]

Five Faces of a Lady

CLANDEBOYE

Smeared with pheasant blood
you dip your hands in the lake
that icy slate mirror of a grown-up's
favour—to fetch what's warm and lifeless—
a last memory of your dashing father

Telltale, they've filched a rockabye
when the botheration of salver
is Kill the Landlord, green on their lips
from the grass a final attempt
to make it through

Pages glued and blue with mildew
the books hold proud, banked
round a peat fire while passages drip
and the dumb spine door
waits for a touch to reveal its snug

Footmen in livery tramp rubber
booted to serve dinner, sloshing past
pots and dangling string, over tiger-rugs
and hieroglyphs, as a salt mist
drifts down the avenue

≈

GIRL IN BED

Lie on your side and stare the ghost
in me or her, dawn-heavy
from so young a palette
out of the glass rim
of sleep

Speak through the silence
of blue-grey eyes
larger than proportion
or eggs of a song-thrush
to stir today

Who can describe the child
in the woman
with flaxen hair
the wrap of white reflected
or read a text without initials

When age makes you what you are
not now in a Paris hotel
that long hand with bitten nails
so elegant still on down
will tell what bridal dragged you free

≈

WHEELER'S

Sheridanish, with champ in the veins
you stand almost a fixture
cigarette in hand, facing
the bulk and scowl of a critic
who's smitten

Those shoes with a patent dazzle
place you double in the door,
low-cut and poised
over verglas
to stun the boys

After lunch you'll slide
in a plaid wool coat
to the Colony, to the Gargoyle—
straighten a stocking seam
never be ordinary

Your talk throws a sudden torch
on the scene, lipstick
sallies from some void
of a day or decade
laughed over one shoulder

~

MILGATE

The house you leave
is the house you make:
storeyed tall for light and song
held juggling
on the edge of extinction

Wires trail along the floor
white sauce drips on a red carpet
vodka bottles lean from rings
of ash, word-fire
spent till the next raid

The muse fills her own
blue exercise books—
great looping letters
that drag an ancestor
by stages into play

Black-lashed slitherer
gazing up from deeps
of magma and kelp, lithe
in the tangle towards
a silver ceiling

~

SAG HARBOR

One of your lamps will jump
off the shelf—as scenes collected
go on rolling an ocean beyond
in a white Venetian whaler's house
where the clocks are still

You shift from the garden
into purple velvet, laces undone
to pique a visitor's eye
a touch awry but ever the deb
through a grander season

Like newspaper slipped across paint
you scrim the truth of truth
twisting was and wasn't
to make the tale that is
a daughter in the mother, never quit

It's the worst
really the worst
you crack with a gleam:
an elm dies from the inside—
just comes toppling down

Gravespeak

To return to all that on the family front
you're after finishing the work
got in the dark some call dawn

    I am the wind that breathes
    I am this dancing wave
    I am fire in the head

You say it's not from father or mother
Trenchmore or *Sellinger's Round*
when the words we bore you use again

    Friends we mustered
    when your lung shrank
    now you'd punish with dye

You'll never shoo the crow away
he'll fly when all is ready
the message in a dream delivered

    A hero turns key-like
    from soldier to cowboy
    bronzed on the outmost plain

Muffle the drum, pipe lowly here
from Lock to St James
rides the chip in your skull

    Is himself within
    tinkling small wires
    under notes of the bass

Through a door I whistle
blurred on the terrace
to secure the grinder's air

Sligo City your mother
catches . . .
via Liverpool and Wales

Know what to follow
where you can't translate
that grim triad to leave and love

André Breton Dreams the Walk
of Charles Maturin

A little before midnight
by the café window
one comes out from a passage
(has that body a wolf's coat?)

greenish smoke wraps the hand
that writes on stained marble
the House must fall
(it doesn't look like a plume
it looks like a dagger)

    three wipes of a rag
    and the menu changes—
    not a flagon to pour
    or a matchstick to chew

    the square piano gives
    a heretic laugh
    no kitchen Richard
    stalks this dame-crossing lane

centuries are marked on the plate
not hours, the pavement staggers
the stamp on a packet, toys salute
as the drain floods back

did I forget to climb the stair
and deliver the text for today—
adventure startles through a ribbon
of little torments
the giant key points how

Spectropoetic

No *we* can be taken for granted, joining
hands did you mean conserve or converse
as the lash of filome dictates. What are
these figures now little now great
said to surround your house and trees.
If it's a dream, why dream this
mass of green piled on one red coat.
The fiddling fancy could be shoved
in a big box or beneath a creepy-stool
but who will resist strong words:

> Sator.
> Arepo.
> Tenet.
> Opera.
> Rotas.

Fragments of forgotten people slip out
in paper covers, wh-is-per a nitty job,
hop down the right side, spit on butter
to steal light or save us from ourselves.
It doesn't seem like a metal engine
drives the play, but a certain record
close to my hand says Iran reads Erin
through *dar* to *darragh*:

> rip-rap
> tip-tap
> iligant
> noetry
> dashes.

She wants to type the story
brought by her Nurse. On the Skelligs
I want to frolic. It would have been different
if I'd been raised by wolves. In fact
I was raised by nuns. Each letter you form
lies like a cross-beam in the jambs.

Irish Melody

Near the end with approaching ease
the keyboard jammmmmmmmmms
as a letter is **HIT** and the writing goes
into « re « verse « `esrever` « servere
deleting ✳✳✳✳✳✳✳✳ vvvv aaaassst
s ~ w ~ a ~ t ~ h ~ e ~ s of *T E X T*

What was that glyph that was
𝔥𝔞𝔯𝔭-𝔰𝔭𝔢𝔞𝔨 under the sea—
a chord plucked from a siren's hair.

The bell in the case cries alarm
now English or Anguish
backup fails in the record file.

Each word you quarry chases another
Bronti the fearless back to Pruntee
told to sing from a mask.

≈

Are you waiting for your people?
It's a proper moonlight evening.

They left a hundred years ago. I don't think
either summer, harvest, or winter moon
will shine on their revels again.

If you disown parents, you must have some
sort of kinsfolk: uncles and aunts?

None that I ever saw.

Lullaby and Nocturne

Shoheen, shoho • word don't say
reed in wind • will quiver
rock you • sliver to rest
shapes what else • are stirred

hammer here • string tinkle
Betty Blue • Doctor Dee
can't strike • the air I sing
hush a-lee • hush a-lo-lee

On sidhe hill • the fairies dance
into night • to seize their own
who'll jump • through trance in a box
stroked alone • on leaning spike

bright as branch • of rowan berries
short you're held • in care
fingers light • stencil echo
if you dare • play this away

Nicola LeFanu:
Clarinet in A and Piano
Cello and Piano

Chinks in the Word Machine

Charcoal appetite this was my breath my alcove. I climb on pendent fragments of beams and girders. Scrabbling in rubble to read a line and a half of twenty years: 'leave it at that. I know now . . . you don't care twopence. If you did you would . . .' Black sheet bedded like a truffle in liver, ghost of a script, stark and familiar, with o's and a's open at the top.

I was tormented by specks dancing—as squares, diamonds, little figures green, blue, yellow, all whispered in one breath, you are the head must carry our likeness even as a carriage rolls.

DARES OWN SERES TREE MUTTER? Every pure trait hangs its bottle of awe posing farces to sheep cheer actor not daintical but fluvey in fastness. Won halve is without stay-in (*sine macula*) and tether is all spiced to embraze polepost. What knot revs a psalm on, jar fellow moon chimes a limb-wreck. Quires do vent the pod agreed vampare, err dent gazed, who pendulous revise/adds the house, sidewise steeped. Veer is di abe sent whiteness or thanotic hand famishes intro itch frame?

The sea I caress I curse. My boat slips through the swell, phosphorescent trail astern, breeze of pine from the hills, all words sewn up in watertight canvas. The barometer falls, waves go leaden, a gale strikes. Wind howls through the rigging, sheets of spray beat the deck, the whole goes over. I swim alone empty of ties, to stare at the room in which I was born.

I was talked into using Ampex tape by some guys who felt it was better because it was limper and gave a better head wrap but as it turned out the 'new' Ampex —red-on-black — was made in the old Shamrock factory and the adhesive that was used to glue the oxide particles on to the backing turned to snot over the years and would rub off on your hands. So all the stuff seemed lost. But someone discovered that if you heat the tape up to about 130°F, the adhesive is reset for a while. The highest frequencies are erased in the cooking because it randomizes the particles but the rest can be recovered. God, you don't get something for nothing.

Castle and Pin

Don't you long when watching the televised Parliament
to see *Sheridan* stand up and really say something, even
perhaps wake up those bland grey-suited mediocrities!
Peter Wood

Do you have your body if the House
declares it forfeit when malversation
shuffles cage and cake? Ninety days
is enough to turn 𝔞𝔩𝔦𝔢𝔫. A may be I
in a little manœuvre, though August
is not April. Between the ribs
some lookout will detect
an urge to hate. Because. Brothers
consort to blast our sacred space.

One furnishes the raw material of fact
the second spins the argument
the third twines up the conclusion.

1. a black drum (smoking)
2. canal water
3. a plaster bird
4. soggy bill (pasted)
5. a fossil name
6. wire mesh hand
7. a bitten plate
8. bent aerial drone

Suppose it common by bad arithmetic
the system locks on receding zero
and the remedy proves the disease. Find
like a germ means armed intent. Gag
upon gag I recognize—who's who
to whom via a paragraph inserted.
Only under battens a slither of truth
emerges. When Mist is prosecuted
call it Fog.

Terror Twilight

Don't need the rattle of bones
      to tell the timer's ticking
Don't need a stain on the rug
      to smell who's been before
Don't need a rusty key
      to scan the hidden passage
Don't need a blank in the mirror
      to feel the stuff drained out
Don't need a lamp in the tower
      to know the planes are coming

There's new killer waste in the living-room
as a genie spins with flicker and static

A cyberspirit crashes the website
pulling his knife on a safety platform

A scratch letter forms on the girth-rim
hissing from ragged gauze

Clutch your mobile, hug the wall
hide bottles and cans

Unplug and tune in
may use data for marketing

The keeper who saves your bacon
is the ogre who steals your face

Jackety Jiggit

When you know the answer you still forget.

What is the secret of the Green Chamber?
Where is the deed in the red box?
How do you move behind stamped leather?
Which is the flower that reduces space?
Why speak French from a spire of hair?
Whose is the face resurrected?

Is there a devil in Deverell?
Suspicions are one thing, certainties another.

SOURCES NOT IDENTIFIED IN TEXT

Page 66 / The Portraits: Thomas P. Le Fanu, *Memoir of the Le Fanu Family*.

71 / Fool of Quality: Henry Brooke, *The Fool of Quality*.

78 / Glass Master: Edmund Spenser, *The Fairie Queene*, *A View of the Present State of Ireland* and *Ruines of Rome*; J.S. Le Fanu, 'The Fortunes of Sir Robert Ardagh'.

84 / Skaldic Manœuvres: *Catalogue of the Library of the Very Rev. Thomas P. Le Fanu, Dean of Emly* (Auction, C. Sharpe, Dublin 1845).

90 / Knowles Knocks: James Sheridan ['Paddy'] Knowles, *The Dramatic Works*; cf. James Joyce, *Ulysses*, 13 (Nausicaa).

93 / Idiogloss: Anon., *The Age; A Poem* (1810), note.

96 / Taking the Stiff: J.S. Le Fanu, letter to 'Richard' (i.e. W.R. Le Fanu), 16 Jan., 1861.

97 / Soul's Ward: J.S. Le Fanu, *Uncle Silas* and 'Spalatro'.

101 / Attic Fits: J.S. Le Fanu, 'A Chapter in the History of a Tyrone Family'; Charlotte Brontë, *Jane Eyre*; J.S. Le Fanu, *The Wyvern Mystery*; Jean Rhys, *Wide Sargasso Sea*.

104 / Autofrag: J.S. Le Fanu, 1858 notebook (meditations after the death of his wife) and 'The Mysterious Lodger'; Jonathan Swift, letter to Hester (Vanessa) Vanhomrigh, 5 July, 1721.

105 / Suspiria: J.S. Le Fanu, *The House by the Church-yard*.

110 / Faded Novel: Fine Again: *The House by the Church-yard*; James Joyce, *Finnegans Wake*.

113 / Casement: Sophia Lee, *The Recess*.

115 / Voltascope: James Joyce, letters; Luke McKernan, 'James Joyce's Cinema' and Kevin Rockett, 'Something Rich and Strange' in *Film & Film Culture* 3 (2004).

117 / Dreor Grammaticus: Carl Dreyer, *Vampyr*; plus script in Dreyer, *Four Screenplays*, tr. Oliver Stallybrass.

119 / Belfast Blues: Big Joe Williams, 'Lone Wolf'.

129 / <u>Mizmaze Mizzard</u>: James Joyce, *Finnegans Wake* (Swiftiana, as noted by Mackie L. Jarrell); P.W. Joyce, *English as We Speak It in Ireland*.

130 / <u>Danespeak to Cellbrook</u>: Jonathan Swift, letters and 'The Description of an *Irish-Feast*'; Charlotte Brooke, *Reliques of Irish Poetry*.

139 / <u>Ars Punica</u>: [Dr Thomas Sheridan], in *A Collection of Scarce, Curious and Valuable Pieces* (1773); cross-checked with the first London edition, J. Swift [sic], *The Art of Punning* (1719).

145 / <u>Chaocipher</u>: J.F. Byrne, *Silent Years*.

148 / <u>Fief dom</u>: Articles and stories from the *Dublin University Magazine* under the editorship of, respectively, Isaac Butt and J.S. Le Fanu.

153 / <u>Hibernia Curiosa</u>: Henry Angelo, *Reminiscences*.

156 / <u>King Tom's Personation of Ulysses</u>: Nicholas Rowe, *Ulysses: a Tragedy*.

159 / <u>Osharidum's Doct'ring</u>: James Boswell, *London Journal*; Thomas Sheridan, *A Course of Lectures on Elocution*.

161 / <u>Chambermade</u>: Alicia Le Fanu (2), *Memoirs of the Life and Writings of Mrs Frances Sheridan*.

166 / <u>Vannummery</u>: National Folklore Collection, MS S772 (published with the permission of UCD School of Irish, Celtic Studies, Irish Folklore and Linguistics); British Library, Add. MS 39839.

167 / <u>Words on the Window Pane</u>: W.B. Yeats, *The Words Upon the Window Pane*, Rapallo Notebook E draft (reproduced in Mary FitzGerald's Cornell Yeats edition); J. Swift, *Journal to Stella*; J.S. Le Fanu, *All in the Dark*.

171 / <u>Name Withheld</u>: J.S. Le Fanu, 'Carmilla'.

173 / <u>Cross Carpet</u>: J.S. Le Fanu, *Haunted Lives*.

174 / <u>Exquisite Corpse</u>: J.S. Le Fanu, 'The Room in the Dragon Volant'; Frances Sheridan, *The History of Nourjahad*.

175 / <u>Ropelight</u>: Henry Angelo, *Reminiscences* (from a section written up for John Bannister's 'Budget' by George Colman jnr.).

183 / <u>Screen Seen</u>: R.B. Sheridan, *The School for Scandal*.

184 / <u>Rivals Interleaved</u>: Frances Sheridan, *A Journey to Bath*; Samuel

Foote, *The Maid of Bath*; R.B. Sheridan, *The Rivals* (mainly Larpent MS version) and *The School for Scandal*.

188 / Duelling Tales: Thomas Moore, *Memoirs of the Life of the Rt. Hon. Richard Brinsley Sheridan* (drawn from accounts by, among others, Lissy and Betsy Le Fanu).

189 / How oft Eliza: Elizabeth Linley, letters to R.B. Sheridan (1772–90); quoted from Matilda Stoker, 'Sheridan and Miss Linley' in *English Illustrated Magazine* (April 1887). But see Percy Fitzgerald, *Sheridan Whitewashed* (1897) for a challenge to their authenticity.

191 / Circumbendibus: Thomas Moore, *Memoirs of the Life of the Rt. Hon. Richard Brinsley Sheridan*; J.S. Le Fanu, *Uncle Silas* and *The Rose and the Key*; R.B. Sheridan, *A Trip to Scarborough*.

194 / Polesden Lacey: R.B. Sheridan, letters, speeches and *Pizarro*.

197 / Lord Edward's Last Goodnight: Thomas Moore, *The Life and Death of Lord Edward Fitzgerald*.

199 / Cavan Cares: J. Swift and Thomas Sheridan, correspondence; B [Rev. R.S. Brooke], 'A Pilgrimage to Quilca in the Year 1852' (*Dublin University Magazine*, Nov., 1852); J.S. Le Fanu, letter to John Forster, 24 Oct., 1864.

204 / Floor Proposition: W.R. Le Fanu, Diary, 1846.

206 / Dobbin Deeds: W.R. Le Fanu, *Seventy Years of Irish Life*.

207 / Eccles Variorum: Ambrose Eccles ed., *King Lear*; W.R. Le Fanu, *Seventy Years of Irish Life*; James Joyce, *Stephen Hero* and *Ulysses*.

209 / Oglio: William Ireland, *Vortigern*, Preface to *The Abbess*, and *Confessions*.

226 / Wander Jar: Charles Maturin, *Melmoth the Wanderer*.

229 / Morphosis: Thomas Moore, *Journal*, 1818–1825.

235 / Hammerish: *Lust for a Vampire* and *Twins of Evil*; Rhoda Broughton, *Cometh Up as a Flower*.

237 / Amarantha Takes: Amarantha Knight [Nancy Kilpatrick], *The Darker Passions: Carmilla*.

246 / Liquid Syntax: J.S. Le Fanu, *In a Glass Darkly*, *A Lost Name*, *The Rose and the Key*, *All in the Dark* and *The Cock and Anchor*.

252 / <u>Catalogue of the Letter M</u>: J.S. Le Fanu, 'Some Account of the Latter Days . . .' (1848) to *Willing to Die* (1873); 'A Chapter in the History of a Tyrone Family' (1839) to 'Laura Silver Bell' (1872).

258 / <u>A Line Through Sheridan's Site</u>: L.B. Alberti, *De re aedificatoria*, Prologue (a passage cited by John Dee); J.S. Le Fanu, *A Lost Name*, 'The Evil Guest', 'A Chapter in the History of a Tyrone Family', *Checkmate* and *Guy Deverell*.

260 / <u>The Formula</u>: Richard Bentley, letters to J.S. Le Fanu and contracts, February 1863 to July 1864; William Tinsley, *Random Recollections of an Old Publisher*; Edmund Downey, *Twenty Years Ago*.

264 / <u>Missing Sprig</u>: 'Railway Wanderer' phrase transposed from letter by Caroline Norton to Emma (Dobbin) Le Fanu, 1856 (?).

265 / <u>Down the Staff</u>: G. Brinsley Sheridan Le Fanu, letters to Edmund Downey, 1892–1916.

268 / <u>Pepper-Box</u>: John Lennon and Paul McCartney, 'With A Little Help From My Friends' (two lines apparently written by Lennon). Both musicians of Liverpool Irish stock.

269 / <u>Smock-Alley Secrets</u>: Harry Houdini, letters to Fred Black, 1925.

270 / <u>Inward Passage</u>: J.S. Le Fanu, 'Passage in the Secret History of an Irish Countess'.

272 / <u>Podcast</u>: Margaret Barry, 'She Moved Through The Fair', recorded at the Bedford Arms, Camden Town (1957/58); text, with overt reference to the 'dead' revenant, adapted from Padraic Colum's reworking of an old ballad; on *The Voice of the People*, vol. 10.

275 / <u>Ghost Workshop</u>: J.S. Le Fanu, 'The Ghost and the Bone-Setter', 'An Account of Some Strange Disturbances in Aungier Street' and 'Squire Toby's Will'.

276 / <u>Skullscape</u>: *The House by the Church-yard*.

280 / <u>Knockabout</u>: *The House by the Church-yard*.

284 / <u>Ready Dupe</u>: Caroline (Callander) Sheridan, *Carwell; or, Crime and Sorrow*.

285 / <u>Cenci Face</u>: Russell Gray [Eleanor Le Fanu], *Never—For Ever* and *John Haller's Niece*; cf. J.S. Le Fanu, *The Tenants of Malory*.

286 / <u>Norton versus Norton</u>: Caroline and George Norton, correspondence; Caroline Norton, pamphlets; George Meredith, *Diana of the Crossways*.

294 / <u>Head-Piece</u>: R.B. Sheridan Knowles, *Glencoonoge*.

295 / <u>Helen's Tower</u>: Harold Nicolson, *Helen's Tower*; cf. Tennyson's poem of the same title, one of several texts displayed on the walls of the top room.

298 / <u>Gray Villanelle</u>: Oscar Wilde, *The Picture of Dorian Gray*.

299 / <u>Lyceum Double (5.72)</u>: Leopold Lewis, *The Bells*; Edward Gordon Craig, *Henry Irving*.

300 / <u>Criss Cross: In Irving's Shadow</u>: Algernon Blackwood, *Tales of the Uncanny and Supernatural*; Bram Stoker, working notes for *Dracula* (in which days and dates correspond to 1893).

303 / <u>Five Faces of a Lady</u>: Caroline Blackwood, *Great Granny Webster*.

307 / <u>Gravespeak</u>: A.P. Graves, *Irish Literary and Musical Studies* and *To Return to All That*; Robert Graves, 'The Poetic State'.

310 / <u>Spectropoetic</u>: Lady Wilde, *Ancient Legends, Mystic Charms and Superstitions of Ireland*; W.B. Yeats, *Uncollected Prose* ed. J. P. Frayne, vol 1 (1886-96).

311 / <u>Irish Melody</u>: Thomas Moore, 'The Origin of the Harp'; Charlotte Brontë, *Jane Eyre*.

313 / <u>Chinks in the Word Machine</u>: Sarah LeFanu, *Rose Macaulay*; Alicia Le Fanu, *Strathallan*; Clare Sheridan, *To the Four Winds*; Owsley 'Bear' Stanley, interview, *Dupree's Diamond News*.

316 / <u>Jackety Jiggit</u>: J.S. Le Fanu, *Guy Deverell*.

Certain of the found texts have been condensed
or lightly treated for emphasis.

REFERENCES, PASSIM, TO THE FOLLOWING WORKS BY J. SHERIDAN LE FANU

The Cock and Anchor [1845] ed. Jan Jedrzejewski (Colin Smythe, 2000)

The Fortunes of Colonel Torlogh O'Brien [1847] (Downey & Co., 1896)

The House by the Church-yard [1863] intro. Thomas Kilroy (Appletree Press, 1992)

Wylder's Hand [1864] (Gollancz, 1963)

Uncle Silas [1864] ed. & intro. W.J. Mc Cormack (Oxford University Press, 1981); intro. Elizabeth Bowen (Cresset Press, 1947); ed. & intro. Victor Sage (Penguin, 2000)

Guy Deverell [1865] (Dover, 1984)

All in the Dark [1866] (Downey & Co., c. 1895)

The Tenants of Malory (Tinsley Brothers, 1867)

A Lost Name (Richard Bentley, 1868)

Haunted Lives (Tinsley Brothers, 1868)

The Wyvern Mystery [1869] (Alan Sutton, 1994)

Checkmate [1871] (Alan Sutton, 1997)

The Rose and the Key [1871] intro. Norman Donaldson (Dover, 1982)

Willing to Die (Hurst and Blackett, 1873)

'The Fatal Bride', *Dublin University Magazine*, January 1848.

'Some Account of the Latter Days of the Hon. Richard Marston of Dunoran', *Dublin University Magazine*, April, May and June 1848

Ghost Stories and Tales of Mystery (James McGlashan / William S. Orr & Co., 1851) [printed by Edward Bull, Dublin]

Chronicles of Golden Friars (Richard Bentley & Son, 1871)

In a Glass Darkly [1872] intro. V.S. Pritchett (John Lehmann, 1947)

The Purcell Papers, with a Memoir by A.P. Graves (Richard Bentley & Son, 1880)

The Watcher and Other Weird Stories [1894] (New English Library, 1974)

Madam Crowl's Ghost and other Tales of Mystery ed. M.R. James (Bell, 1923)

Best Ghost Stories of J.S. Le Fanu ed. E.F. Bleiler (Dover, 1964)

Ghost Stories and Mysteries ed. E.F. Bleiler (Dover, 1975)

The Illustrated J.S. Le Fanu selec. & intro. Michael Cox ((Equation, 1988)

Borrhomeo the Astrologer: A Monkish Tale [1862] ed. W.J. Mc Cormack (Tragara Press, 1985)

Spalatro: Two Italian Tales [1843 & 1862] ed. Miles Stribling (Sarob Press, 2001)
Schalken the Painter and Others: Ghost Stories 1838-61 ed. Jim Rockhill (Ash-Tree Press, 2002)
The Haunted Baronet and Others: Ghost Stories 1861-70 ed. Jim Rockhill (Ash-Tree Press, 2003)
Mr Justice Harbottle and Others: Ghost Stories 1870-73 ed. Jim Rockhill (Ash-Tree Press, 2005)

The Poems of Joseph Sheridan Le Fanu ed. [with an introduction] A.P. Graves (Downey & Co., 1896)

PROLOGUE: SELECT SOURCES

Anon., *The History of the Theatre Royal, Dublin, From its Foundation in 1821 to the Present Time* (Ponsonby, Dublin, 1870)

Aspinall, A., ed., *Mrs Jordan and her Family: being the Unpublished Correspondence . . .* (Arthur Barker, 1951)

Auerbach, Nina, *Our Vampires, Ourselves* (University of Chicago Press, 1995)

Bingham, Madeleine, *Sheridan: The Track of a Comet* (George Allen & Unwin, 1972)

Blackwood, Caroline, *Great Granny Webster* (Duckworth, 1977)

Breton, André, 'Limits not Frontiers of Surrealism', in Herbert Read ed., *Surrealism* (Faber & Faber, 1936)

Broughton, Rhoda, 'Behold it was a Dream', *Temple Bar* (Nov., 1872); collected in *Tales for Christmas Eve* (1873) and *Twilight Stories* (1879)

Cole, John W., 'Irish Theatricals', *Dublin University Magazine*, Mar., 1850
—— 'The Theatre Royal, Dublin, from 1830 to 1851', *Dublin University Magazine*, Oct. & Nov., 1868, Jan., 1869

Craig, Maurice, *Dublin 1660-1860* (Allen Figgis Ltd., 1969)

Ellis, S.M., *Wilkie Collins, Le Fanu and Others* (Constable, 1931)

Fitzgerald, Percy, *The Lives of the Sheridans* (Bentley & Son, 1886)
——*Memoirs of an Author* (Bentley & Son, 1894)

Foster, Roy, *W.B. Yeats: A Life: I. The Apprentice Mage 1865-1914* (Oxford University Press, 1997)

Foucault, Michel, 'Language to Infinity', in *Language, Counter-Memory, Practice* (Blackwell, 1977)

Igoe, Vivien, *A Literary Guide to Dublin* (Methuen, 1994)

Jarrell, Mackie L., 'Jack and the Dane' in A. Norman Jeffares ed., *Fair Liberty Was All His Cry* (Macmillan, 1967)

Keats, John, letter to Richard Woodhouse, 27 Oct., 1818

Kemble, John Philip, Professional Memoranda [MS journal]

Laing, Cecil Y., ed., *The Swinburne Letters*, vol 1: 1854-1869 (Yale University Press, 1959)

Le Fanu, Elizabeth, letter to Thomas Wilkie, 11 Nov., 1821

J.S. Le Fanu, 'I'm here but to claim your kindness . . .' in 'Garrison Amateur Theatricals', *Freeman's Journal* Supplement, 29 Feb., 1860
——Letter to Brinsley Le Fanu (c/o Rev. R. Allen), 11 June, 1870

Le Fanu, Thomas Philip, *Memoir of the Le Fanu Family* (Manchester, 1924)

Le Fanu, William Richard, letters to Lord Dufferin, 1 Apr., 1870 and 15 Sept., 1891

Levey, R.M. & O'Rorke, J., *Annals of the Theatre Royal, Dublin from its Opening in 1821 to its Destruction by Fire, 1880* (J. Dollard, Dublin 1880)

Mc Cormack, W.J., *Sheridan Le Fanu and Victorian Ireland* (Oxford University Press, 1980)

—— *Dissolute Characters: Irish literary history through Balzac, Sheridan Le Fanu, Yeats, and Bowen* (Manchester University Press, 1993)

Morgan, Lady Sydney, *Memoirs: Autobiography, Diaries and Correspondence* ed. W.H. Dixon (W.H. Allen, 1862)

Moynahan, Julian, *Anglo-Irish: The Literary Imagination in a Hyphenated Culture* (Princeton University Press, 1995)

Norton, Caroline, *The Sorrows of Rosalie: A Tale, with Other Poems* (John Ebors & Co., 1829)

O'Toole, Fintan, *A Traitor's Kiss: The Life of Richard Brinsley Sheridan* (Granta, 1997)

Pritchett, V.S., *The Living Novel* (Chatto & Windus, 1949)

Quinn, David B, *The Elizabethans and the Irish* (Cornell University Press, 1966)

Rogers, Samuel, *Recollections of the Table-Talk of Samuel Rogers* (D. Appleton, New York, 1856)

Ryan, W.P., *The Irish Literary Revival: its History, Pioneers and Possibilities* (Dulwich, 1894)

Sage, Victor, *Le Fanu's Gothic: The Rhetoric of Darkness* (Palgrave Macmillan, 2004)

Shaw, Bernard, Preface to *Immaturity*, in *The Matter with Ireland* ed. D.H. Greene & D.H. Laurence (Rupert Hart-Davis, 1962)

Sheridan, Thomas the elder, 'Tom Punsibi's Letter to Dean Swift' in *The Poems*, ed. R. Hogan (University of Delaware Press, 1994)

Sheridan, Thomas the younger, *The Life of the Reverend Jonathan Swift*, vol 1 of [Swift's] *Works* (C. Bathurst, 1784)

Spenser, Edmund, *A View of the Present State of Ireland* ed. W.L. Renwick (Oxford University Press, 1970)

Sullivan, Kevin, 'Sheridan Le Fanu: The Purcell Papers, 1838-40', in *Irish University Review* 2 (1972)

Whyte, Sam[uel], *Poems* (R. Marchbank, Dublin 1792)

Note on the authorship of *Lucy Osmond* (G. and J. Robinson, 1803)

This work has been attributed to Alicia Le Fanu the elder[1] but an article by William Chamberlaine states that Elizabeth Le Fanu is 'the elegant authoress of *Lucy Osmond* and *The India Voyage*' (*Gentleman's Magazine*, Supplement to Part 1, 1824). Chamberlaine was Betsy's cousin and his remarks, sent to the editor shortly after Christmas 1804, were published retrospectively to coincide with the appearance of Alicia the younger's biography of Frances (Chamberlaine) Sheridan. The article includes part of a letter by Betsy to William, in support of the argument that she is a reliable assessor of artistic talent. Chamberlaine seems to have been well-informed about the literary activities of the Le Fanus, supplying details to the *Gentleman's Magazine* on at least one other occasion. The editor, John Nichol, was evidently an acquaintance of both Chamberlaine and John Robinson. Author of *Literary Anecdotes*, he had an unrivalled knowledge of the publishing world.

The title page of *The India Voyage* (G. and J. Robinson, 1804) states that its author is Mrs H. Lefanu (i.e. Betsy). *Lucy Osmond* was published anonymously, although the introduction speaks of the author's name as not 'unsettled in the rolls of fame' and the first two lines of the prologue to *The Discovery* form the book's epigraph: 'A Female Culprit at your Bar appears/Not void of Hope, nor destitute of Fears'.[2] The French edition, *Lucie Osmond* (Paris: 1804), merely indicates that the translator is 'A*** P*** P***'. A substantial part of the book is set in Devon, near Woodley, which, if it is a version of Woodleigh, was close to Betsy's home at this point: Kingsbridge. The other locations in the novel all coincide with Betsy's places of residence: Bath, London, Surrey and Kent. Furthermore, the romantic hero travels to India. Lucy's father is a Captain who has pecuniary worries, like Henry Le Fanu. The satirical portrait of Mrs Gray in Bath is reminiscent of vignettes in Betsy's journal, and the author admits that she has 'described characters that have come within [her] own observation'. It was common for novels to be published without the author's name at this point. Betsy may have suppressed her authorship in order to deflect attention from real-life equivalents and to avoid censure in the case of the book being poorly received.

Counter-evidence emerges from a letter by Lady Morgan to Alicia Le Fanu the elder, dated December 9th, 1803. She says: 'I read your little secret memoir with much the same species of emotion as Uncle Toby listened to Trim's account of Le Fevre, for more than once I wished I was asleep.' This allusion to *Tristram Shandy* establishes the pathetic quality of whatever piece of writing is under discussion. Morgan mentions Alicia's reference to Ellen [i.e. Helen] Maria Williams, in the context of imprudent conduct. The latter's notoriety on account of her liaison with a divorced (or possibly still married) man bears some relation to Lucy's 'unshackled sensibility', yet there is no mention of Williams in the novel.

If Alicia is the author of *Lucy Osmond*, we must conclude that she and her sister allowed their cousin to think that the work was by Betsy. However, given the latter's record as a writer of fiction and the fact that Chamberlaine's assertion of 1804/1824 remained uncorrected, it is reasonable to assume that Mrs H. Le Fanu is indeed the author of the novel.[3]

---

1. R.A. Peddie & Q. Waddington, *English Catalogue of Books 1801-1836* (1914); S. Halkett & J. Laing, *Dictionary of Anonymous and Pseudonymous Literature*, vol 9: Addenda (1962). No author is listed in the *New London*, *London* and *English* catalogues of books for the years 1805-1820, or in the Robinsons 1804 catalogue. Many standard reference works confuse the two Mrs Le Fanus, Alicia and Elizabeth, with each other, and Alicia with her niece, Betsy's daughter.

2. *Lucy Osmond* received notices in the *Monthly Review*, *Critical Review* and other journals in 1803-4.

3. It is not clear which 'Mrs Lefanu' features as an example of 'the illustrious obscure' in the Preface to *Adonais* (1821), which angles at those puffed by critics in the *Quarterly Review*. Possibly, as a poet and recent recipient of laudatory reviews (for fiction), *Miss* Alicia Le Fanu is the object of attention. Alternatively, Shelley may be recalling praise of *The Sons of Erin* or of Betsy's work. Yet none of these authors has any evident connexion with the *Quarterly Review*. The Le Fanu reference (along with the names of E.S. Barrett and J.H. Payne) was removed, at Mary Shelley's request, from the Galignani edition of *Poetical Works . . .* (1829), but reinstated by her in the 1839 text. It is perhaps relevant that Godwin was entertained by Joseph and Alicia the elder in Dublin in 1800, and that Shelley himself may have encountered them there in 1813.

PERSONALIA

AIKIN, ANNA LAETITIA (later Barbauld) 1743-1825: daughter of Dr Aikin, whose radical Dissenting views she sustained; friend of Joanna Baillie and Maria Edgeworth; essay 'On the Pleasure Derived from Objects of Terror' included in *Miscellaneous Pieces, in Prose* (1773), written with her brother John; edited *The British Novelists* (1810); critic, poet and educationist.

ANGELO, DOMENICO 1717-1802: father of Henry; husband of Elizabeth (née Johnson), Irish friend of Frances Sheridan; ran School of Arms in Soho; taught R.B. Sheridan to ride and fence; regarded by George II as 'the finest horseman in the world'; before marriage, had affair with Peg Woffington.

ANGELO, HENRY 1756-1835: friend of the Sheridans; tutored by Thomas (2) and R.B. Sheridan; fencing master to, among others, Lord Byron; acted in private theatricals at Brandenburgh House, including *Nourjad* [sic] in which he played the role of the prince opposite Elizabeth Craven.

ARNOLD, SAMUEL JAMES 1774-1852: son of composer Samuel Arnold, who collaborated with Thomas Linley on music for Drury Lane; dramatist and proprietor, 1809-41, of the Lyceum [English Opera House], the first theatre to be lit by gas (1817); business partner of Thomas Sheridan (3).

BACON, FRANCIS 1909-92: friend of Caroline Blackwood and Daniel Farson (Bram Stoker's great-nephew); born and brought up in the street where Stoker lived for a period in the 1870s; South Kensington studio re-created at the Hugh Lane Gallery, Dublin.

BARNES, WILLIAM 1801-86: invited to Frampton Court after poems had been published in the *Dorset County Chronicle*; befriended and encouraged by Caroline Norton, for whom he wrote a sonnet.

BARRINGTON, SIR JONAH c.1760-1834: as young adult lived with family in Merrion Square; removed to France to escape creditors c. 1815; wrote *Personal Sketches* in exile; narrative technique, ear for colloquial idiom and taste for the macabre, in vivid tableaux, influenced J.S. Le Fanu; grotesque humour also appealed to Yeats and Joyce, who reworked stories and details; lawyer, politician and memoirist.

BENNETT, GEORGE (1) 1777-1856: father-in-law of J.S. Le Fanu and grandfather of Rhoda Broughton; leading QC on Munster circuit.

BENNETT, GEORGE (2) 1846-1916: grandson of George (1) and husband of Emma Le Fanu (2); classics scholar and headmaster of Sutton Valence School, Kent.

BENTLEY, RICHARD 1794-1871: with son GEORGE (1828-95), publisher and correspondent of J.S. Le Fanu; also published Rhoda Broughton and Eleanor Le Fanu.

BESSBOROUGH [DUNCANNON], LADY HARRIET (née Spencer) 1761-1821: lover of R.B. Sheridan, who swore to be with her after death, eyes looking 'up at the coffin-lid as brightly as ever'; collaborated with sister Georgiana on play based on Harriet Lee's 'Kruitzner'; mother of Lady Caroline Lamb.

BLACKWOOD, ALGERNON 1869-1951: great-grandson of Henry (brother of Hans, Price Blackwood's father); hence related to both Sheridans and Le Fanus; met Bram Stoker in New York, 1893; visited Clandeboye, 1925; novelist and short story writer.

BLACKWOOD, LADY CAROLINE 1931-96: great-great-granddaughter of Helen Dufferin; wife of Lucian Freud and Robert Lowell; novelist and short story writer; presents fictionalized portrait of life at Clandeboye in *Great Granny Webster*.

BLACKWOOD, FREDERICK, LORD DUFFERIN 1826-1902: son of Helen (Sheridan) Dufferin and Price Blackwood, Lord Dufferin; cousin of J.S. Le Fanu; built house at Clandeboye, Co. Down, where visitors included Caroline Norton, J.S. and W.R. Le Fanu; diplomat and author.

BLACKWOOD[-]PRICE, HENRY N. fl. 1877-1923: friend of James Joyce; preoccupied with cure for foot and mouth disease, as relayed in *Ulysses*, and with Blackwood ancestry; part-model for Mr Deasy; assistant manager of Eastern Telegraph Company in Trieste; engineer with 'fund of useful information [on] electrical branches'; designed a selenium relay.

BOADEN, JAMES 1762-1839: theatre historian, dramatist and journalist; adapted M.G. Lewis's *The Monk* [*Aurelio and Miranda*] and Ann Radcliffe's *Romance of the Forest* [*Fountainville Forest*] for the stage; edited Garrick's *Private Correspondence*.

BOSWELL, JAMES 1740-95: sometime theatre critic, protégé and friend of Thomas Sheridan (2); remembered by Betsy Le Fanu, from Soho 1769, as 'a thin eager-looking man, in black'; biographer of Dr Johnson.

BOUCICAULT, DION 1820-90: nephew of George Darley; helped to launch career of Henry Irving by assigning him role of villain in two dramas; friend of Bram Stoker; playwright, manager and actor; invented fireproof scenery; developed techniques which anticipate cross-cutting, tracking and panning; adapted Polidori's *The Vampyre* for stage; *London Assurance* (1841) is the main bridge between Sheridan's and Wilde's comedies.

BOWEN, ELIZABETH 1899-1973: early experiences of Dublin recalled in *Seven Winters*, where Merrion Square's transition from 'stylish half-savagery' to 'sombre, solid propriety' is noted; family house Bowen's Court in Co. Cork demolished after sale in 1959; novelist, short-story writer and essayist; influenced by Anglo-Irish 'peculiarities' of Le Fanu and Barrington.

BRETON, ANDRÉ 1896–1966: saw the Gothic as a precursor of surrealism, as outlined in essay included in *Surrealism*, ed. Herbert Read (1936); wrote preface to the French translation of *Melmoth the Wanderer* (1954).

BRONTË, CHARLOTTE 1816–55: daughter of Patrick Brunty from County Down; 'constant and grateful reader' of the *Dublin University Magazine*; may have absorbed the account of the concealed first wife in J.S. Le Fanu's 'A Chapter in the History of a Tyrone Family' (October 1839) and developed the idea in *Jane Eyre*.

BROOKE, CHARLOTTE 1740–93: daughter of Henry Brooke; friend (affectionately 'cousin') of Alicia Le Fanu (1); translator of Gaelic literature, poet and anthologist; argued for a fusion of ancient Irish and younger English linguistic/cultural expression; *Reliques of Irish Poetry* (1789) was the first printed anthology of Irish vernacular verse to draw a significant readership.

BROOKE, HENRY 1703–83: friend of Thomas Sheridan (1); was born and lived at Rantavan, Co. Cavan, near Quilca; 'a patriot to excess'; plays banned on two occasions, in London and Dublin; borrowed the Ned Warner episode from *Memoirs of Miss Sidney Bidulph* for *Juliet Grenville*; defended Sheridan's hospitality against Swift's strictures; novelist, poet and dramatist.

BROOKE, REV. RICHARD SINCLAIR 1802–82: descendant of Henry Brooke's uncle, Alexander; contributed literary and topographical essays to the *Dublin University Magazine*, including the article on Quilca (1852); author of *Recollections of the Irish Church*, which names many of the anonymous contributors to the magazine, and *The Story of Parson Annaly*, a novel partly serialized therein.

BROOKE, STOPFORD 1832–1916: son of R.S. Brooke; father-in-law of T.W. Rolleston; friend of A.P. Graves; wrote reviews for the *Dublin University Magazine*; delivered inaugural lecture ('The Need and Use of Getting Irish Literature into the English Tongue') to the Irish Literary Society; preacher and man of letters.

BROUGHTON, RHODA 1840–1920: daughter of Sue Le Fanu's sister Jane; granddaughter of Sir Henry Delves-Broughton; friend of Mary Braddon and Henry James; novelist whose frank treatment of female emotion, with racy narrative and colloquial dialogue, excited controversy; *Cometh Up as a Flower* dedicated to J.S. Le Fanu, who assisted with publication, in magazine and book form, of this and other work.

BUCKINGHAM, LORD GEORGE (GRENVILLE) 1753–1813: took lessons in elocution from Thomas Sheridan (2), 1770–72, and was cured of a chronic stammer; Lord Lieutenant of Ireland in 1780s; brother, Thomas Grenville, one of R.B. Sheridan's greatest friends.

BUTT, ISAAC 1813-79: friend of J.S. Le Fanu; writer, lawyer and politician; founder and editor of the *Dublin University Magazine* 1834-38; founder of Irish Home Rule movement; lived at 64 Eccles Street.

BYRON, LORD GEORGE GORDON 1788-1824: friend of R.B. Sheridan, whose work in various genres he considered 'the *best* of its kind'; wrote 'Monody on the Death of R.B. Sheridan', recited at Drury Lane, 1816; friend of Thomas Moore and George Colman (2); much concerned with the state of English drama; wrote the Address for the reopening of Drury Lane, 1812; on managing committee, 1815; author of seven plays.

CALLANDER, COL. GEORGE 1770-1824: half-brother of Caroline; hence Tom Sheridan (3)'s brother-in-law; son of James Callander (later Sir James Campbell); married daughter of advocate Henry Erskine, whose subsequent legal action in George's name, pursuing an entail on the Craigforth estate (south-west of Strathallan), threatened the rights of Sir James; due to bitter dispute, father and son never reconciled.

CAMPBELL, SIR JAMES [FORMERLY COL. CALLANDER] 1745-1831: son of antiquary John Callander of Craigforth; father of George and Caroline; stationed in Ireland 1776-85; married Elizabeth MacDonnell, daughter of Earl of Antrim; owned house in Merrion Square where Caroline born; succeeded to estate of cousin (Campbell of Ardkinglas) 1810; adventurous life from Seven Years' War to detention by Napoleon, with romantic and legal wrangles, described in *Memoirs* (1832).

CANNING, MEHETABEL (née Patrick) d. 1831: wife of banker Stratford Canning; R.B. and Eliza Sheridan's most loyal friend; letters to Betsy Le Fanu, used by Moore, testify to Sheridan's anguish and kindness at Eliza's deathbed.

CHAMBERLAINE, WILLIAM 1752-1822: nephew of Frances Sheridan; regarded by his cousin Betsy Le Fanu as excessively 'sentimental', but championed Alicia the younger's work; spent nine years in Jamaica, where his father had also gone (from Dublin); settled in London as surgeon and apothecary; author of various medical works.

COBB, JAMES 1756-1818: author of operas and farces; *The Haunted Tower* was a prodigious success at Drury Lane; with music by Stephen Storace, it was partly a parody of Gothic motifs; auditor of the East India Company.

COLE, JOHN WILLIAM [J.W. CALCRAFT] 1793-1870: actor-manager of Theatre Royal, Dublin 1830-1851; Dublin debut as Joseph Surface, 1824; later played second male lead to Macready; secretary to Charles Kean; dramatized *The Bride of Lammermoor* (1823); frequent contributor to the *Dublin University Magazine*.

COLMAN, GEORGE (1) 1732-94: friend and correspondent of Joseph Le

Fanu (1); commentator on the latter's work; letters to Dublin intricately cross-written; lawyer, playwright and theatre manager.

COLMAN, GEORGE (2) 1762-1836: son of George (1); portrait hung at 18 Merrion Square supposedly the model for that of Uncle Silas in J.S. Le Fanu's novel; playwright, theatre manager and—against the tenor of his writings and behaviour—censor.

CRAVEN, LADY ELIZABETH, MARGRAVINE OF ANSPACH 1750-1828: playwright and society beauty; adapted, produced and played the lead female role in a version of *Nourjahad* at Brandenburgh House, Hammersmith (1803).

DE RENÉVILLE, MARY MARGARET MOTLEY (née Sheridan) b. 1912: daughter of Wilfred and Clare Sheridan; travel writer and memoirist.

DOBBIN, ORLANDO THOMAS 1807-90: Rector of Killochonnigan, Meath; contributed numerous essays to the *Dublin University Magazine*; author of *A Plea for Toleration towards [those] in Ireland who profess the Roman Catholic Religion* (1866) and other works; consulted by Gladstone on Irish affairs.

DOBBIN, DR WILLIAM 1733-1823: grandfather of J.S. and W.R. Le Fanu; rector of St Mary's, Dublin; friend and comforter to the Sheares brothers before their execution, 1798; would-be confessor to Robert Emmet before his execution; lived at 33 Eccles Street, from the balcony of which the Le Fanu boys watched George IV's procession into Dublin, 1821.

DOWNEY, EDMUND [F.M. ALLEN] 1856-1937: worked for Tinsley Brothers; subsequently published J. S. Le Fanu's work under own imprint; novelist and short story writer; based in London 1878-1906, then returned to birthplace, Waterford.

DREYER, CARL 1889-1968: Danish director of *Vampyr* (1932), which conflates motifs from *In a Glass Darkly* so as to (re)present a version of 'Carmilla'; coincidentally, perhaps, the ruined factory, river and mill locations resemble those at Chapelizod; the film was actually shot near Paris.

DUFFERIN, LORD: see Blackwood, Frederick.

DUFFERIN, LADY HELEN (née Sheridan) 1807-67: granddaughter of R.B. Sheridan and sister of Caroline Norton; cousin of J.S. Le Fanu; wife of Price Blackwood; poet; set texts by herself and Caroline to music; stayed latterly at Clandeboye, where her son erected a tower in her honour.

ECCLES, AMBROSE d. 1809: son of Mrs Delany's friend Hugh Eccles, whose wife's maiden name was Ambrose; produced variorum editions of *King Lear*, *Cymbeline* and *The Merchant of Venice*, in the former two transposing scenes which he considered wrongly placed; Dublin street named after the family estate in the northeast quadrant.

EDGEWORTH, MARIA 1768-1849: friend of Thomas Moore, whom she re-encountered at Bowood, the Lansdowne estate; shared mutual friend with Alicia Le Fanu (1); friend of Mrs S.T. Hall; father defended Pamela de Genlis in the House of Commons; novelist and writer of tales for children.

ELLIS, STEWART M. 1878-1933: relation of George Meredith and friend of Montague Summers, who admired his meticulous research; essayist, critic and biographer; source for life of J.S. Le Fanu, via A.P. Graves, Edmund Downey and Brinsley Le Fanu; article in *The Bookman* (1916), reprinted 1925 and extended 1931; also wrote *The Life of Michael Kelly*.

ELLISTON, ROBERT WILLIAM 1774-1831: first comedian of his day; excelled in part of Charles Surface; managed Drury Lane, 1819-26; opened library and assembly room in his preferred retreat, Leamington Spa, where he also leased the theatre from 1817 onward; sometimes served readers at the library; son Henry was organist at All Saints Church; both would have known Betsy Le Fanu and family.

FARREN, ELIZABETH (later COUNTESS OF DERBY) 1759?-1829: daughter of Cork surgeon who had turned strolling actor; succeeded Mrs Abington as lead comedic actress on stage at Drury Lane (1782-97); Berinthia in *A Trip to Scarborough* and Helen in *The Iron Chest*; particularly celebrated as Lady Teazle.

FITZGERALD, LORD EDWARD 1763-98: lover of Elizabeth Linley (Sheridan) in the last two years of her life; married Pamela de Genlis in Tournai, 1792, after R.B. Sheridan had escorted her, as *his* fiancée, to Dover; prominent member of United Irishmen; captured and mortally wounded in Dublin, 1798; in Fitzgerald's death 'a complete history of the fatal policy of England towards Ireland, through a lapse of more than six centuries, may be found epitomized' (Moore).

FITZGERALD, PAMELA (née Sims) 1776?-1831: daughter of Philippe 'Egalité', Duc d'Orléans; adopted by Madame de Genlis, rumoured to be her actual mother; bore striking resemblance to Elizabeth Linley; supposedly engaged for a brief period to R.B. Sheridan but married Lord Edward Fitzgerald; in 1798 given sanctuary at Moira House, where Fitzgerald occasionally visited her while on the run from the authorities.

FITZGERALD, PERCY 1834-1925: friend of J.S. Le Fanu and Dickens; biographer, novelist, theatre historian and sculptor; writings reflect his Catholic background; settled in London but maintained strong links with Dublin; disputed provenance of the Linley letters used by Matilda Stoker, arguing that they emerged via a dubious path and might be forgeries.

FOOTE, SAMUEL 1720-77: acted at Smock Alley under Sheridan (2), 1757; wrote *The Maid of Bath* (1771), which depicts Elizabeth Linley (Kitty Linnet), Captain Mathews (Major Rackett) and the elderly, wealthy Walter

Long (Solomon Flint), to whom Elizabeth had been promised by her parents; specialized in satirical comedy, featuring topical people and events; also wrote *The Devil upon Two Sticks*, a satire on the medical profession built around his own disability; actor-manager and playwright.

GARRICK, DAVID 1717-79: invited by Thomas Sheridan (2) to perform for a season in Dublin, 1745-46; played opposite Sheridan in *The Discovery* at Drury Lane (1773) and revived the play as a rival attraction to *The Duenna*, then a hit at Covent Garden, in 1775; on retirement from stage, sold share of Drury Lane to R.B. Sheridan, Thomas Linley and Dr Ford; despite tensions with Sheridan (2), regarded R.B. as natural successor.

GODWIN, WILLIAM 1756-1836: father of Mary Shelley; met Sophia and Harriet Lee in Bath; proposed to the latter in 1798; friend of R.B. Sheridan and one of the few who attended his funeral; friend of George Robinson; radical thinker and Gothic novelist whose *Caleb Williams* was dramatized by George Colman (2) as *The Iron Chest*; diary records contact with the Le Fanus in London and Dublin, 1798-1811; corresponded with Alicia (2?), possibly about *Rosara's Chain* (reminiscent of *Nourjahad*); saw *Sons of Erin*, 1812.

GOLDSMITH, OLIVER 1728-74: Sheridan's 'twin' as writer of comic drama; *She Stoops to Conquer* (1773) and *The Rivals* (1775) shared many of the same actors; circumbendibus motif in *She Stoops . . . or, The Mistakes of the Night* reused in several works by J.S. Le Fanu; probably the first editor of *Mother Goose's Melody*, which contains nonsense verse.

GOSSE, EDMUND 1849-1928: befriended by Sheridan Knowles in Torquay, c. 1860; editor (of among others T.L. Beddoes); introduced Ibsen's work to the British public; instrumental in securing a grant from the Royal Literary Fund for Joyce in Zurich but later tried to stifle his growing reputation; 'gosse' means youngster or boy in French/Swedish; critic and poet.

GRAHAM, LADY FANNY (née Callander) 1795-1857: youngest daughter of Sir James Callander; wife of Sir James Graham, who became Caroline Norton's legal adviser; with sister Georgiana, took care of nieces Caroline and Georgiana Sheridan while parents abroad 1813-16; R.B. Sheridan's letters to the Callander sisters show great fondness for his grandchildren.

GRAVES, ALFRED PERCEVAL 1846-1931: father of Robert Graves; friend and posthumous editor of J.S. Le Fanu; contemporary of Bram Stoker at Trinity College; poet, authority on Celtic literature and music, and inspector of schools; involved with cousin T.W. Rolleston, Stopford Brooke and W.B. Yeats in the activities of the Irish Literary Society; known affectionately as 'Irish Graves in England', after the work by Michael McDonagh.

GRAVES, ROBERT 1895-1985: a more original and skilful poet than his father but owed much to the latter's lyric impulse and knowledge of Celtic folklore, which fed into *The White Goddess* and ballad work; disparaged this inheritance in *Goodbye to All That*, provoking corrections in A.P.'s auto-biography; suffered shell-shock and lung damage in World War I; alludes to his 'father's trade' in 'The Poetic State', which refers to a Gaelic triad that was *not* one of those translated by A.P. for *The Book of Irish Poetry*.

GRIMALDI, JOSEPH [JOE] 1778-1837: regular performer at Drury Lane, taking 'straight' comic parts as well as the role of Clown; appeared in *Hamlet* (as Second Gravedigger), *Robinson Crusoe* (Friday) and *Blue Beard*; at times worked a double shift, running between Sadler's Wells and Drury Lane; first appeared at the Wells as a monkey; later played Acres in *The Rivals*; the greatest clown of English pantomime; melancholic, as expressed in his pun: 'I am Grim all day but I make you laugh at night'.

GUINNESS, RICHARD 1755-1829: husband of Mary Darley (related to the poet George); cousin of Arthur, founder of brewing firm; friend of Joseph and Alicia Le Fanu; also knew J.P. Kemble; poems appeared in Joshua Edkins ed., *A Collection of Poems* (1789-90), along with work by Alicia Le Fanu, R.B. Sheridan and Samuel Whyte; lived in Mercer Street.

HALL, ANNA MARIA (née Fielding) 1800-81: with husband SAMUEL C. (1800-89), entertained J.S. Le Fanu in London; toured parts of Limerick with Le Fanu and his brother as guides; received much advice on antiquarian lore, this being included in *Ireland, its Scenery, Characters &c* (1841-43); lived at The Rosery and Bannow Lodge, Old Brompton, likely models for Laura Gray's house in *Haunted Lives*; Irish authors and folklorists.

HARDY, THOMAS 1840-1928: friend of Mary Sheridan and regular guest at Frampton Court where, in 1889, he asked one of the Sheridan daughters to sing the favourite song of his youth, 'How oft Louisa' from *The Duenna*; he was shocked to discover she had never heard of it; Emma Hardy's last horse-ride was to Frampton Court.

HOLLAND, LORD HENRY 1773-1840: nephew of Charles James Fox; life saved by mother in house fire shortly after birth; friend of Sheridan; Whig politician and author; active in support of the rebuilding of Drury Lane; not to be confused with his namesake, architect of the 1794 theatre; wife Elizabeth Vassall (formerly Lady Webster), stigmatized for adulterous relationship before their marriage, presided over circle of wits and statesmen at Holland House.

HOUDINI, HARRY [Ehrich Weiss] 1874-1926: magician, escape artist and collector of theatre MSS. and memorabilia, including the only surviving copy of Peter Le Fanu's *Smock Alley Secrets*; poached Harvard scholar to catalogue library; owned a copy of the rare *Ghost Stories and Tales of Mystery* (1851); shared with J.S. Le Fanu a fascination with the device of the (apparently) sealed chamber.

HUTTON, LAURENCE 1843-1904: theatre historian, critic and collector of portraits in plaster; owned death mask of R.B. Sheridan, now in Princeton University Library.

HUXLEY, ALDOUS 1894-1963: adapted Frances Sheridan's *The Discovery* for performance at the 300 Club, London, in 1924, providing a new ending.

IRELAND, WILLIAM HENRY 1777-1835: forger of Shakespearean manuscripts, including a transcript of *King Lear* and the self-composed *Vortigern and Rowena*, performed at Drury Lane, with Kemble and Jordan in the cast, in 1796; after exposure and confession, made career as Gothic novelist.

IRVING, SIR HENRY 1838-1905: played Captain Absolute in *The Rivals* at Theatre Royal, Dublin, 1867, a performance seen by Bram Stoker; first met the latter, as drama critic, at Shelbourne Hotel, 1876; interviewed by Algernon Blackwood, in Stoker's presence, New York, 1893; based at Lyceum Theatre 1871-1902, the first acclaimed production being *The Bells*.

JAMES, HENRY 1843-1916: story 'The Liar' (published 1888, immediately after 'The Aspern Papers') mentions 'the customary novel of Mr Le Fanu' as 'the ideal reading in a country house for the hours after midnight'; the narrator is sufficiently diverted to be late for dinner; motifs tied to the lying Colonel's consciousness include a haunted room, a person buried alive then resurrected, and a threatening portrait which is slashed to rags.

JEPHSON, ROBERT 1736-1803: friend of Horace Walpole, whose *Castle of Otranto* he dramatized as *The Count of Narbonne*; Master of the Horse in the Viceregal establishment in Dublin; playwright, poet and satirist; Thomas Sheridan (2) edited *The Law of Lombardy* for performance at Drury Lane.

JOHNSON, ESTHER [STELLA] 1681-1728: fellow member with Swift of Sir William Temple's household; moved to Ireland in 1701; recipient of the letters collected as *The Journal to Stella*, first assembled in full by Thomas Sheridan (2); thought by Sheridan to have been secretly married to Swift in 1716; jealous of Swift's relationship with Vanessa.

JORDAN, DOROTHY [DORA] (née Bland) 1761-1816: daughter of Grace Phillips, who acted at Smock Alley under Thomas Sheridan (2); friend of Alicia Le Fanu (1); consort of the Duke of Clarence, later William IV; took prominent roles in many plays at Drury Lane, including *Pizarro* and *The Castle Spectre*; actress.

JOYCE, JAMES 1882-1941: practitioner of the art of punning as set forth by Dr Sheridan and devotee of J.S. Le Fanu's *The House by the Church-yard*, one of only four books in the childhood home; alludes to *William Tell* and *The Daughter*, by J.S. Knowles, in *Ulysses*; founded Dublin's first cinema, the Volta Cinematograph, at 45 Mary Street, adjacent to St Mary's Church; thought by Frank O'Connor to suffer from 'associative mania'.

KEAN, CHARLES 1811-68: son of Edmund Kean; husband of Ellen Tree;

after early phase in which his acting tended to be over-expressive, settled into a more restrained style which, paradoxically, suited melodrama; managed Princess's theatre (1851-62) where new work by writers such as Boucicault alternated with Shakespeare and Sheridan revivals, all lavishly staged.

KEAN, EDMUND 1787-1833: first appeared on stage as Cupid in *Cymon*, an opera produced by Sheridan in 1791; selected for that role on account of his fine black eyes; performed regularly at Theatre Royal, Dublin in the 1820s, at one point with his son Charles (1829); combined naturalistic touches with an older rhetorical tradition; played Mortimer in *The Iron Chest*.

KELLY, MICHAEL 1762-1826: actor, vocalist and composer; encouraged Sheridan to stage grand, spectacular pieces at Drury Lane; wrote the music for Colman's *Blue Beard* and for Samuel Arnold's *Illusion; or the Trances of Nourjahad*, based on Frances Sheridan's romance.

KEMBLE, CHARLES 1775-1854: actor at Drury Lane and Covent Garden; appeared regularly in Dublin, where he was an effective Charles Surface; played a greater range of parts than any actor except Garrick, excelling in comic roles; premièred role of Alonzo in *Pizarro*; manager of Covent Garden (1822-32).

KEMBLE, FANNY 1809-93: daughter of Charles Kemble and Maria de Camp; actress and writer; friend of Caroline Norton; played alongside her father and J. S. Knowles in the latter's *The Hunchback* (1832), and with Macready in *Macbeth* (1848); provides vivid account of the Sheridan family, c. 1829, in *Records of a Girlhood*.

KEMBLE, JOHN PHILIP 1757-1823: grandson of Irish actor John Ward from whom the 'Kemble style' may partly derive; brother of Sarah Siddons and Charles Kemble; manager of Drury Lane under R.B. Sheridan, 1788-1802, and subsequently of Covent Garden; tragic actor and arranger of plays; acclaimed as Rolla in *Pizarro*; learned profession in Dublin and remained a regular visitor at the Le Fanu house in Cuffe Street; model for hero of Inchbald's *A Simple Story*.

KENNEDY, PATRICK 1801-73: friend of J.S. Le Fanu; second-hand bookseller and collector of Irish folklore; premises at 8 Anglesea Street.

KNIGHT, AMARANTHA [Nancy Kilpatrick] b. 1946: author of *The Darker Passions* series in which classic horror tales are reworked as erotic novels; one of these is a version of 'Carmilla' (1997).

KNOWLES, HESTER (née Sheridan) fl. 1730-66: named after Swift's Stella; younger sister of Thomas Sheridan (2); mother of Frances (Fanny) and James Knowles; ran girls' boarding-school in York Street.

KNOWLES, JAMES 1756-1840: father of J.S. Knowles; lexicographer, whose pronouncing dictionary was based largely on that of his uncle, Thomas Sheridan (2); Knowles began work on this at the age of seventy.

KNOWLES, JAMES SHERIDAN [PADDY] 1784-1862: grandson of Hester Sheridan and nephew of Fanny Knowles, wife of Peter Le Fanu; actor-dramatist, radical newspaper editor, and latterly lay preacher; given early encouragement by Edmund Kean, fellow member of Cherry's acting company in Waterford; friend of Hazlitt; buried in Necropolis, Glasgow.

KNOWLES, JOHN fl. 1752-59 : husband of Hester, Thomas Sheridan (2)'s sister; assistant treasurer, Smock-Alley Theatre; because of joint liabilities, had to flee to the Isle of Man when Sheridan himself departed.

KNOWLES, R.B. SHERIDAN 1848-1931?: grandson of J. Sheridan Knowles; civil servant, essayist and novelist; Catholic (like father, R.B. Knowles) and, implicitly in *Glencoonoge* (1891), critic of English policy in Ireland; the narrator's beloved, in this novel, is called Alicia, perhaps in homage to the Sheridan/Le Fanu forename.

LAMB, WILLIAM, LORD MELBOURNE 1779-1848: husband of Lady Caroline (d. 1828) from whom he separated; friend of Thomas Sheridan (3) and close friend of the latter's daughter, Caroline Norton; Irish secretary, then prime minister; chief political adviser to the young Queen Victoria; part-model for William Clavering in Norton's 'The Woman's Reward' (1835).

LEADBEATER, MARY (née Shackleton) 1758-1826: friend of Joseph Le Fanu (1)'s eldest son, who encouraged her to publish work; corresponded with Melesina Trench, Maria Edgeworth and George Crabbe; ran the post office in Ballitore, Co. Kildare; account of the political violence of 1798 included in *The Leadbeater Papers* (1862); poet and recorder of Irish customs.

LEE, HARRIET 1757-1851: sister of Sophia and acquaintance of Betsy Sheridan; novelist, dramatist and joint-author (with sister) of *The Canterbury Tales*; 'The German's Tale: Kruitzner', by Harriet, was dramatized by Byron as *Werner*.

LEE, SOPHIA 1750-1824: author of Gothic novels, plays and short stories, notably *The Recess*; adapted *The History of Nourjahad* as a musical drama; acquaintance of Betsy Sheridan; ran girls' school in Bath; parents, John and Anna Lee, acted with and for Thomas Sheridan (2) in Dublin.

LE FANU, ALICIA [LISSY] (1) (née Sheridan) 1753-1817: sister of R.B. Sheridan and wife of Joseph Le Fanu; grandmother of J.S. Le Fanu; playwright and drama enthusiast; adapted mother's novel *Eugenia and Adelaide* as comic opera for Dublin stage; *The Sons of Erin* staged at the Lyceum, 1812; hosted literary gatherings in Cuffe Street; also entertained at 'country' cottage in Glasnevin; wrote account of her brother's elopement and the Mathews affair which Moore subsequently drew upon; buried at St Peter's, Aungier St; remains reinterred in the crypt of St Luke's in the Coombe (1980/81).

LE FANU, ALICIA (2) 1791-1867: daughter of Betsy (Sheridan) Le Fanu; prolific novelist and biographer of Frances Sheridan; published first book, *London; or, the Gift Revoked*, at the age of twelve; a moral tale in verse, *Rosara's Chain: or, the Choice of Life*, was issued by Godwin's Juvenile Library (1812); born in Dublin; lived with parents in various places including Northampton; after father's death dwelt in Leamington Spa until at least 1851; died at Chipping Norton, where she lodged with the Bowen family.

LE FANU, CATHERINE FRANCES 1813-41: eldest child of T.P. (1) and Emma Le Fanu; suffered from poor health; lived with parents in Dublin, Phoenix Park and Abington, Co. Limerick; occasional writer.

LE FANU, ELEANOR/ELLEN FRANCES ['RUSSELL GRAY'] 1845-1903: eldest child of J.S. Le Fanu; married Lieutenant (later Lt.-Colonel) Patrick Robertson of the 92nd (Gordon Highlanders); based in the Punjab and Afghanistan 1872-81, where six children born; subsequently lived near Peterhead; her comedy, *A Daughter of Erin*, performed at Theatre Royal, Dublin; novelist.

LE FANU, ELIZABETH [BETSY] (1) (née Sheridan) 1758-1837: wife of Henry Le Fanu and sister of Alicia (1); novelist and author of the diary letters known collectively as the *Journal*; supplied Moore with material for the Life of Sheridan; led a wandering life, dictated initially by her father's needs and then by her husband's career; lived in Bath, Dublin and London, then Kingsbridge (Devon), Northampton and Leamington Spa.

LE FANU, ELIZABETH BONNE (2) 1787-1828: daughter of Alicia and Joseph (1); niece of Betsy; 'lively and most engaging' (Mary Leadbeater); died at Bath.

LE FANU, EMMA LUCRETIA (1) (née Dobbin) d. 1861: wife of Thomas Philip and mother of J.S. Le Fanu; lover of poetry and the supernatural; nationalist sympathizer; essayist; biographer of Dr Orpen (founder of the Institution for the Deaf and Dumb, Dublin); slept on a mattress containing Lord Edward Fitzgerald's dagger.

LE FANU, EMMA LUCRETIA (2) [EMMIE] 1846-93: second daughter of J.S. Le Fanu; married her cousin George Bennett (2); left Dublin 1874; lived in Plymouth 1877-83, then at Sutton Valence, Kent.

LE FANU, REV. FLETCHER 1860-1939: second son of W.R. Le Fanu (1); vicar of Lissadell, Co. Sligo; rector of St John's, Sandymount, Dublin; met Yeats when the latter stayed with the Gore-Booths in 1894; officiated at the marriage of Constance Gore-Booth and Count Markiewicz, 1900.

LE FANU, G. BRINSLEY SHERIDAN [BRIN] 1854-1929: youngest of J.S. Le Fanu's four children; book illustrator and painter; worked on many of the titles in Stead's series of children's classics, including a Sheridan selection and a version of *Bluebeard*; friend of Edmund Downey, who commissioned pictures for three Le Fanu books; lived by Chelsea Bridge in a flat adjacent to that of J.K. Jerome (with a view stretching to the Surrey hills), then in Lavender Hill; own children died in infancy.

LE FANU, CAPTAIN HENRY [HARRY] 1747-1821: son of William [Guillaume] Le Fanu and husband of Betsy Sheridan; officer in 56th Foot; made heroic journey by row-boat from Faro to Gibraltar after assuming disguise; returned to Dublin; spent early years of marriage in Bath; ironically, given R.B. Sheridan's opposition to the barrack system, Le Fanu then became a Barrack Master, at Steyning, Birmingham, Northampton and elsewhere; died aged 74 while still so employed.

LE FANU, JOSEPH [JOE] (1) 1743-1825: son of William [Guillaume] Le Fanu and husband of Alicia Sheridan; grandfather of J.S. Le Fanu; Clerk of the Coast in Ireland; amateur actor and author of at least twelve plays, six of which are extant; friend of George Colman (1), whom he probably met through the bookseller/publisher William Johnston (see infra: Robinson); enthusiastic patron of the London theatre during visits, 1772-82; particularly admired Colman's *The Fatal Curiosity*; after wife's death lived in Molesworth Street (close to what is now the Buswell Hotel), then in Leeson Street.

LE FANU, JOSEPH (2) 1793-1833: son of Joseph (1) and Alicia; had particular interest in books and pictures; owned Quilca estate, subsequently passed down to J.S. Le Fanu.

LE FANU, JOSEPH SHERIDAN [JOE] 1814-73: great-nephew of R.B. Sheridan; grew up in Phoenix Park and Limerick; lawyer manqué; proprietor of journals and newspapers, including the *Dublin University Magazine*; custodian of family relics such as letters by Swift, Betsy's Journal and a host of portraits; inherited Sheridan's edition of Swift's *Works* from his father; novelist, poet and short story writer.

LEFANU, NICOLA FRANCES b. 1947: great-granddaughter of W. R. Le Fanu (1); composer and professor of music, York University; 'Lullaby' and 'Nocturne' were composed in 1988 for the Mühlfeld Trio, which performed the pieces at the Purcell Room, London.

LE FANU, REV. PETER 1749-1825: youngest son of William [Guillaume] Le Fanu and husband of Fanny Knowles (daughter of Hester Sheridan); amateur actor and playwright whose *Smock Alley Secrets* was known to Harry Houdini; house in Charlemont Street used for private performances by, among others, Sheridan Knowles; next home in Camden Street close to the Bleeding Horse inn, featured in *The Cock and Anchor*; noted for his vivacity and French manners.

LE FANU, PHILIP [PHILIE] 1847-79: elder son of J.S. and Susanna Le Fanu; aberrant spirit; inherited the Quilca estate on the death of his father but, debt-ridden, disposed of it two years later; suffered severe concussion in fall from carriage shortly after father's demise.

LEFANU, SARAH b. 1953: great-great-great-granddaughter of Peter Le Fanu and Frances Knowles; writer and broadcaster.

LE FANU, SUSANNA [SUE] (née Bennett) 1823-58: wife of J.S. Le Fanu; daughter of George Bennett QC, whose house, 18 (now 70) Merrion Square, became the Le Fanu home, c. 1850; aunt of Rhoda Broughton; mother of Eleanor, Emma, Philip and Brinsley Le Fanu.

LE FANU, VERY REV. THOMAS PHILIP (1) 1784-1845: son of Joseph Le Fanu (1); chaplain to the Hibernian Military School, Phoenix Park; then dean of Emly and rector of Abington, Co. Limerick; father of J.S. Le Fanu; scholar, harpist and book collector; library sold after his death to liquidate debts.

LE FANU, THOMAS PHILIP (2) 1858-1945: eldest son of W.R. Le Fanu (1) and father of W.R. LeFanu (2); author of memoir of the family (1924), based largely on materials collected by W.J.H. Le Fanu; worked at Dublin Castle; subsequently Commissioner of Public Works, like his father; one of the few top civil servants invited to stay on after the formation of the Irish Free State; lived at house called 'Abington' in Bray.

LE FANU, VICTOR 1865-1939: fifth son of W.R. Le Fanu (1); schoolmaster at Sutton Valence, then land agent and J.P., Co. Wicklow; lived near Bray with two sisters; 'inherited something of his father's charm and wit, also his great frame and presence'; poet, known for nonsense verse and translations of Horace; reported favourably on Dubliners MS when consulted by Joseph Hone of Maunsel & Co., c. 1909.

LE FANU, WILLIAM [GUILLAUME] 1708-97: husband of Henriette Raboteau de Puygibaud; wine merchant; trustee and banker of Thomas Sheridan (2); managed the latter's affairs with care after the Sheridans fled abroad; bought Quilca estate, which he had previously stewarded for Sheridan, 1788; resided on the west of Stephen's Green, known as French Walk on account of the number of Huguenots dwelling there.

LE FANU, WILLIAM RICHARD (1) 1816-94: brother of J.S. Le Fanu; husband of Henrietta (Banky) Barrington; railway engineer; Commissioner of Public Works in Ireland, and by association overseer of Lunatic Asylums; office in Merrion Street; as adult lived in Dublin, Cork and Kingstown; made frequent trips to England, overseeing transport-related bills in committee; attended to the welfare of many family members, including his brother's children; author of diary and memoir.

LEFANU, WILLIAM RICHARD (2) 1904-95: grandson of W.R. Le Fanu (1); husband of Elizabeth Maconchy and father of Nicola LeFanu, both wife and daughter being composers; medical historian, keeper of family documents and editor of Betsy Sheridan's *Journal*.

LEWIS, LEOPOLD 1828-90: adapted *Le Juif Polonais* as *The Bells*, which ran at the Lyceum from Nov. 1871 to May 1872 and laid the foundation for Henry Irving's rule; solicitor and dramatist.

LEWIS, MATTHEW G. [MONK] 1775-1818: friend of Byron, for whom he translated parts of *Faust*, and of Scott; Gothic novelist and dramatist whose plays, including *The Castle Spectre*, were popular at Drury Lane; drew on *Memoirs of Miss Sidney Bidulph* for certain incidents in *The East Indian* (1799); inherited estates in Jamaica (1812) and tried to improve the lot of his slaves; died on second passage home, supposedly after promising liberty to these 'black brethren' after his death; author of *The Monk* (1796).

LINLEY, ELIZABETH 1754-92: daughter of Thomas Linley; first wife of R.B. Sheridan, with whom she eloped to France, and mother of Thomas (3); singer and musician; depicted by Reynolds as St Cecilia; early experience of courtship depicted in Samuel Foote's *The Maid of Bath* and in *The Rivals*; had affair with, and bore son to, Lord Edward Fitzgerald, whom she apparently advised to marry Pamela Sims after her own death.

LINLEY, MARY [POLLY] 1758-87: sister of Elizabeth, wife of Richard Tickell and friend of Betsy Sheridan, to whom the Tickell apartment at Hampton Court was lent after her marriage to Henry Le Fanu; comic actress and talented soprano; appeared regularly with sister in Bath; sang in father's Drury Lane oratorios; gave up career upon marriage; after death, children entrusted to her sister's care.

LINLEY, THOMAS (1) 1733-95: father-in-law of R.B. Sheridan; family described by Dr Burney as 'a Nest of Nightingales'; composer and conductor, based in Bath, then London; manager of oratorios and joint patentee, Drury Lane; wrote music for *The Duenna*.

LINLEY, THOMAS (2) 1756-78: son of Thomas (1) and brother of Elizabeth; composer and violinist; wrote music for *The Duenna*, including a setting of 'How oft Louisa' to the Scottish tune 'The Birks of Endermay'; drowned in boating accident; praised posthumously by Mozart as 'a true genius'.

MACREADY, WILLIAM 1793-1873: son of Dublin actor who moved to England; tragic actor, at Covent Garden then Drury Lane; rival of Edmund Kean but shared reaction against the Kemble style; took lead role in *Virginius* and other plays by Knowles; as manager, restored Fool to *King Lear*.

MANGAN, JAMES CLARENCE 1803-49: worked as scrivener (and may have lodged) in York Street, near Maturin's house; much affected by *Melmoth*; published an account of Maturin in 1849; frequented the Bleeding Horse tavern; work published regularly in *Dublin University Magazine*; poet and essayist.

MATHEWS, CAPTAIN THOMAS 1744-1820: visitor to Linley household in Bath; married man whose unwelcome attentions to the young Elizabeth Linley seem to have precipitated the elopement of this 'syren' or 'angel' and R.B. Sheridan; fought two duels with Sheridan over questions of status and honour; these events and the behaviour of the three parties have provoked varying interpretation; leading authority on the game of whist.

MATURIN, REV. CHARLES 1780-1824: Curate of St Peter's, Aungier Street, where he officiated at the burial of Alicia Le Fanu, 1817; lived in York Street, close to Cuffe Street; great-uncle of Oscar Wilde; novelist and playwright who influenced J.S. Le Fanu; theorist, in *The Milesian Chief*, of Irish Gothic; *Bertram* staged at Drury Lane 9 May, 1816; this year is also the present time of *Melmoth the Wanderer*.

MELBOURNE, LORD: see Lamb, William.

MEREDITH, GEORGE 1828-1909: met Caroline Norton in the 1850s and used her as the model for Diana Merion in *Diana of the Crossways*; novelist and poet.

MIST, NATHANIEL d. 1737: ran anti-government journal which, probably under Charles Molloy's editorship, reprinted pieces from *The Intelligencer*, notably Dr Sheridan's account of Ireland (no. 6), which resulted in the arrest of the printer; after its prosecution and closure, *Mist's* was replaced by *Fog's Weekly Journal*.

MOORE, GEORGE 1852-1933: son of Irish MP; studied painting in Paris (1873-79) where he came to know Manet and Zola and met Brinsley Le Fanu (a link probably furthered by joint experience of Charles Lutyens's London studio); Paris phase described in *Confessions of a Young Man* (1888); afterwards lived in London and Dublin; presents decay of Merrion Square as index of corruption in *A Drama in Muslin* (1886); author of *Esther Waters* and *The Lake*; novelist, essayist and short-story writer.

MOORE, THOMAS 1779-1852: friend and biographer of R.B. Sheridan; poet whose *Irish Melodies* were influenced by Sheridan's lyrics; sang with Caroline Norton at parties and dedicated 'Summer Fête' to her; born above shop in Aungier Street; lived at Sloperton, near Devizes, from 1817; strong nationalist, as evinced by *Memoirs of Captain Rock* and *Life of Sheridan*; MS of *Journal* rediscovered in a metal chest at Longmans, 1967.

MORGAN, LADY [SYDNEY OWENSON] 1776-1859: daughter of actor Robert Owenson; friend and protégée of Alicia Le Fanu (1); influenced the work of Charles Maturin, a regular visitor to her salon in Kildare Street; friend of Thomas Moore; possible model for Thackeray's Becky Sharp; fought for Catholic emancipation and Irish independence; novelist and woman of letters; presented fictional portrait of Lord Edward Fitzgerald in *The O'Briens and the O'Flaherties*.

MURRAY, JOHN 1824-94: maternal grandfather of James Joyce; lived at Church House (or the Grey Stone House), Chapelizod; previously ran a pub, The Eagle House, in Roundtown (now Terenure).

NORTON, CAROLINE ELIZABETH (née Sheridan) 1808-77: granddaughter of R.B. Sheridan and cousin of J.S. Le Fanu; godmother of Brinsley Le Fanu; 'Diana Merion' in Meredith's novel (cf birthplace of mother); part-model for Lady Montfort in Disraeli's *Endymion*; campaigner for improvement to the rights of married women; novelist and poet.

NORTON, HON. GEORGE CHAPPLE 1800-75: husband of Caroline; brother of Lord Grantley; barrister and magistrate; appointed to latter office through recommendation of Lord Melbourne, the man he later cited as having had 'criminal conversation' with his wife; called 'the late' at school because both slow and lifeless.

NUGENT, LORD ROBERT 1702-88: described by Betsy Le Fanu as an 'Old admirer' of Alicia; accumulated wealth by marrying rich widows (hence Walpole's coinage 'to Nugentize'); 'a jovial and voluptuous Irishman, who had left Popery for the Protestant religion, money and widows' (Glover); friend and patron of Goldsmith; MP, vice-treasurer for Ireland and poet.

PEAKE, RICHARD BRINSLEY 1792-1847: son of Richard Peake (treasurer of Drury Lane and R.B. Sheridan's friend); engraver, dramatist and treasurer of the Lyceum Theatre; adapted *Frankenstein* for the stage; adapted Frances Sheridan's *The Discovery* (with added material from Steele) as *Court and City*.

PETITJEAN, ARMAND 1913-2003: son of perfumer of same name; perhaps no relation of Matilda Stoker's husband Charles; friend of James Joyce; translated parts of *Finnegans Wake* and wrote essays on Joyce and myth; also published a study of Swift (1938); philosophical essayist.

RAMSDEN, LADY GUENDOLEN (née Seymour) 1846-1910: daughter of Lady Georgiana and Lord Edward Seymour; granddaughter of Thomas Sheridan (3); novelist, artist and editor of family correspondence; the climax of *Speedwell* (1894) involves the gutting of a theatre when scenery catches fire.

ROBINSON, GEORGE 1736-1801: after working for Wm. Johnston set up own firm; in partnership with brother John and son George, published works such as *The Mysteries of Udolpho*; J. and G. jnr. issued *Lucy Osmond* and *The India Voyage*; business collapsed after fire in printing office, 1804; John then went into partnership with George Wilkie, publishing inter alia *Canterbury Tales*, vol. 5 and *Zastrozzi*.

ROBINSON, MARY (née Darby) 1757-1800: of Irish descent; actress at Drury Lane during early years of Sheridan's tenure; played Amanda in

A Trip to Scarborough and Perdita in *The Winter's Tale*; found Sheridan 'strikingly and bewitchingly attractive' but became mistress of the Prince of Wales and later Charles James Fox; friend of fellow opium-eater, Coleridge, and of Wollstonecraft and Godwin, whose radical views she shared; died in poverty; poet and Gothic novelist.

ROGERS, SAMUEL 1763-1855: friend of Sheridan, Byron, Moore and of Caroline Norton, who often acted as hostess at his dinner and breakfast parties; noted for acerbic wit and flair as raconteur; table-talk and recollections (1856/59) constitute important record of era; banker and poet.

ROLLESTON, THOMAS W. 1857-1920: husband of Maud, daughter of Stopford Brooke; founded *Dublin University Review* (1885); first secretary of the Irish Literary Society (1892-93); poet, journalist and editor.

ROSS, ROBERT [ROBBIE] 1869-1918: friend and lover of Oscar Wilde; joint-author of the memoir of Maturin in the 1892 (Bentley) edition of *Melmoth the Wanderer*; literary journalist and art critic.

ROWE, NICHOLAS 1674-1718: dramatist, poet and editor of Shakespeare; plays, including *Ulysses*, performed by Thomas Sheridan (2); *The Fair Penitent* and *Jane Shore* held the stage for well over a century, as noted by Hazlitt.

SEYMOUR, LADY JANE GEORGIANA, DUCHESS OF SOMERSET (née Sheridan) 1809-84: third daughter of Tom and Caroline Sheridan; probably named after her aunt, Georgiana Callander (who was named after *her* godmother, Georgiana, Duchess of Devonshire); married Lord Edward Seymour, whose duel with Sir Colquhoun Grant, with preceding business, was reminiscent of *The Rivals*.

SHELLEY, MARY 1797-1851: daughter of William Godwin and Mary Wollstonecraft; friend of Thomas Moore, Lady Morgan and Caroline Norton; having experienced threat of separation from son, contributed advice for Norton's pamphlet *Observations on the Natural Claim of the Mother*; worked on the expanded version of *Frankenstein* in the house next to the Grand Pump Room, Bath, 1816-17; read *Strathallan* and *Helen Monteagle*, 1817-18.

SHELLEY, PERCY BYSSHE 1792-1822: husband of Mary; supporter of Catholic emancipation in Ireland but opponent of church misrule; stayed in Cuffe Street, 1813; author of *The Cenci*, from which Joyce quotes in *Giacomo Joyce*; a film version of the story, *Beatrice Cenci*, was included in the opening programme at the Volta Cinematograph, 20 December 1909.

SHERIDAN, ALGERNON 1845-1931: great-grandson of R.B. Sheridan; owner of Frampton Court, demolished after his death; wife Mary (d. 1918) a close friend of Thomas Hardy.

SHERIDAN, CAROLINE HENRIETTA (née Callander) 1779-1851: wife of

Thomas Sheridan (3) and mother of Helen Dufferin and Caroline Norton; born in Merrion Square; after husband's death lived in apartment at Hampton Court; 'lovely . . . engaging and interesting beyond measure' (R.B. Sheridan); novelist whose work was admired by Disraeli.

SHERIDAN, CHARLES FRANCIS 1750-1806: son of Thomas (2) and Frances Sheridan; politician and writer; supposed by the family to be the model for Joseph Surface in *The School for Scandal*.

SHERIDAN, CHARLES BRINSLEY 1796-1843: son of R.B. and Hecca Sheridan; shared house with niece Caroline Norton after her re-emergence following the Melbourne trial; hellenist and classicist.

SHERIDAN, CLARE (née Frewen) 1885-1970: wife of William [Wilfred] and mother of Dick and Mary Margaret Sheridan; sculptor and journalist.

SHERIDAN, ELIZABETH [PONSY] (1) (née MacFadden) 16?-c.1736: wife of Thomas Sheridan (1); known for sharp tongue; Quilca estate inherited from her father Charles, although it seems to have passed to the Sheridans with accompanying debts.

SHERIDAN, ELIZABETH (2) c. 1716-96: daughter of Dr Sheridan and Elizabeth MacFadden; 'maintained that the Banshi of the Sheridan family was heard wailing beneath the windows of Quilca before the news arrived from France of Mrs Frances Sheridan's death at Blois, thus affording them a preternatural intimation of the impending . . . event' (Alicia Le Fanu [2]); schoolmistress.

SHERIDAN, ELIZABETH [BETSY] (3): see Le Fanu, Elizabeth (1).

SHERIDAN, ESTHER [HECCA] (née Ogle) 1776-1817: second wife of R.B. Sheridan; as part of the marriage settlement, Polesden Lacey, Surrey, was purchased in 1797, the estate being held in trust for Hecca and their son Charles.

SHERIDAN, FRANCES (née Chamberlaine) 1724-66: wife of Thomas Sheridan (2); friend of Richardson and Johnson; novelist and playwright; wrote in secret, initially, to avoid disapproval of father and husband; work, once published, widely admired: 'every body has read her *Nourjahad*' (Boaden); *Sidney Bidulph* is 'the best novel of our age' (C.J.Fox).

SHERIDAN, MARY MARGARET MOTLEY: see de Renéville.

SHERIDAN, RICHARD BRINSLEY [SHERRY] 1751-1816: son of Thomas (2) and Frances Sheridan; baptized at St Mary's church; briefly a law student; playwright, politician and poet; proprietor of Theatre Royal, Drury Lane; company based at Lyceum Theatre, 1809-1812; at a point between Elizabeth Linley's death and his marriage to Esther, supposedly engaged to Pamela de Genlis; close to two United Irishmen; vigorous and eloquent opponent of repressive legislation such as the Seditious Meetings Act.

SHERIDAN, R. BRINSLEY (2) 1806-88: brother of Caroline Norton;

owner, via wife Marcia, of Frampton Court, Dorset, where Sheridan MSS were kept, including versions of *The School for Scandal*.

SHERIDAN, R. BRINSLEY (3) [DICK] 1915-36: grandson of Algernon and son of Wilfred and Clare Sheridan; lost MSS of Sheridan plays when his boat was wrecked off the Algerian coast, 1935; sailing enthusiast and adventurer.

SHERIDAN, DOCTOR THOMAS (1) [TOM PUN-SIBI] 1687-1738: friend and correspondent of Swift, his partner in language games; their journal *The Intelligencer* notable for its critique of English policy in Ireland; country residence at Quilca, Co. Cavan, passed down through the family to J.S. Le Fanu; classicist, schoolmaster and poet; influence on Joyce indicated by reference to 'Sharadan's *Art of Panning*' in *Finnegans Wake*.

SHERIDAN, THOMAS (2) 1719-88: son of Doctor Thomas (1); father of R.B., Lissy and Betsy Sheridan; manager of Smock Alley Theatre, 1745-56; driven by creditors into exile; returned to Dublin stage frequently, 1763-77; projector of academy for recitation in Bath, 1770; joint-manager with son of Drury Lane, 1778-80; actor (ranked second to Garrick as tragedian in Churchill's *Rosciad*), playwright, lexicographer and elocutionist; biographer of Swift; called 'King Tom' in satiric pamphlets.

SHERIDAN, THOMAS (3) 1775-1817: son of R.B. Sheridan; father of Helen Dufferin and Caroline Norton; playwright; manager of Drury Lane and joint-proprietor of Lyceum; Paymaster General at the Cape of Good Hope; jested about the family name and situation, 'who has a greater right to the "O" . . . ? for we *owe* every body' (*Angelo's Pic Nic*).

SIDDONS, SARAH (née Kemble) 1755-1831: career promoted by Thomas Sheridan (2), who saw her in Bath; leading tragic actress of her time, at Drury Lane and subsequently Covent Garden; played Julia in *The Rivals* and Elvira in *Pizarro*; despite stage success, suffered from R.B. Sheridan's disinclination to pay regular salaries, his pocket being in her words 'that dreadful gulf from which no plea of right or justice can save its victims.'

SMITH, CHARLOTTE 1749-1806: after Scott, novelist most strongly represented in Dean Le Fanu's library (8 titles plus *Elegiac Sonnets*), perhaps reflecting taste of wife and mother; one book, *Desmond*, published by G. & J. Robinson (1792); poet and novelist who harnessed gothic romance to radical social ideals; corresponded with Dublin antiquarian Joseph Walker (see infra).

SPENSER, EDMUND 1552-99: undertaker of colonial development whose experience of landscape and political-religious tension intersects with that of the Le Fanu family: Kilcolman is less than 30 miles from Abington; poet and commentator on state of Ireland; Aikin's edition of *Works* (1802) in Dean Le Fanu's Library; R.B. Sheridan could recite whole cantos of *The Faerie Queene* and quoted Guyon's reply to Mammon in a Westminster Hall speech of 1794.

STEAD, WILLIAM 1849-1912: social reformer and publisher; edited the *Review of Reviews*; published the 'Books for the Bairns' series (continued by his daughter Estelle) which, with 'The Penny Poets' and 'Penny Popular Novels', provided the main inspiration for Allen Lane's Puffin Books.

STOKER, BRAM 1847-1912: drama critic/commentator for the Dublin *Evening Mail* and *The Warder*, formerly owned by J.S. Le Fanu; clerk in Petty Sessions office, beside Bedford Tower, Dublin Castle; secretary/manager to Henry Irving; novelist and short story writer, influenced by Le Fanu.

STOKER, MATILDA (later Petitjean) 1846-19?: sister of Bram; author of article which printed for the first time (1887) many of Elizabeth Linley's letters to R.B. Sheridan, supposedly found in cellars adjoining Drury Lane, where they had been deposited during the fire of 1809; writer and painter.

SUMMERS, MONTAGUE 1880-1948: expert in occult lore and Restoration drama; author of *The Gothic Quest: a History of the Gothic Novel*, *The Vampire: His Kith and Kin* and 'Joseph Sheridan Le Fanu and His Houses' (1932); knew Edmund Gosse and S.M. Ellis ('one of my closest . . . friends').

SWIFT, JONATHAN 1667-1745: friend, reciprocal-author and sometime critic of Thomas Sheridan (1); guest at Quilca, where parts of *Gulliver's Travels* written; godfather and occasional tutor to Thomas Sheridan (2); wrote a version of the Gaelic poem 'O'Rourke's Feast', which he supposedly heard, sung to Carolan's music, at a country house in County Cavan; entwined with two [H]est[h]ers.

SWIFT, THEOPHILUS 1746-1815: son of Deane Swift; lawyer and self-deluded, rival suitor for the hand of Emma Dobbin; published *The Touchstone of Truth*, an account of his rejection in favour of Thomas Le Fanu.

SWINBURNE, ALGERNON 1837-1909: admirer, with qualifications, of Sheridan Le Fanu's work, as evinced by letters to George Powell.

TERRY, ELLEN 1847-1928: of Irish descent on father's side; joined Charles Kean's company, with father and sister, as a child; Henry Irving's leading lady at the Lyceum; probably also his lover; mother of Edward Gordon Craig; actress and author.

TICKELL, THOMAS 1686-1740: grandfather of Richard Tickell; friend of Swift and Delany, protégé of Addison and Chief Secretary for Ireland; poet.

TICKELL, RICHARD 1751-93: husband of Mary Linley; close friend and brother-in-law of R.B. Sheridan, his partner in pranks from Bath period onward; fell, perhaps deliberately, to his death from a parapet next to his apartment at Hampton Court; political satirist and dramatist.

TINSLEY, WILLIAM 1831-1902: publisher of J.S. and Eleanor Le Fanu, Wilkie Collins, Thomas Hardy and Percy Fitzgerald; theatre-addict; laissez-faire in business habits but ready to gamble on unknown property; went bankrupt 1878; seen as gullible and sloppy by George Moore but defended by Edmund Downey as 'a Bohemian publisher' with a remarkable memory.

TONE, THEOBALD WOLFE 1763-98: born in (former) Stafford Street, opposite St Mary's church; agnostic from Protestant background; co-founded Society of United Irishmen, in Belfast then Dublin; captured during 1798 rebellion; denied a soldier's death, committed suicide; writer and republican hero.

TRENCH, MELESINA (née Chenevix) 1768-1827: born in Dublin; of Huguenot descent like second husband, Richard Trench; travelled extensively on the Continent; diarist, author and letter-writer.

VANHOMRIGH, HESTER [VANESSA/HESSY] 1688-1723: daughter of King William's Muster-Master-General, a merchant and Lord Mayor of Dublin; met Swift during period in London when he was a regular family guest; became increasingly intimate with the latter, as suggested by 'Cadenus and Vanessa'; from 1714 lived at Marlay Abbey, Celbridge; depressed by Swift's reluctance to commit himself to her alone.

VESTRIS, MADAME ELIZA (née Bartolozzi) 1797-1856: wife of Charles Mathews, with whom managed the Lyceum (1847-55); actress and first female manager of London theatre (1830); premièred role of Catherine in Knowles's *Love* (1839).

WALKER, JOSEPH COOPER 1761-1810: acquaintance of Alicia Le Fanu (I) and friend of the Brooke family; pioneer in Irish antiquities; authority on poetry, music and drama; published Charlotte Brooke's early translations and the first genuine ossianic poem to appear in print; influenced work of Lady Morgan, who had made contact via Alicia.

WHYTE, SAMUEL [SAM] 1732-1811: illegitimate son of Captain Solomon Whyte (uncle of Frances Sheridan); ran school in Grafton Street attended by R.B. and Alicia Sheridan, and subsequently by Thomas Moore; friend of Alicia and her husband Joseph Le Fanu; author and elocutionist.

WILDE, LADY JANE F. (née Elgee) 1821-96: wife of Sir William and mother of Oscar; niece (by marriage) of Charles Maturin; author of two collections of Irish folklore, partly derived from her husband's researches; translated Meinhold's *Sidonia the Sorceress*; poet and essayist.

WILDE, OSCAR 1854-1900: spent most of childhood in family house on the opposite side of Merrion Square from J.S. Le Fanu's residence; occasional playmate of Le Fanu's children; subsequently met Bram Stoker, a regular visitor to the Wildes' home in the 1870s; became close to, perhaps semi-engaged to, Florence Balcombe, before she became Stoker's wife; continued friendship with the Stokers in London, partly through involvement with theatre; went into exile under the alias Sebastian Melmoth (see above: Maturin).

WILDE, SIR WILLIAM 1815-76: father of Oscar; acquaintance of J.S. Le Fanu and Bram Stoker; eye and ear specialist; archaeologist and folklorist; wrote study of the skulls of Swift and Stella; acquired the former's death-mask.

WILKIE, THOMAS 1759-1824: son of John Wilkie, who published the first edition of *The Rivals* and the song lyrics from *The Duenna*; brother of George, who issued the first edition of *A Trip to Scarborough*; made agreement with Sheridan to publish 'authentic copies' of his plays (1809), a plan which was finally realized in conjunction with John Murray, 1821.

WOFFINGTON, MARGARET (PEG) 1714-60: leading actress in London and Dublin; friend of and joint performer with Thomas Sheridan (2); played Penelope opposite Sheridan's Ulysses at Smock Alley in 1753; only female member of the Beefsteake Club; had three-year affair with Garrick.

WOLLSTONECRAFT, EVERINA 1765-1843: sister of Mary Wollstonecraft; friend of Alicia (1), Joseph and Peter Le Fanu; ran school in Dublin with sister Eliza; presented Catherine Le Fanu with a copy of *Original Stories*, 1817; regular dinner guest at Cuffe Street.

YEATS, WILLIAM BUTLER 1865-1939: co-founder of Irish Literary Society, through which he may have encountered Brinsley Le Fanu; initially *The Words Upon the Window Pane* had a character who is J.S. Le Fanu's great-nephew; references to *In a Glass Darkly*, *Uncle Silas* and Swedenborg establish a context for the 'spirit' re-enactment of relations between Swift, Stella and Vanessa; knew Blackwood, whom he introduced to the Order of the Golden Dawn, and Stoker, whose *Dracula* he read in 1915; refers to Alicia Le Fanu's 'banshi' anecdote in *Fairy and Folk Tales of the Irish Peasantry*; lived at 82 Merrion Square (1922-28).

ACKNOWLEDGEMENTS

For permission to quote unpublished writings by and correspondence to members of the Le Fanu family: Nicola LeFanu; for research funding: Arts Council England; for archival assistance: Rosalind Moad and Elizabeth Pridmore, King's College, Cambridge; for other research assistance: National Library of Ireland; the Royal Irish Academy; Trinity College Library, Dublin; National Folklore Collection, University College Dublin; Public Record Office of Northern Ireland; Bodleian Library; British Library; Brotherton Library, University of Leeds; National Film and Television Archive; University College (London) Library; University of London Library; Victoria and Albert Museum; Gordon Highlanders Museum; Huntington Library.

For help of various kinds: Mike Ashley, Peter Beresford Ellis, Roy Clements, Steve Clews, Mary Cloake, Gary Crawford, Kathleen Dickson, Chris Edgson, Paul Ferguson, Alun Ford, Sarah George, Harry Gilonis, Tom Hall, Alan Halsey, Andrew Hambling, Judith Harridge, Frank Harte, Michelle Hoctor, Elizabeth James, Robert Jenkins, Noel Kissane, Patrick Lee, Nicola and Sarah LeFanu, Rolf Loeber, Gerry Long, Denis McCarthy, Bill Mc Cormack, Dona and Barney McCullagh, Murdo MacDonald, Patricia McGuire, Luke McKernan, George MacLennan, Catherine Maxwell, Jim Mays, Anthony Mellors, James Morwood, Hovhanness Pilikian, Robin Porteous, Raymond Refaussé, Meg Rich, Gayle Richardson, Jim Rockhill, Dawn Ryans, Victor Sage, Maurice and Mary Scully, Clare Selerie, Brian Showers, Peter Simon, Bill Smith, Colin Smythe, Diane Towe, Michael Trimble, Siân Truszkowska, David Watson, Timothy Webb, Peter Williams, Marilyn Wood; for personal and artistic support: Frances Presley. 'Tomogram' is dedicated to Glenn Storhaug, in appreciation of his skills as designer and typesetter.

Some of these texts have been published in: *Advent, Angel Exhaust, Boxkite, CCCP Review* (2006), *Chicago Review, Fire, The Gig, Great Works, Gut Cult, In the Company of Poets, Litter, Kore Broadsheets* (TCD), *Openned, Poetry Ireland Review, Poetry Salzburg Review, Sentence, Shearsman, Stride magazine, Tears in the Fence*. Thanks are due to the editors.